TWAYNE'S WORLD AUTHORS SERIES
A Survey of the World's Literature

SOUTH AFRICA

Joseph Jones, University of Texas
EDITOR

William Charles Scully

TWAS 490

William Charles Scully

WILLIAM CHARLES SCULLY

By JOHN ROBERT DOYLE, JR.
The Citadel

TWAYNE PUBLISHERS
A DIVISION OF G. K. HALL & CO., BOSTON

PR
9369
.3
.S35
Z6

Copyright © 1978 by G. K. Hall & Co.
All Rights Reserved
First Printing

Library of Congress Cataloging in Publication Data

Doyle, John Robert, Jr.
  William Charles Scully.

  (Twayne's world authors series ; TWAS 490 : South Africa)
  Bibliography: pp. 214–217.
  Includes index.
  1. Scully, William Charles, 1855-1943—Criticism and interpretation.
PR9369.3.S35Z6   828   78-127
ISBN 0-8057-6331-7

MANUFACTURED IN THE UNITED STATES OF AMERICA

To
Reinhardt Eybers
Who has made my South African books
better than they would have been
without his help
and
In Memory of
Frances Willard Eybers
Whose friendship, together with that of
her family, contributed much to my year
in South Africa

Contents

About the Author
Preface
Chronology
1. From Tipperary to South Africa Is a Long Way   17
2. In the Service of Government   31
3. Poems Came First   46
4. Prose Stories   62
5. Reaction to Experiences in the Desert   81
6. Autobiographical Writing   123
7. Opposite Worlds   131
8. The Painful Growth of a Nation   143
9. After Retirement from the Civil Service   152
10. Conclusion   194
    Notes and References   206
    Selected Bibliography   214
    Index   219

About the Author

A native Virginian, John Robert Doyle, Jr. attended Randolph-Macon College, the University of Virginia, the Bread Loaf School of English, and the University of North Carolina. He has taught in Virginia, North Carolina, Missouri, and South Carolina. Over a period of years, he has published a number of critical essays, most of them dealing with twentieth-century literature. *The Poetry of Robert Frost*, a full length study, was published simultaneously in South Africa and the United States. He is the author of books on the life and works of the South African-English poet, novelist, short-story writer, biographer, editor, and librettist William Plomer; South African poet, short-story writer, novelist, and editor Francis Carey Slater; Scottish-South African poet and prose writer Thomas Pringle; and English-Rhodesian missionary poet and prose writer Arthur Shearly Cripps.

For four years he was drama critic for *The Evening Post*, Charleston, South Carolina, and reviewed poetry and criticism for both *The Evening Post* and *The News and Courier*. At The Citadel he taught modern poetry, poetry writing, literary criticism, the modern novel, and American literature. He was the founding editor of The Citadel Monograph and founding director of The Citadel Fine Arts Series.

Visiting Professor of American Literature at the Universities of Cape Town and the Witwatersrand, he also lectured at other South African universities. His essays have been published in a number of South African periodicals.

Recently he retired from The Citadel as Professor Emeritus, but at his home in Virginia he continues his research and writing.

Preface

William Charles Scully deserves to be remembered because chronologically he holds a crucial position in South African literature, and because he has recorded many facts about the country, facts which otherwise would have been lost, and because of the intrinsic worth of his writing as an interpretation of the human spirit. Arriving from Ireland early enough to experience life in South Africa before the discovery of diamonds and gold changed its direction among the nations of the world, he was late enough to be able to examine the resulting civilization and compare it with what preceded.

South African literature in English had started with Thomas Pringle. Pringle, 1789–1834, (TWAS 238) coming from Scotland, reached the Cape in 1820 and saw South Africa as a land with agricultural and herding potentials. He was also concerned with a pagan civilization which presented missionaries millions of souls which they hoped to save. Francis Carey Slater, 1876–1958, (TWAS 173) South African born and South African in outlook, started life on a farm and moved into a banking system which stationed him at intervals of several years in small towns throughout the Cape, until he terminated his banking career in Grahamstown and his years of retirement in Cape Town. Slater knew the native peoples, especially the Xhosa, but essentially in an agricultural and domestic situation. William Plomer, 1903–1973, (TWAS 54) belonged to the generation that reversed the direction of author movement. Born in the Transvaal, he, with Roy Campbell (TWAS 439) and Laurens van der Post (TWAS 68), left South Africa in his youthful days. Only one of the three ever returned except for visits. When Plomer departed from the land of his birth, his poems, and stories, and novels no longer employed South African materials. Rapidly he developed into an international literary figure.

Considered in the company of Pringle-Slater-Plomer, Scully not only represents a different period of time, but he knew places, and types of people, and events outside of the range of experience of the others. Pringle lived two years on the frontier and after that was a librarian and editor in Cape Town during the brief period he remained in South Africa. A cripple throughout the whole of his life, Pringle experienced from the back of a horse much of what he saw of the Cape. He knew the territory better than its varied inhabitants. Slater's boyhood was spent on a farm, but his mature life was passed in the employment of the Standard Bank of South Africa. Here he met many people, but predominantly those who might have business on the inside of a bank. Though at a later time, Plomer's father had known South Africa in something of the same way as Scully, and the young William got close to certain aspects of native and rural life in South Africa for a very brief period before he sailed off to Japan in his early twenties. Thus, wherever a reader turns, he discovers that William Charles Scully has something to offer not found elsewhere in South African literature.

Taken collectively as complementary authors, Pringle-Scully-Slater-Plomer afford an admirable sampling of South African literature. This is not to say that other writers need not be examined. It does imply, however, that the four present a solid representation of what has been done during a hundred and fifty years. Some of the materials a reader will find if he expands his investigation are revealed when he examines Scully beside his poetic contemporaries. In *South African Verse*, 1945, Francis Carey Slater represented eight poets born in the same decade as Scully. Of these eight, only half are named in the Miller and Sergeant *Survey of South African Poetry in English*, 1957. From these four, the authors indicate only one other than Scully as having written poems worthy of permanent recognition. Herbert Tucker, they claim, "Within his own narrow field [a passionate response to 'sun and wind, seascape and mountain, dawn and sunset'] . . . has achieved a special quality by the completeness of his surrender to his experience." When the drastically restricted performance of Tucker is placed beside the rich diversity of Scully, a reader immediately understands something of his value as a representative of the period. Perhaps it should be noted that, according to Miller and Sergeant, after Pringle only three poets of the nineteenth century are to be given serious attention: William Rodger Thomson (1832–1867), William Elijah Hunter (1839–1913), and William Charles Scully (1855–1943). In addition to sharing the name "William," the three shared a love of South Africa. Thomson, born in South Africa, was the son of a Scottish missionary; Hunter was of English birth; and Scully was Irish. To Thomson goes the distinction of having written the first poem expressing a passionate desire to be in South Africa when far distant from its shores.

Preface

More important than anything already said about Scully as a poet is the value that can be credited to him as a prose writer. Here he made a far greater contribution to South African literature and history than in his poetry. At the age of thirty-seven, after two published volumes, he turned from verse to prose. Three collections of short stories, four novels, six volumes of nonfictional prose, and miscellaneous pieces give both in quantity and quality a writing achievement which cannot be ignored.

Of greater significance than the poets were several prose fictionists who appeared during the period to stand beside Scully and represent South Africa during the nineteenth century. Among these was Olive Schreiner (1859–1922), daughter of missionaries, the father German and mother English, with some Jewish blood. In her early twenties, Olive wrote *The Story of an African Farm* (1883) while she was a governess on a sheep farm in the Karroo (vast arid plateau, interior of the Cape Province). Despite its genuine South African setting, the novel was universal in its principal concern, childhood and youth, the process of human growth. Ill health and various complications perhaps account for the lack of the author's continued creativity. Publishing at the same time as Olive Schreiner was Sir Henry Rider Haggard (1856–1925), whose novels, among other things, present the times of Chaka, the Zulu chieftain, and an extended consideration of Zulu life. The novels span the period from 1885 to 1917. The most intense years of Scully's fictional creativeness were from 1895 to 1898, which saw the publication of two volumes of stories and two novels. At that point, the South African War broke the flow of his work.

Moving into the twentieth century, a reader finds the situation very different from that suggested for the nineteenth. The development of the international reputation of William Plomer was parallel to that of Roy Campbell and Laurens van der Post. The three friends were joined and followed by others and still others. Pauline Smith's (TWAS 80) *The Little Karroo* (1926) and Herman Charles Bosman's *Mafeking Road* (1947) are individual collections of stories which are not likely to be forgotten, even in a world where many books are insisting upon attention. No longer is there need to feel that South Africa has no literature, either in quantity or quality. This twentieth-century growth makes significant all efforts to determine the nature of the foundation upon which the present has been brought into being.

JOHN ROBERT DOYLE, JR.

Acknowledgments

The author offers grateful acknowledgment to the following:

Reinhardt Eybers, who located and sent all of the long out of print primary materials for this study and assisted with the secondary materials of various kinds.

Professor A. C. Partridge, who introduced me to Mrs. Betty Gray, youngest daughter of William Charles and Honoria Emily Richards Scully.

Mrs. Betty Gray (Mrs. William Quiller Orchardson Gray), who not only contributed to the accuracy of the chronology and bibliography but generously supplied facts about her father's life and work, details unavailable from any other source. She also furnished the best of the Scully portraits, the one used in this book. Finally, I am indebted to her for giving me an impression of her father and mother, which only one very close to them could offer. The final draft of the body of my book had been completed before I received the first letter from her. The attitudes and ideas I have advanced are my own, not anything for which she can be held responsible. With her permission, I have inserted details at various points in the text, always over her name.

Gerald Creigh Scully and the Scully family for permission to quote from the books of William Charles Scully.

The National English Documentation Centre, Grahamstown, South Africa, for copies of papers giving information about William Charles Scully and for permission to quote from these papers.

Chronology

1855   Born on Gardiner Street, Dublin, October 29, though the family lived in Cashel until the early 1860s, when they moved to Springfield.

1867   In November embarked at Dublin for Falmouth and from there sailed for the Cape, reaching Table Bay in the middle of December and then passed on to Port Elizabeth and inland to Grahamstown.

1868   After six weeks in Grahamstown, the Scullys moved to King William's Town. Several months later the father hired a farm near Maclean. Farming having proved unprofitable, the family returned to King William's Town and for slightly more than half a year William was placed in school.

1869   In June, William undertook his first South African adventure, an expedition to the Transkei. For a brief time, William with one helper was placed in charge of his father's sheep. Next, for one month, he worked for a trader near Sandile's kraal. Soon after the discovery of diamonds, he started for the fields.

1871   Had enteric fever. Returned home for medical care; upon his recovery, he went back to Kimberley.

1872   In diamond fields, messed for about a year with the Rhodes brothers—Cecil John, Herbert, and Frank.

1873   Rich alluvial gold reported near Lydenburg. Scully decided to go to the scene of the discovery.

1874   In June joined an expedition to Delagoa Bay, organized to transport materials for war against the Baphedi Chief, Sekukuni. (Also Bapedi or Pedi and Sikhukhuni or Seccocoeni.)

1875   Started April 5 into the Low Country (from Pilgrim's Rest); four of the five making the attempt died of fever. Scully alone survived. Made a prospecting trip into Swaziland. Struck camp Christmas Eve, and departed from Pilgrim's Rest, January 3, 1876.

1876   Worked for Boat Company in East London. Joined Cape Civil Service and was assigned to Tarkastad. Reported May 28 but official date of starting work was June 1.

WILLIAM CHARLES SCULLY

1877   Latter part of September, transferred to Graaff Reinet.
1879   Sent to Aberdeen. For a brief period became an officer in the Tembu War.
1882   Early part of year went to Seymour, district of Stockenstrom. Late in year, transferred to Cape Town. During period in Cape Town married Ellen Doveton, who died at the time of the birth of the first child, Elaine, 1883.
1883   Returned to Seymour.
1884   Serious insomnia. Became a relieving officer. First place he was sent was Colesburg.
1885   Appointed magistrate at Springbokfontein in Namaqualand.
1886   Published *Wreck of the Grosvenor and Other South African Poems*. Next appointment was to Oudtshoorn and from there sent again to Seymour.
1889   While at Fort Beaufort married Honoria Emily Richards.
1890   As preparations for the 1891 census were being made, Scully was sent to Namaqualand for taking the census in that vast area.
1892   At the end of the year appointed Resident Magistrate and Civil Commissioner at Peddie. Published *Poems*. First son, Gerald Creigh, born.
1893   Late in the year a second son, Ernest Richards, born.
1894   Delivered lecture on "The Native Question" before the Lovedale Literary Society, February 23. Sent to Mount Frere, on the edge of Pondoland.
1895   "After a little more than a year and a half spent at Mount Frere . . . transferred to Nqamakwe, the largest and richest district in the Transkei proper. . . ." Remained about four years. A daughter, Miriam Power, was born in 1895. Published *Kafir Stories*.
1896   During summer had a vacation of several weeks at the seaside, near the mouth of the Kobonqaba River.
1897   Acted as chairman of the first district council set up at Nqamakwe under the Glen Gray Act. This was the terrible rinderpest year. Published *The White Hecatomb and Other Stories*.
1898   Volunteered to take charge of the Emjanyana Leper Asylum for a time. Ordered by his doctor to proceed to Europe and consult a specialist. Early in the year left Cape Town for England. Returned to Nqamakwe, after an absence of seven

Chronology

	months, in the (southern) spring of 1898. Published *Between Sun and Sand* and *A Vendetta of the Desert*, first novels.
1900	During the early years of the new century held appointments at Bredasdorp and Caledon.
1901	A daughter, Lilla Lucy Madeleine, was born.
1907	Published *By Veld and Kopje*, short stories.
1909	Last child, Ethne Elizabeth Emily, was born in February, soon after the family reached Port Elizabeth, Scully's last appointment.
1910	Published *Unconventional Reminiscences* in *The State*, 1910–1912.
1912	Publication of *The Ridge of the White Waters*, nonfiction.
1913	Published *Reminiscences of a South African Pioneer* and *Further Reminiscences of a South African Pioneer*.
1914	Retired from the Cape Civil Service at the end of the year.
1915	In the New Year Scully and Lilla joined Mrs. Scully and Betty in England. The family group crossed the Atlantic to the United States. After reaching Vancouver, Scully left the family there and went alone to South America. Rejoining the family in Victoria, he proceeded with them through the Canadian provinces and sailed for England and soon after for South Africa. Publication of *A History of South Africa* and *Lodges in the Wilderness*, nonfiction.
1917	Settled in Queenstown after returning from the longest of all the family journeys. Became acting magistrate at Lobatse, in Transvaal.
1919	Scully purchased land and built a house at Somerset Strand.
1921	Published *The Harrow*, novel, and *Sir J. H. Meiring Beck*, biography.
1923	Published *Daniel Vananda*, novel. Moved to Kimberley.
1937	Published *Scopalomine in Africa, Or Pharmacy and Politics*, satire.
1938	Honorary doctorate in literature from the University of Stellenbosch.
1940	Moved to Umbogintwini.
1943	Published *Voices of Africa*, poems and stories, which appeared before his death. Died at Umbogintwini, August 25.

CHAPTER 1

From Tipperary to South Africa Is a Long Way

THROUGH his poems, short stories, novels, and nonfictional prose, William Charles Scully, a thoroughly assimilated South African, revealed the impact of his varied experiences and his reaction to human existence as he understood it. Following his birth and childhood in Ireland, the future author entered a country far more interested in pioneers than poets. In 1867, at the age of twelve, he came to reside in a land as yet little influenced by the modern doctrine of progress. This condition was soon to change, under the shock of violent actions and reactions. Of these changes Scully was intensely aware. Having reached that time of life when a man dares look back upon his days and ways, he wrote, in the prefatory statement for his *Reminiscences*, "The period mainly dealt with is that magical one when South Africa—unnoted and obscure—was startled from the simplicity of her bucolic life by the discovery of gold and diamonds. This was, of course, some years before the fountains of her boundless potential wealth had become fully unsealed."[1] That William Scully was eminently qualified to present this era is elaborated upon by Field-Marshal Jan Christiaan Smuts in an introduction to a collection of Scully's stories and poems, published in 1943. Of the now retired elderly magistrate and author, Smuts wrote,

No one is more competent than he to interpret Africa to the reading public; no one has had a more varied and vivid and intimate knowledge of her ways of living and thinking. He has spent a lifetime in African administration; he has followed the absorbing trail of gold and diamonds; he has studied its native peoples with the curious and deep interest of a lover. He has felt the appeal of its scenery, of its tropical forests and jungles alternating with its grim deserts, its towering mountains, its vast curves of salubrious high table-lands and low malarial basins.

Above all he has felt, as few have felt, its intense human appeal—the immemorial past persisting unchanged through thousands of years, and confronted and disturbed to-day by the onrush of the newer currents of history; an aggressive Western civilisation impinging with rude awakening on the sleep of the ages from which the African peoples are only just emerging.[2]

Nothing said here would have availed had Scully not carried within himself one further quality. He possessed what was required to transform "varied and vivid and intimate knowledge" into poems and stories and novels—and finally into factual accounts of his experiences.

How thoroughly equipped W. C. Scully was as a writer can be estimated from the reviews of one of his fictional efforts. The following comments on *Between Sun and Sand* (1898) reveal an emphatic agreement about Scully as a novelist. "The innumerable writers with whom salvation by local colour is an article of faith should strive to discover from this book the way it is done." "He is master of the art of calling up for us the unknown as a visible, sensible presence that is not to be put by, but absorbs us and abides." "The most experienced reader will find the interest of absolute novelty." ". . . can be recommended to any one who appreciates the art of a well-written vigorous narrative." "Mr. Scully lavishes on his book a wealth of local colour, one-tenth of which would be a gold-mine to the average stay-at-home automatic novelist." "Apart from his exceptional gift of description, he can tell a story. . . . " 'Between Sun and Sand' is one of the most enthralling tales we have read in recent times."[3] Even had the reviewers quoted here been totally prejudiced in Scully's favor because of his subject matter, there is no reason for them to praise his literary methods.

I Down Irish Paths

Though William Charles Scully was born in Dublin, the family appears to have resided in County Tipperary since the seventeenth century.[4] His date of birth is given as October 29, 1855, and the place a house on Upper Gardiner Street.[5] Scully explains that the residence in Dublin was owned by a maternal uncle-by-marriage. His father was John Joseph Scully, of a family that had been landed gentry in Tipperary for many generations; his mother was Elizabeth Mary Creagh, of County Clare, the family being "reckoned among the leading gentry."[6] The boy's first recollections were of Abbeyview, near Cashel, where the Scullys lived until the early sixties. Ruins of the Abbey and its renowned "Rock" were visible from the front window of the Scully home. From Cashel the family moved to Springfield, located in a rugged pass of the Wicklow hills, south of Dublin.

When of school age, William was not allowed to attend because of "weak health," which persisted to within a year of the Scullys' departure for South Africa. At the age of seven, the boy learned to read but as yet could not write. Evidence, however, of an active young mind is suggested by his interest in playing chess—an addiction which led to more than one unusual childish adventure. As if playing chess, along with various childhood activities, were not enough, the ten-year-old boy decided that he wished to join the Royal Navy. Not only did he conceive the idea but acted upon it and offered himself to the Admiralty as a midshipman, albeit at the time he still could not write, and had to request an acquaintance to make the application for him. Undoubtedly it was his release from the normal inschool life of a growing boy that directed him into more than the normal number of youthful escapades.

Very early the traits which were to make Scully a poet and fictionist began to appear in his attitudes and activities. By the age of eleven, he had explored in the Wicklow environs any locality to which legends were attached. Later he wrote that "Every storied spot fascinated me. . . ."[7] His interest, however, in stories and the legendary materials of the area was even in childhood balanced by a careful attention to realistic detail. The family of his closest friend was sorely poverty-stricken, and William made every effort to increase the food supply of Jimmy Kinsella. The process showed not only a humanitarian attitude but also a simple awareness of the flora and fauna of his region. Hazelnuts were collected and stored. In season he gathered mushrooms, wild strawberries, blackberries, vegetables from the Scully garden, rabbits snared in the woods, and on rare occasions one of Lord Powerscourt's pheasants. Then, too, there were fish from the lake and streams. All of this distinctly foreshadowed his interest in similar features of the regions of South Africa to which he soon was to be introduced.

In Scully's childhood the desire for solitude as well as the more normal actions of men were also manifested. As an adult he was strongly attracted to the desert areas of the Cape, very especially the Bushmanland desert, which became very important in two of his novels and one nonfictional volume. As boys, attempting to escape from civilization, he and Jimmy secretly constructed a hut in one of the remote areas of a Wicklow larch wood. This they stocked with cooking and eating utensils. When all was ready, they disappeared one afternoon and assumed residence in their hideaway. Their hopes, however, were frustrated. One of Jimmy's brothers tracked them during their preparations and now revealed the information. Thus, about midnight of their first evening alone, William was awakened when the glare of a lantern held by his father was put close to his eyes. On this occasion, he was forced to return to the abode of conventional beings. In South Africa, he was at times to be more successful in his escapes.

An interest in experiment and adventure was revealed when, after reading about volcanoes, young William became anxious to construct one. He and Jimmy carried this project to completion in the Scully toolhouse. Almost a pound of gunpowder was placed in a can to which they attached a fuse. Around this they built a volcanic cone of wet clay. The center hole was filled with dry sand and fragments of brick. From one point of view, the experiment was a total success: a frightful explosion occurred. All windows were knocked from the toolhouse; the boys were thrown against the wall; bits of brick had to be picked from the face of each. As an adult, Scully engaged in a more controlled use of gunpowder—though he carried the experimental spirit with him through a long life.

II *To the Cape*

At this period of history it was not unusual for English, Scottish, or Irish families to emigrate for economic reasons. The Scully family was one of these. William explained that "In 1867 a disastrous lawsuit with the Marquis of Bute over some mining rights in Wales almost brought ruin to our door."[8] Several parts of the world were considered, but South Africa was selected as their new home. Of the three daughters, only the oldest went to the Cape. The other son, younger than William, remained behind in school. Early in November 1867, the Scullys left Dublin on a small steamer named *Lady Eglinton*, bound for Falmouth, from which they sailed on the *Asia*. The weather was excellent as they moved through the Bay of Biscay, but as the ship passed the Cape of Finisterre a gale struck, and the ship "behaved like a drunken porpoise."[9] The storm did not abate until they reached the vicinity of the Madeira Islands. Later Scully recorded that he had never forgotten "the enchanting prospect which Funchal afforded as . . . [the ship moved to its] anchorage in the early morning. The misery of the previous week was forgotten in the rapture of a moment. . . . What joy the first sight, smell, and taste of the tropical fruits brought."[10] Passing to the west of the Canary Islands in perfectly clear weather, the ship offered an excellent view of Teneriffe, over twelve thousand feet above the sea. Scully observed that "The recent storms encountered by us had extended far to the south; consequently the great peak was clothed in dazzling snow to an unusual distance below its summit. The impression left on my memory by that mountain mass, with the snow-mantle glowing in the rose-red light of sunset, will never fade."[11] All went well until they approached the Cape. Then a violent southwest gale struck and battered the ship for two days, but finally the "poor old tub" steamed into Table Bay. It was mid-December, summer at the Cape. Scully was impressed with the variety of fruits available in the market, the strange dress of the Malays, and the unknown languages around him. After about a week in Cape Town, the ship sailed on to Port Elizabeth, their destination, which was reached on Christmas Eve. The Scullys were carried ashore through the surf, a normal process here.

What William remembered most favorably about the first days in Port Elizabeth was South African hospitality. He felt that the friendliness with which they were received was genuine rather than conduct guided by form or dictated as a duty. Grahamstown, however, was their ultimate goal; so, after a brief time in Port Elizabeth, an ox-wagon was engaged for the trip. Six days were needed to bring them to the City of Saints and Settlers. During their first week in Grahamstown, they were the guests of Judge and Mrs. Fitzpatrick. When young men together in Dublin, the elder Scully and the present judge had occupied chambers together. William recorded his admiration for the excellence of the judge's orchard, especially the apricots. In addition to fine fruits, this family also produced one of the most widely read and loved books in South African literature. *Jock of the Bushveld* (1907) by Sir Percy Fitzpatrick, is the story of a dog who goes with his owner on transport journeys in the Old Transvaal and is important for the creation of the physical aspects of the country at that time.

The Scullys moved to King William's Town when they were unable after six weeks to secure a suitable farm in the Grahamstown area. Ultimately a farm called "Sunny Slope" was hired near Maclean Town and stocked with eight hundred sheep and a few cattle. It did not require long for the new arrivals to understand that they were not likely to be successful as farmers. Conditions at the moment were not favorable, nor did the family have the needed agricultural or herding experience. Thus the farm was given up, and the Scullys returned to King William's Town. The sheep, however, were not sold, their market value having declined since the time of purchase. Arrangements were made for pasturage some five miles from town. William was placed in school, where he remained for something more than half a year. The lower school at that period was under the direction of G. McC. Theal, who later became widely known for his studies in South African history. This brief period was to be the extent of William's formal education.

During the June holidays, 1869, William with Mr. Samuel and two school fellows undertook what he considered his first South African adventure, an expedition into the Transkei. While making a visit to the mission station of Tiyo Soga, at Tutura, the party was invited to go with the Sogas on their annual holiday at the seaside. The group accepted and started for a spot at the mouth of the Kobonqaba. William rode most of the way beside Tiyo Soga himself and listened to him recite Wordsworth, especially "The Excursion," when passages from that particular poem appeared appropriate in relation to the country through which they were travelling. The author to be had never heard of Wordsworth, but here as he rode through one of the areas of Africa he was being introduced to the poet of the English lakes by a man who had emerged from a tribal civilization. One wishes Wordsworth could have known of the episode. Among the various experiences of this holiday, the one perhaps farthest from Wordsworth was Scully's first sight of a pack of the wild dogs of Africa.

When William returned home after his vacation, he learned that the sheep needed attention which they were not receiving. His father hired a farm some ten miles from town and accepted his son's offer to take charge of the flock. The boy was not yet fourteen, but the task for which he had volunteered was the work of a man. It was at this moment that William Scully abandoned his childhood and turned towards whatever adult life might hold for him in Africa. There was no house to receive the new master of the flock; so a tent had to serve. The labor force was composed of one Kaffir boy named Toby, who was identified by lips that "resembled sausages strung across his face. . . ."[12] All went well while novelty remained as a companion. Following the departure of this visitor, monotony arrived and took up permanent residence. Soon everything came to an end, not merely monotony. One day William went out with the sheep and left Toby to cook dinner. There was too much wind to light an outside fire; so

From Tipperary to South Africa Is a Long Way

William consented to Toby's suggestion of a fire in the tent, though the cook was warned of the danger. The warning was wise but did not prevent everything being converted into a pile of ashes. Toby resigned his place without notice and allowed William to discover the disaster. Thus ended W. C. Scully's first experience in the adult world. His second was of even shorter duration, working for a trader whose post was near the kraal (tribal village) of the widely known Chief Sandile, the Gaika Reserve, in the vicinity of Tembani. Young Scully was discharged as incompetent. Later he accepted the evaluation as just, but he was probably wrong. Actually it was not so much incompetence as a total lack of interest in the mercantile processes. What he brought away with him was a memory of Sandile, a memory later converted into a character sketch worthy of being recorded.

. . . Sandile, who possessed enormous influence with his powerful and warlike tribe, was a man utterly wanting in dignity. He was club-footed, and consequently went very lame. I remember being once sent on a message to his kraal. He came to know that I had a threepenny-piece, so began begging for this. He paid no heed to my refusal, but clung to my stirrup-leather and dragged himself after me for nearly half a mile, begging in the most abject terms. I am glad to be able to say that I kept the coin. But Sandile was a brave man; he died the death of a soldier in the Gaika Rebellion of 1878.[13]

Within this brief passage several of the characteristics that make writing effective, whether fiction or nonfiction, will be found. The sketch is developed from the claim that Sandile lacked dignity. The mere assertion is then supported by the use of a specific incident, which is given a setting. Thus a reader knows where he is and exactly what is happening. The author ends the action by ascending the abstraction ladder, with the word "abject." Then he presents another aspect of Sandile's character. The contrast assures a reader of the genuineness of the portrait, for Sandile possesses inconsistency. As Scully closes the passage, he descends to the foot of the abstraction ladder to give the place, time, and circumstances of Sandile's end. Methods enumerated here were employed regularly by Scully in both fiction and nonfiction.

III *Sparkling Elusiveness*

While not indifferent to the economic aspects of acquiring such stones as diamonds, emeralds, and rubies, man is perhaps guided more by his imagination than his reason in seeking to possess these small exquisite packages created in the depths of the natural world.

Thus, when word that diamonds had been found went out across the South African bergs and veld, the imagination of thousands turned in the direction of a locality soon to be spoken of as Kimberley. Many only speculated upon what it would be like to find a diamond of many carats; others built or bought a wagon and started for the "fields." The assortment of humanity soon assembled in the mining area was extensively depicted by Scully in his *Reminiscences*. He himself represented one category—a boy of fourteen, recently out from Ireland, with no skill or experience, but with an active imagination. Though William was there without his family, he calls attention to the presence of many families. Thus, in the evenings, there were girls in print dresses, coffee and rusks, music from various instruments and also the human voice—indeed, a scene very different from that usually associated with a mining camp. Certainly many very strange characters appeared, but not as yet an influx of evil men. Inevitably these would arrive, but the percentage was much higher in the gold mines of the Rand than the diamond diggings or when gold was found in the Lydenburg area. In the very early days, the search for diamonds was often made by small groups, frequently only two men in partnership. For a while, at least, the integrity of the whole was maintained by the integrity of the individuals, many of them recently from the homesteads of the veld.

As might be expected, one of the most serious problems of life in the mining area was a lack of simple sanitation—closely related, of course, to a scarcity of doctors, nurses—and water. In the summer of 1871, William (along with many others) had enteric (typhoid) fever. Convinced that he would die if he could not get away from the fields, the boy took a coach to Queenstown. He collapsed on the journey, but kind passengers cared for him until he arrived. After several days of rest, he was able to take the postcart for King William's Town. Several weeks at home brought him out of danger, and soon he was ready for a return to the fields. This time he purchased his own wagon and equipment. As he travelled back to the diggings, he transported a load of onions for sale once he arrived, since fresh food was always in demand.

When William reached the fields, he was the guest of Major Drury, formerly of the Cape Mounted Riflemen. Messing together at this time were Major Drury, Dr. Thorne (formerly of Queenstown), George Paton (afterwards the representative in Parliament of Barkly West), H. C. Becher (subsequently well known in Hatton Gardens), and Cecil John, and Herbert Rhodes. Soon a third Rhodes brother arrived. This was Frank, now sixteen. Of him Scully later wrote, "I have never met any one possessing such charm of manner as did Frank Rhodes at this period."[14] Camped a few yards from the mess tent used by the above group were Norman Garstin and "Tommy" Townsend, his partner. Garstin later became a noted painter. Others with whom Scully became acquainted at this time were H. C. Seppings Wright, who became an artist on the staff of the *Illustrated London News;* Archibald Campbell, later distinguished in the Russo-Turkish War; and Reginald Fairlie, who became a painter. These and others formed an amazing collection of men occupying a very small plot of ground at Kimberley in the early 1870s.

Even in his teens, Scully was aware that Cecil Rhodes was concerned with things outside of all that was physically present around them. He has left the following paragraph as evidence of his early observation.

. . . After dinner it was his wont to lean forward with both elbows on the table and his mouth slightly open. He had a habit, when thinking, of rubbing his chin gently with his forefinger. Very often he would sit in the attitude described for a very long time, without joining in whatever conversation happened to be going on. His manner and expression suggested that his thoughts were far away, but occasionally some interjection would indicate that, to a certain extent, he was keeping in touch with the current topic. Indeed, it often seemed to me that the larger part of his brain was dealing with something of which no one else had cognizance. Mr. George Paton used to banter him severely for this peculiarity, but the banter was always taken in good part.[15]

Scully's account of settling the price of a wagon he had furnished for an expedition led by Herbert Rhodes is much more homely. William insisted on £30; Cecil offered £25. Finally they decided to determine the price on the basis of a game of euchre, the best two of three hands. A bag of mealie meal was used as a table, and the players sat on the ground. At Groote Schuur in 1894, Scully reminded Rhodes of the incident and found he remembered every detail.

Preserving stories of this kind is important as a balance to the later conduct of Rhodes, when he was much better known to the world. Twenty years after the period at Kimberley, Scully reported on the situation in the following manner.

Mr. Rhodes, during his Premiership of the Cape Colony, annexed Pondoland, the last independent native state south of the Zambezi. This happened in 1894. I was offered a magistracy in the Native Territories, but although I had for long taken a keen interest in all branches of Native administration, I declined the offer. My main reason for so doing was that I did not wish to take my family to regions so remote from civilization. . . .

However, Mr. Rhodes called me to Cape Town, and there he persuaded me to fall in with his wishes. He promised that if I would enter the Native Department he would, at the first opportunity, advance me to a Chief Magistracy. He was, he explained, unable to do so just then on account of the jealousy such an appointment would cause among my seniors. . . .

One night when dining at Groote Schuur, the conversation turned to the subject of Native administration. I expressed an opinion adverse to that advanced by Mr. Rhodes on a certain point, and he at once became extremely rude. Next morning Sir Sydney Shippard, who had been present, spoke to me about the matter. He condemned our host's conduct in most unmeasured terms, and added:

"As a matter of fact Rhodes has been for so long surrounded by men who defer to him in every way, and hang on his every utterance as though it were that of an oracle, that he can no longer brook even a difference of opinion."[16]

Though Scully accepted the appointment, he sent his family to Fort Beaufort before starting to the scene of his new activities, which were to become very important to him in many ways.

IV *When Gold Glitters*

Life at Kimberley had filled Scully's head with stories that sparkled more brilliantly than did his coffers with diamonds. Therefore, in 1873, when gold was said to have been discovered in the Lydenburg area, he started for Pilgrim's Rest hoping to acquire more of the "precious bane" than he had of the precious gems at Kimberley. Again Fortune was not kind, but his life became rich in experiences. At the site of the diamond diggings and the gold mines, he was able to witness crucial events in the growth of South Africa. As an Irish lad he brought to the situation somewhat greater detachment than might have been possible had he been South African born or even of English birth.

Careful distinction should be made between the gold-mining activities at Pilgrim's Rest in the early 1870s and what the world remembers when gold was discovered on the Witwatersrand in the middle 1880s. The search at Pilgrim's Rest very much resembled what had happened during the early days of the diggings at Kimberley. Groups of miners were small, and the human situation was similar. Scully is very definite about the life which he observed around him.

Pilgrim's Rest, during the first few years after gold had been discovered there, was an interesting and delightful place. Those whose experience of mining camps is limited to ones in which the syndicate or the company holds sway, can form no idea of the life of a community where the individual digger is dominant. I am prepared to maintain that life was healthier, saner, and on the whole more generally satisfactory at Pilgrim's Rest in the early seventies than it is in any South African community to-day. There was, of course, the inevitable percentage of loafers, idlers, and scoundrels, but these were kept in their proper place. Public opinion was a very effective force; in matters affecting the general welfare of the community, opinion quickly translated itself into action when the occasion demanded it. Thus the blackguards knew perfectly well that if official justice occasionally halted, its unofficial equivalent was apt to be short, sharp, and decisive in its operation.[17]

During his years in the gold fields, Scully was on more than one occasion passed over by Fortune. The irony of one of these rejections is rather special. At the time, William's tent covered the gold he sought—indeed, the legs of his bunk were apparently sunk in the gold for which he was digging elsewhere. Because of his yielding to a request that he remain a little longer in the employ of a group for which he was working and because of a technicality concerning the registration of a claim while connected with a company, he lost the area upon which his tent stood—and gold amounting to some £4,000.

Scully does not appear to have been embittered by his "ill fortune in not finding diamonds or gold." In truth, though he may not have known it at the time, he seems to have been too deeply concerned with the country and the people with whom he was associated to give much time to brooding over his lack of funds. It has already been twice observed that Scully was very fond of fresh fruit. Thus he would certainly be expected to grow ecstatic over the plentiful quantities of wild peaches discovered in the vicinity of the gold mines. Immediately he begins to speculate upon the origin of superior peaches on the flats of Pilgrim's Creek, along the Blyde River terraces, and in many of the valleys. The locality and arrangement of the trees excluded the possibility of conscious planting. Their presence must have resulted from chance; here Fortune had been thoughtful in affording mankind so much luscious fruit, just where it was useful and would be appreciated.

Never satisfied until he knew what was beyond the next mountain ridge, Scully soon began to use his weekends for exploration. From Pilgrim's Rest to the divide was a hike of several hours. Here he would camp Saturday night and at dawn move on to the edge of the cliffs. Visibility across the Low Country was always limited. Once, on an especially clear day, he had a glimpse of the Lebomba Range. In the seventies little was known of this region. No maps existed, and thus knowledge of its geography was vague. There were great rivers, yes—Crocodile, Komati, Olifant, Letaba, and Limpopo. An infinite variety of big game inhabited the region, but so did fatal fevers, from November to May inclusive. Man, as usual, had to learn by experience the presence of danger. Scully reports that in 1873 thirty-five men descended to the Low Country during the hot season. Only eight lived to remember the experience. Today some of the land Scully tried to see through its constant haze has become part of the great Kruger game reserve. Here the animals live in the habitat intended by nature, and man is excluded for more than half the year. The new arrangement has proved wiser than the old one.

Near the end of his gold-mining days, Scully made the most extensive of all his early expeditions. With one companion and two bearers, he started from Pilgrim's Rest with Swaziland as his destination. He was following the trail of a group of Australian prospectors who had gone to the land of the Swazis in 1875. This undertaking became a genuine adventure. There were rugged mountain areas to be "negotiated" and flooded rivers to be crossed. The Crocodile River almost took the life of his companion, who had to be left to recuperate, while Scully moved on with only his bearers. One day, when the group had travelled until dark, they stopped on a steep slope. The space was filled with a dense white mist. When morning came and a breeze from the west cleared the mist, they discovered themselves on the northern verge of the Great Kaap Basin. Across the valley were the mountains of Swaziland. Having reached the other side of the Basin at the end of the following day, Scully camped beside a peak of granite which turned out to be inhabited by a pack of baboons. At intervals during the night, there were skirmishes and at times general fights among the animals. When this happened, stones came crashing down and endangered the camp. Entering Swaziland, he followed the trail of the Australian prospectors until the direction turned suddenly westward. William concluded that the party had abandoned its quest and decided to return through a part of the Transvaal known as New Scotland.

Disappointed in his own fruitless search, Scully began retracing his steps towards the Crocodile River, where he had left his companion. He stopped at the kraal of an induna (headman or councilor) named

'Ntshindeen, who had been kind to him as he entered the country. Physically exhausted and almost starved, he paused for more than a week. Here he was treated as if he were a person of importance. He thought perhaps the attention shown him resulted from his very youthful appearance. Finally, however, the host suggested to his guest that he was in danger because of a deadly enmity existing between the Swazis and the Bapedi tribe—to which his bearers belonged. The warning was wise, for Scully had to lead his two bearers away from the kraal with his gun raised, both barrels cocked and obviously trained upon their adversaries. That his danger was not imagined was confirmed when soon after this a prospector had his two Bapedi boys killed in his presence.

Several days were required to reach the Crocodile River, where he joined his companion. After some exploration in the river valley, the partners started in the direction of Pilgrim's Rest, having been deserted by their bearers. For some days Scully had felt that he was developing a case of fever. Before he reached Pilgrim's Rest he was taken in by Mr. (later Sir Drummond) and Mrs. Dunbar and nursed until he was out of danger. The trip brought no gold, but he had learned much about the country and about human beings. Of the Swazis as a tribe, he wrote, "After a somewhat wide experience I can truthfully say that the Swazis, at the time I knew them, were the finest savages I ever came in contact with."[18]

Only gradually as his strength returned was he able to do the work of digging and panning for gold. Then, however, he located a spot which would have produced gold had there been water for the washing process. Awaiting the rain normally expected at this season of the year, he built a reservoir with trenches leading to a sluice box. Everything was ready for the rains, but no rains came. Days became weeks, and weeks months, but no rain fell. On Christmas eve he struck his tent and descended the mountain. The spot upon which he had expended this great labor later became known as the Theta Mine, one of the best of those belonging to the Transvaal Gold Mining Estates Company. This time an enormous fortune had escaped him because of the weather. Scully decided to leave the gold fields and return to the Cape, through Natal. Travelling as a tramp, he started southwest on January 3, 1876. At this moment he was nearer his twentieth than his twenty-first birthday. After twenty-four days and more than twenty-four adventures he entered Durban late in the afternoon of January 27. Three weeks of searching for work in Durban brought no success. At this time he went to the agent of the Union

Line, told him his situation, and asked that he be given on credit a deck passage to East London, upon a promise to pay out of the first money he could earn. The agent knew the Scully family and let William have the ticket on credit. The next day he left on the *Basuto* and reached East London the following afternoon. He was united with his family and soon found work with the Boating Company. The work was hard and dangerous. Moreover, he suffered constantly from seasickness. After some four months, he was unexpectedly relieved of his job. A letter from the Civil Commissioner asked him to call at the office. When Scully appeared before this government official, he was offered a place as "clerk on probation to the Resident Magistrate of Tarka." The salary was set at £120 per year. Scully explains that the offer was made because his "father and the then Lord Carnarvon, who happened to be Colonial Secretary, had been friends in the old days. Lord Carnarvon wrote to Government House, Cape Town, asking that something might be done for us. My father was beyond the age-limit; I, clearly, was not. . . ."[19]

During the months with the Boating Company, Scully had worked each day in a copybook, making every effort to improve his handwriting. He confessed, however, that his hand still held a trigger or a pick with more ease than a pen. His spelling, he says, was phonetic. Though he knew by heart most of Shakespeare's sonnets, he did not know any of the rules of English grammar. Yet he decided to accept the offer, saying, "I had faced lions on the Lebomba and crocodiles in the Komati; why should I quail before a mere magistrate?"[20] Acting upon this reasoning, Scully left East London May 22, 1876, and arrived in Tarkastad May 27. He assumed his duties June 1.

CHAPTER 2

In the Service of Government

WHEREVER William Charles Scully went, he found people interesting to him and conversely people interested in him. The first category was always more numerous. Even before he was conscious of it, his life was being devoted to a study of human beings and their total environment. During the years at Kimberley and at Pilgrim's Rest, most of his physical effort, though never most of his conscious mind, was focused upon diamonds and then gold. After reaching Tarkastad, as soon as he was able to understand the nature of this new work in the Cape Civil Service and came to perceive what was expected of him, he began to look around at the inhabitants of the community. Slowly he sensed an attitude he had never before encountered. "My experiences," he wrote, "had made me different from those among whom I lived, and, quite involuntarily, they disliked me. . . ."

> For years past I had been dealing with the sternest realities of life; I had been face to face with danger in various forms, and the discipline I had undergone was searching and severe. I had had to grapple with almost elemental forces, to fight battles in which the mere doubtful grace of survival was the only prize of victory. But all this had left me utterly ignorant of the amenities of any communal life except that of the strenuous fabric of which I had been such an insignificant strand. And this community was so utterly different; its members seemed to be steeped in triviality and unreason. Nevertheless, I longed with all my soul to be on friendly terms with those among whom I lived. But the more I strove in this direction the more cruelly I was rebuffed. . . .
> In those dark days I often longed passionately for the old, hard life. . . .
> I felt like a wild hawk penned in a poultry yard, with talons clipped— exposed to the peckings of a lot of corn-fed roosters.[1]

Nothing here suggests an injured ego, merely a natural desire for human companionship. Scully immediately did one thing that was needed, and when occasion permitted, he performed an action which established his popularity, especially with the men. First, since there was ample time, he began to read and study with the intention of compensating for his lack of formal education. Once started, his studies never ceased, since the passion for knowledge was as intense as that for adventure. Studies, however, were not likely to increase his popularity in the village. If anything, they would have the opposite effect. The lonely young man had to await developments. Soon an opportunity came. New Year's Eve was the occasion selected for Scully's disgrace, but events did not develop as the enemy planned. A group of the men invited the new clerk to a party at the local hotel. It was to be an alcoholic affair. A trusted friend warned Scully what to expect. He was to be insulted and drawn into a fight. Even the man to do this had been selected. He was large and powerful; Irish William was small and certainly not a person of great strength. Yet, with advance information, he was able to consider what he might do to protect himself. Not a drinker (indeed, this was one of the grievances against him), at the celebration he carefully managed to dispose of his drinks without consuming them. Then, too, he had observed his opponent enough to know that while he was powerful, he was not very alert in his movements. Though Scully noted that on this particular evening he was throwing his drinks in the fire, the new arrival had lived long enough in Tarkastad to have learned that dissipation on the part of this person was likely to mean he was not in good physical training. Scully was aware that he himself was quick on his feet, tough, had good wind, and was accustomed to tests of endurance. Thus he planned the encounter as one of delaying action. As midnight approached, the enemy proceeded almost with the regularity of the ticking clock in the "big room" of the hotel. As twelve sounded, the company hailed the New Year. Scully, wishing everyone the greetings of the season, started towards the door. As he expected, the man chosen as his opponent intercepted him and called him a foul name. Scully accepted the challenge, and everyone followed the combatants into the street. There was a full moon, and New Year's in South Africa meant the middle of the summer.

As Scully had anticipated, his adversary came at him like an angry rhino making a charge. Each rush, the quicker, smaller man evaded. Soon the challenger was breathing hard. Now Scully began to execute the second phase of his plan—first, four swift jabs to the nose; later, a blow on the ear, which dropped the big man to the ground. Scully now offered to stop the proceedings, but his opponent refused. Later, when Scully was fouled, he turned what he had considered a contest into a genuine fight. Finally, he left his insulter down and in a state almost beyond recognition. Weeks under the care of a doctor were required to restore him to normal. Meanwhile, an inspection of the post office, where the man was in charge, revealed an irregularity. He was dismissed and the place given to Scully, along with the £36 a year. The reason for recalling this whole story is to mention the effect on the community. Seemingly the loser took his defeat as he assumed a sportsman should; and the town which had rejected a serious, clean-living, hard-working young man now accepted the same person for winning a completely unnecessary fight. This was perhaps the first event to teach the new Civil Servant the ways of "civilized man."

How William Charles Scully managed to hold his position during the early years of his thirty-eight with the Cape Civil Service is at least one of the minor mysteries of life. Bureaucratic methods disturbed him beyond endurance. Very early in his career, while for a brief period he was acting magistrate, he was reprimanded by telegram for allowing the Excise officer to receive large sums of money. Scully replied that this person had not received a single sixpence of the reported revenue. Next a telegram came asking why this lowly officer had signed the monthly abstract reporting the revenue received. Scully replied that this man had not signed the abstract and in the reply requested that the papers be returned to him for inspection. When the materials arrived, he verified the fact that he himself had signed the abstract as acting magistrate and the Chief Constable, according to law, as Excise officer, had signed the certificate (added to the abstract) indicating that any spirits on which duty had been paid was not in excess of the "proof" specified. Scully marked each signature with a large "X" in red ink and returned the report. Now by post he was informed that the abstract had been received; a letter explained "that the misunderstanding arose owing to the illegibility of his [the Acting Magistrate and Civil Commissioner] signature and the consequent difficulty of distinguishing it from that of the Excise officer."[2] Scully observed that the signature of the Excise officer, who had signed the certificate, was in a flowing hand which filled the page from one side to the other, while his own "W. C. Scully" would have fitted inside one of the flourishes of the other signature. It must be added that examples of Scully's signature show that it was quite legible. Behind this story there is a delightful bit of irony. The office from which all of the queries originated was presided over by a man whose signature was indeed illegible. Scully himself was unaware of this gentleman s identity until an associate told him from whose hand the signature had come. This was the first, but not the only, time that Scully reminded headquarters of how stupid it could be. He found great difficulty in accepting the practice which proclaimed the superior officer was always right and headquarters was guilty of no errors.

Studies that Scully had initiated in East London and Tarkastad were at least in the beginning elementary, but very important mental stimulation came two years later when he was assigned to Graaff Reinet. There he met a man, Charles Rubidge, who was, Scully believed, the first original thinker he had known. Though half a century separated the two, the younger man took delight in the relationship. In early life Charles Rubidge had secured a piece of desert land at the foot of the Sneeuwberg Range and by an ingenious use of dams had provided water with which to become a successful farmer, orchardist, breeder of fine sheep, and a conservationist of wild life. He was widely read and interested in ancient writing as well as modern developments of practical value to him. He told William that he had always been intellectually lonely. If Scully ever looked back upon his days and some of the events in Tarkastad, he now understood better his first experience of isolation from society. Charles Rubidge taught him that "Loneliness is the heavy penalty which Nature imposes upon originality."[3]

Scully immediately began a study of botany under Professor P. MacOwan when he was sent in 1882 to Cape Town as a clerk in the Colonial Secretary's office. The junior clerk used his lunch hour for this instruction and found the professor not only a competent scientist but "the wisest and sanest man with whom [he, Scully, had] ever come into contact, and he generously placed his ample store of sound, human philosophy at [his] disposal."[4]

Both happiness and sadness attended Scully during this period of his life. Here he married Ellen Doveton, who died at the birth of the first child, Elaine, in 1883. For this crucial period, his wife had gone to be with her family. Scully was never to see Ellen again. Elaine was raised by her aunts. When his first volume of poems was issued in 1886, it was dedicated to his wife who, he wrote, changed life from "grief to joy." Yet her passing from the mortal scene returned him to days of grief. Though at all times Scully avoided the presentation of family affairs, even in his autobiographical writing, he felt free to use in his poems that which was closest to him. The child playing beside the mother's grave in "Traditur dies die" would seem to present

Elaine and Ellen Scully in the Cape Town setting, though this must have been imaginative. There is also a sonnet "To Elaine," the final three lines of which state,

> I wait thy waking smile that, sure, will bring
> A message from the loved lips of the Dead,
> And on us both a spirit's sheltering wing.[5]

From Cape Town Scully was transferred to Stockenstrom, where he knew he would find ample opportunity to use in the field what he had learned as a student under Professor MacOwan. All available hours were employed in exploring the mountains for rare flora, and specimens were sent to Professor MacOwan for distribution to herbaria in Europe and America. In this same period, to G. F. Scott Elliott, naturalist and traveller in Africa and South America, he supplied specimens of rare plants. It was through him that he sent to the University of Edinburgh a valuable collection. Afterwards Scully was made an honorary fellow of the University. From all that is said here, it might appear that he was interested only in flora that were collected and classified. Quite the opposite is true. Of his explorations at Stockenstrom, he wrote, "Many days I spent wandering in the fairyland of the then unspoiled Katberg forests, gathering ferns, orchids, and other floral treasures. What a joy it was to find, deep in the remotest fold of some craig-surrounded, forest-filled valley, the wonder of some rare, seldom-flowering gardenia, and to gather into one's nostrils the lavished richness of its unparalleled perfume. . . ."[6] Nor was he attracted only to wild nature. When opportunity permitted, he planted at Nqamakwe both an orchard and a flower garden. The former contained the most improved varieties of fruit trees, and his rose garden displayed more than eighty kinds.

With the extra money Scully received from the post office appointment at Tarkastad, he was able to purchase a pony and gun. The area abounded in the various buck of South Africa, and the young clerk seems to have kept the magistrate in ample supply of his favorite meat. At Aberdeen he found hares by the thousands, together with partridges, korhaan, and steenbok. While at Colesberg, he added wild geese and duck to the list of game he had been hunting. When he was appointed to Fort Beaufort, he found awaiting him such a plenitude of game that at one time he counted sixteen different varieties in his pantry. Though Scully had hunted most of the game of South Africa, both large and small, he considered the chase of the oryx an experience above all others. This noble animal he pursued in the Bushmanland desert. He spoke of the chase of the oryx as a "transcendent experience." *Lodges in the Wilderness* offers a detailed account of a hunt in which he participated—with success, it should be noted. (See Chapter 7.)

Because Scully had brought charges against the magistrate under whom he worked at Aberdeen, he created a very difficult problem for headquarters to handle. During this period it was the routine practice to make all decisions in favor of the superior officer of a district and against anyone under him. In this situation, however, the charge was serious and proof conclusive. Headquarters was saved by an unexpected turn of events. Opportunely, Major Nesbitt requested that Scully accept a commission as lieutenant in his corps, then at the front in the Tembu war. The young clerk agreed and soon was enrolling men for "Nesbitt's Horse." Before him now lay an entirely new series of adventures.

Having collected his men and given them at least some training, Scully moved into the Transkei and ultimately joined Colonel Wavell in Tembuland, near Bashee Hoek. Very little fighting was necessary, and upon the cessation of the conflict he was ordered to join Carrington in Basutoland. At this juncture Colonel Wavell received a dispatch informing him that two hundred men of "The Cape Town Rangers" had refused to march. They were located at Clarkbury, about forty miles to the rear. Knowing that Scully had legal knowledge and experience, his commanding officer selected him to return and preside at the court-martial. The young lieutenant-judge found the situation a chaotic one. The men were drunk and still armed. Nor were the officers sober enough to help. Any attempt to reason with the men failed. Scully spent most of the night drawing up the necessary legal documents, and next morning arraigned the men before him—with packing-cases serving as the judge's bench. He read the charges and then heard evidence from the soberest of the officers. Two officers were named to serve with Scully on the court. One of these fell over, half-asleep, on his packing-case, the other wept. At the conclusion of the trial, Scully pronounced all the men guilty and sentenced them to six months at hard labor. With his horse saddled and ready, the judge did not remain at the scene of these special activities. He rode to the nearest telegraph office, filed his report, and asked for an armed guard to convey the men to prison. The guard was sent, and the mutineers served the sentence imposed.

Returning to the Civil Service, Scully held appointments at

Seymour, Cape Town, and Colesberg and was then assigned as Resident Magistrate to Namaqualand. He went by ship from Cape Town to Port Nolloth and then by rail to the O'okiep copper mines. Five miles beyond was the residency, at Springbokfontein. Here he was to have an opportunity to explore the very special qualities of the Bushmanland desert. Not only was he able to collect for Professor MacOwan specimens enough to fill seven large packing-cases but his experiences (together with those of a second period a few years later) resulted in three of his finest books. Yet Namaqualand also held for him an ordeal which he called "the grimmest and most appalling experience of my official career. I little expected, when I assumed duty at that remote village among the granite mountains, that within three days I would touch the skirts of terror and tragedy, and that for the following three months I would be preoccupied in the investigation of a series of horrors of their kind more piteous than anything else that the tragic annals of South Africa record."[7]

Within hours after the assumption of his duties, he realized that there was something very strange about the conduct of his jailer (gaoler). On the second morning evidence began to rush towards him after the loosening of one rock started a mountain slide. The crucial rock was pried loose in the form of an unlocked door. In making the routine inspection he always performed when he came to a place, the magistrate approached a locked cell, isolated from the main yard. He instructed the jailer to open the door but was rudely told that the cell was empty. Nevertheless, insisted the magistrate, he had to inspect every area before he could take charge; therefore, he demanded that the door be opened. The jailer protested that he did not have the key. Then the key must be produced at once. Under what the jailer now understood as an official order, he brought the key and unlocked the door. No previous experience had prepared the magistrate for the scene before him.

The season was winter; the day was cold and damp. The south-west wind was blowing up scud, but there were occasional bursts of sunshine. Just then the sun was shining, but the walls of the yard were high, and it was only on one of the lintels of the cell door that the sunlight struck. Leaning against the doorpost, in an endeavour to get as much of the sun's heat as possible to his body, was a tall, elderly coloured man of mixed race. He wore only two garments—a short pair of breeches . . . and a very small jacket. . . . The man was attenuated almost to a skeleton, and was covered from head to foot with scars and ulcers. The tears were streaming down his haggard cheeks; his teeth were chattering, and he trembled from head to foot. As I gazed, spellbound, at this tragic figure, it collapsed in a huddled heap to the floor, and there lay, motionless.[8]

To the magistrate's demand for an explanation, the jailer replied that the prisoner was a lunatic. This was not a reason, the magistrate said, for keeping an ill man out of the hospital. The jailer's defense was that he had been an attendant at Robben Island and knew how to treat lunatics. The magistrate rejected this point of view and removed the prisoner to the hospital. Four months of special care were necessary to enable the man to rise from his bed. Recovery revealed not an insane person but a prisoner being tortured and starved. Jail records showed that fourteen had died during the preceding eight months of the current year. This figure put the jail Scully had just inherited in a position of having forty-two times as many deaths as comparable places throughout the Cape. Scully learned that no inquests were held and no medical examination made when a prisoner died, though not previously reported sick. The first "case" the new magistrate encountered had not been recorded as sick.

On the third day, as he arrived at the jail, he discovered that all of the prisoners had been sent out to gather firewood. On his orders they returned and were assembled for inspection. When he explained that they could say whatever they wished with safety, "Some of the prisoners flung up their hands and began to laugh wildly; others sank to the ground and wept. A heap of them flung themselves about my knees, clasping my legs and shrieking."[9] It became necessary for the magistrate to retreat to his office and interview the men singly. As the testimony of depraved brutality accumulated, the questioner found that any belief in a hell here-after had become completely unnecessary. It was spread before him. When he called the doctor who was substituting for the District Surgeon, at present on leave, Scully discovered he was dealing with a character who was as insensitive in one way as the jailer was depraved in another. Asked why he had failed to investigate any of these deaths, the doctor said, "My dear Mr. Scully, when I was with Lopez, in Paraguay, I often, as I sat drinking my coffee at sunrise, saw five-and-twenty men marched out together to be shot. I don't value human life at *that*."[10] The *that* was indicated by a snap of the fingers.

Interrogation led to three grave sites where the evidence was buried. The case ultimately went before the Supreme Court, where the jailer was "defended by the most gifted member of the Cape Town Bar."[11] Though convicted, the defendent was sentenced to only one year imprisonment.

Several questions immediately suggest themselves. One instinctively asks how a man of the jailer's character (and the doctor's) came to be where he was? Or, if he was placed in such a position, how could he retain it? Inextricably linked to the first question is a second, an inability to understand how any magistrate ignored or failed to see what he had in this man. Of the jailer, the departing magistrate had told Scully, "You will find him a rough diamond. His manner is brusque . . . but he is a splendid officer."[12] It is to be feared that this speech reveals more about the magistrate than it does about the jailer. A final question, in which Scully had a deep interest, was a query about the condition of the courts—where a trial was a contest, a game of wits between lawyers, not an attempt to establish the truth or falsity of charges made and the defense presented. Here again, what happened in Cape Town revealed much more about the judicial system than about the events in Namaqualand.

Some years after the death of his wife Ellen, while he was attending a recital at Grahamstown, Scully was seriously attracted by a brilliant pianist, Honoria Emily Richards. His pursuit of the lady resulted in an engagement. However, a quarrel led to a breaking off of the intended union. Scully, in an effort to change defeat into victory, appeared on the steps of the Richards' home in Fort Beaufort. Intimidated by Emily's unrelenting demeanor, the suppliant requested an interview with her father. Mr. Richards told his daughter to "Ask Scully to come and smoke a pipe with me in the study." According to a daughter, Mrs. Betty Gray, "Mother drew herself up to her 5 feet nothing, and said to Father, whom she had left on the doormat, 'Mr. Scully, my father says will you come and smike a pope with him!' After a stunned silence, they both laughed—so that was that." Indeed, "that was that" for more than half a century. The marriage (1889) became an extremely successful one. When separated, they wrote to each other every day. Once when Scully was exploring the inaccessible areas of South America, no letters arrived for six weeks. Then one day a parcel came—bringing all of the letters written but unposted. When death finally dissolved the union, only ten weeks divided the departure of husband and wife from an earthly life. Returning home from their mother's funeral, Gerald said to his sister Betty, "Can't you imagine the Old Man arguing with St. Peter, and refusing to enter the Gate, unless Mother was brought to him at once?"[13]

The Cape was preparing for a census at the beginning of the last decade of the nineteenth century. The general enumeration was to begin in April 1891. Scully was sent back to Namaqualand, certainly one of the most difficult portions of the Colony to handle. One specific problem was that a very large area of the region had never been mapped. In addition, Scully had to handle the census in the Port Nolloth district, since the magistrate there proved incapable of doing the work. No one could ever accuse William Charles Scully of avoiding labor, but a part of what had to be done in Namaqualand became one of the greatest joys of his life—exploring the Bushmanland desert. Determining the limits within which the nomads of the district wandered and drawing charts of the area were necessary details; living with and assessing the spirit of the desert was an experience which Scully carried with him to the end of his life. He admitted that "It was with a somewhat sad heart that I used to leave the clean, strong, strenuous life of the wilderness, with its healthgiving hardships, and return to mix with the turgid society that stagnated around the copper-mines."[14] Scully looked upon O'okiep as the most unpleasant community in South Africa. The local head of the Cape Copper Company he suggested was "pompous as a groceralderman and as touchy as a cuttle-fish. It was not alone that one had to give him precedence in everything—that I never objected to doing; but he expected you to approach him with abject homage—to crawl on the ground before his hobnailed feet."[15] Scully discovered that he was supposed to accept without cost the house in which he lived, the courtroom in which cases were tried, the jail in which prisoners were confined, the only water available, a cart and horse for travel, fuel, light, and even postage stamps. As the chief judicial and administrative representative of the Cape government, Scully refused to be under obligation to a powerful economic interest. His independence brought him into great disfavor. While he was completely capable of defending himself, the situation became difficult for his family. After he had completed the special work for which he was sent, he accepted a transfer, at the end of 1892, to Peddie, in the Eastern Province.

Certainly, by this period in his career, it should have become clear that Scully had developed into an extremely useful civil servant. Use him the authorities did. At this particular time (1894), they sent him to the Native Territories, the magistracy at Mount Frere, on the north western boundary of Pondoland. Having settled his family at Fort Beaufort, he started on the two-hundred-mile journey to the new post. As strong ponies drew his cart along, Scully thoughtfully considered the duties toward which he moved. "I felt the burthen and the spur of responsibility; I had to think and to contrive, to deal with elemental conditions, to rule thousands of barbarians by moral force. I had to endeavour to adjust the life of an ancient people, the central and controlling influence of whose ethical system we had destroyed, to our very imperfect civilization."[16]

The Bantu constitute South Africa's foremost problem regardless of how the situation is approached. Leaving out all other considerations, the problem is one of numbers. The Bantu, then as now, outnumber the combined forces of the Dutch, English, Bushmen, Hottentots, the Coloureds (inhabitants of mixed blood), Indians, Jews, and all others. Scully was early aware of many of the issues involved, and on February 23, 1894, delivered a paper on the subject before the Lovedale Literary Society. On that occasion at Lovedale, he said, "Up to the present, the Aryan race has never secured a permanent footing on the African continent." After enumerating the failures, he continued, "Our experiment is on a larger scale than any of these, but its ultimate success is by no means yet assured." Following a detailed consideration of many of the problems, he makes a statement of the spirit in which the situation must be approached. "Our measure of success in dealing with the Native Question depends largely upon the spirit in which we begin our work. If we want to succeed, we must regard the Native's, [sic] welfare as our definite object,—we must not try to work for our own ends alone. If we do, we shall surely fail. 'Whoso loveth his life shall lose it.' Let this text be our motto in the crusade against the growing evil; it embodies a truth deeper than the depth of all philosophies, wider than the mind of man has searched, save His mind who uttered it."[17]

Offering a doctrine of calm moderation, Scully knows how little chance he has of receiving a hearing. He notes in his lecture that great questions which develop violent oppositions make it difficult for the man of moderate views to be heard. This is the man who, knowing that both extremes are simultaneously right and wrong, is seldom given a chance to discuss the situation. Yet he is almost always nearer right than those holding the extreme opinions. "The Natives," Scully says, "have been unfortunate in the intemperate nature of the advocacy exercised on their side. Exaggeration, which sometimes succeeds for a season, generally fails for a century."[18] As he has already warned, he does not accept the opposite position because he has rejected the extreme supporters of the natives. The attitude he holds is unspectacular, and all of his suggestions are simple. He starts with the assumption that the ancient tribal system has already been lost (or is being lost) as a stabilizing force. The native is living in an environment which he does not understand on the basis of anything from his past. Stated in another way, he is living in a vacuum, at least a partial one. This must be filled, and it is not only to the advantage of the native but also the Dutch and English elements of the population to fill this void with that which is good rather than that which is evil.

As, years later, he looked back upon his experiences with the Bantu, he wrote,

> I lived six years in the Native Territories, surrounded by so-called savages—men of wrath—heathen and unredeemed. Yet during the whole of that time I never locked a door or barred a window at night. . . .
> The Natives are, or were, the easiest people in the world to govern. I managed forty thousand of them for four years with the assistance of seven policemen, the latter locally enrolled. . . .[19]

Scully believed that two things were absolutely necessary in all relations with the natives—sympathy and understanding. The first was necessary before a person was likely to seek working information. The information would then become the basis for understanding. One example he gives will make clear the principle guiding hundreds of other situations. Scully had before him a native woman who denied that she knew a man about whom she was being questioned. The magistrate happened to be aware that for years she and the man had lived a few hundred yards from each other. Nothing could change her insistence that she had never heard the man's name. A native clerk solved the difficulty by whispering to the magistrate the word *inhlonipu*. The man about whom she was being questioned was her husband's uncle. Custom forbad her to admit the existence of any male relative of her husband, in the ascending line. To have called the man's name would have brought her into disgrace. Arguing the absurdity of the custom is of no avail. All civilizations have customs by which they live. These appear absurd only from the *outside*.

Perhaps the most spectacular achievement during the first half of Scully's career in the civil service was his work in fighting the great outbreak of rinderpest (an acute cattle disease) in 1897, while he was at Nqamakwe. There were about eighty-thousand head of cattle in the district. When the disease was first detected, it was in the very center of the area—not having started from an edge, as expected. Though the Koch discovery of inoculation was in the testing stages, Scully proposed to the authorities that the method be introduced. The government agreed to this procedure, as long as no pressure was exercised. Ignoring the official warning, for months Scully was a fervent evangelist advocating salvation through inoculation. Slowly what had been an uncertain process became an almost certain protection against the disease.

Soon the serious need was for supplies, not willingness of the natives in his district to have their cattle treated. Emerging from all of the grim tragedy was one bit of comedy. A desperate shortage of syringes was about to create a crisis. Scully had sent telegrams in every direction begging for supplies, but to no avail. With only three syringes left and a large group of cattle ready for treatment, he went to the post office, there to await the opening of the mail bag, just on the chance, the slightest chance. . . . As he sat on the counter, the contents of the bag were emptied on the floor. There in the midst of the pile was a box of the type in which syringes were always sent. With the alacrity of a hungry leopard, Scully jumped in the direction of the parcel and was already running to his horse as he called to the postmaster that he would sign later. Only when he started to open the parcel did he notice that it was addressed to a district nearly two hundred miles away. For once Fortune was on his side.

Finally the day of agony was over. All of the uninoculated cattle were dead, but through his efforts Scully had saved some twenty thousand. In surrounding districts nearly all of the cattle had died because inoculation had not been pressed.

During the epidemic no wagon was allowed across the line between the Colony and the Territories, going in either direction. On the day the restriction was removed, Scully had forty wagons drawn by rinderpest-proof oxen ready to cross the Kei River. From the other districts not a single wagon was present. Soon the forty wagons returned with desperately needed loads, not only for themselves but for other districts. When plowing time came, they made their oxen available to other areas. Slowly a land of death began to live again. How the people came to think of their magistrate is illustrated by one simple event. Scully, relative to some administrative business, had sent a message to a particular location requiring attendance at his office. He received the following answer: "We have no time to go and see you, for rain has fallen and we are busy cultivating. All you have to do is let us know what the order is. We will obey it—even if it be that we are to send our ears in a basket."[20] What greater confidence can a people have in a leader?

Emerging from this experience with the rinderpest epidemic was a short story, "Noquala's Cattle," (see Chapter 5) and a poem, "The

Prayer of the Cattle." Working week after week with the suffering, silent creatures, Scully took it upon himself to speak in verse for them. Here are three of the ten stanzas he wrote:

> Men crucified Thee; men to-day
>   Defile Thy all-embracing Church.
> We know not sin; our humble way
>   Leads not e'en to Thy temple's porch.
> We are as those Thy kind Hand raised,
> Thy poor, that hence Thy Name have praised.
>
> Ours is the meekness that endures;
>   Our patience, like a steadfast tree,
> Stands in the torrent-pain that pours
>   And sweeps all else to some dark sea.
> The patient bovine race unblest
> Is earth's sad, dumb, pathetic guest. . . .
>
> The hour is late, our sun sinks low
>   Beneath a storm-red western cloud.
> Though Death be swift, his steps seem slow;
>   Pain wraps us in a burning shroud.
> Plead for us, O compassionate—
> Plead for us, Christ—the hour is late.[21]

Despite the unquestioned feeling Scully had for the thousands of cattle (and their owners) he was trying to save, he here revealed much about his own beliefs and attitudes. Patience, humbleness, meekness were qualities of which he approved—whether in cattle or men.

Knowing the life that Scully led makes it difficult to think of him as a poet, novelist, and short-story writer. Not until page three hundred and fifty of the second volume of *Reminiscences* did he refer to authorship. At the end of the rinderpest year his health was completely broken. He was ordered to leave for Europe and consult a specialist. This he did, and the result was satisfactory. As his strength increased, he was able to make visits to places of interest and to meet various people. It is at this point that he admits having written several books. "During the three years previous to my visiting London for the first time, I had published a few books.[22] These, although they never attracted the public to any great extent, were remarkably well received by the critics, and were the means of my obtaining introductions to many interesting people belonging to literary and artistic circles."[23]

Following an extended stay in London (first for medical reasons), Scully and his wife visited Ireland in order to see relatives and to recall the experiences of his early childhood at Cashel and his youth in Springfield. He visited Killarney—which he had never seen, in addition to Tipperary and the Wicklow regions. All went well except in Dublin. He was shocked by the slums. Of them he said, "Here I saw the most debased specimens of humanity it has ever been my misfortune to look upon. The degraded remnants of the South African Bushmen were, by comparison, clean, wholesome, and comely. . . . I gasped and fled from the horrid sight, and had the greatest difficulty in keeping from being violently ill. . . . I wondered why people subscribed money for the purpose of sending missionaries to the foreign heathen, when they have domestic heathen festering in a lower Phlegethon-pit than I, who had spent more than half a lifetime in uncivilized Africa, had deemed could possibly exist."[24] While reading this passage, it should be recalled that Scully's life in Africa had been the complete opposite of a sheltered one.

After visiting Ireland, the Scullys spent several weeks on the Continent and returned to South Africa in the Southern spring of 1898. His health was restored, and he resumed his duties at Nqamakwe. Soon, however, because of the growing children, he requested a transfer to the Colony. The request was granted. Thus ended another very important phase of his life. War could already be seen on the horizon.

CHAPTER 3

Poems Came First

REGARDLESS of how strange it may appear, poems often come first in the writing life of authors who later devote themselves so completely to prose that their early verse is totally forgotten. This is actually very natural because poetry is the most elemental form of literary expression. Following the usual sequence, Scully began to write verses as his experiences prompted him to record the images that were forming. His poems, however, were not impressionistic jottings, for he always imposed upon himself the execution of some pattern. Various lyric forms were employed, and not infrequently he attempted sonnets. South Africa's first English poet of substance was Thomas Pringle, who came to the Cape with a university background and a volume of poems published before leaving Scotland. Scully sailed for his new home at the age of twelve, having previously attended no school at all. Yet regardless of the conditions under which he wrote, the Irish youth persevered, and as the years passed his collection began to assume the proportions of a book. Finally, he decided that publication was desirable. The volume, which appeared in 1886, though little noticed at the time, was a significant event in South African literature.

I *Poetry as an Art*

Ostensibly writing in praise of Thomas Pringle as the father of South African poetry in English, William Charles Scully revealed an important aspect of his attitude towards the art itself. The proper things, of course, were said about Pringle and his experiences. Yet ultimately Scully had his attention focused upon the art of poetry and not merely another author. There is nothing original about what he says. In fact, all he suggests had been a part of Western tradition for more than two thousand years before he put it into his lines honoring the little Scot who reached the Cape in 1820. Yet glimmering through certain lines is a hint that the youthful Irishman, like the son of

Poems Came First

Scotland before him, wanted to leave something by which he might be remembered on earth after his death. Pringle had expressed the desire explicitly; Scully was far more reticent, offering it implicitly under the traditional generalizations. Yet what goes before and what comes after shows that he is thinking of himself as well as Pringle.

> Death can still
> All life save that of song; his mouth, the Grave,
> Still swallows all his hunter, Time, runs down—
> But Song than Time is swifter; she can weep
> O'er peoples crumbled into ruin, smile
> When nations blossom from the fallowed world,
> And shout from age to age her words of truth
> That roll as flames from lips white-hot with fire
> That God enkindles when He makes a singer.[1]

Actually it can be argued that in this passage Scully was remembering Pringle far less than the Psalms, the Prophets of Israel, and Shakespeare. Coming to literature after his years at Kimberley and Pilgrim's Rest, Scully went directly to the great writers for his delayed education. Perhaps, among other things, it developed in him the desire to be a poet, not merely a South African poet. One effect of this attitude was to help him avoid feeling self-conscious when he employed local materials. Conversely, when the poem is distinctly not about South Africa, he uses quite freely and accurately environmental details which attach the lines firmly to the country of his adoption.

Several characteristics of *The Wreck of the Grosvenor and Other South African Poems*, Scully's first book, 1886, are unusual. To begin with, first collections of verse are seldom so long, eighty-four poems, a hundred and thirty-four pages. Most young writers are ready to publish when they have accummulated twenty titles. Another characteristic of some importance is the presence of an eighteen-page verse drama. Since the coming of Romanticism to European literature, beginning poets have had a tendency towards the subjective, but here Scully is using a historical event which occurred ninety-six years before the publication of his account. Third, though the volume was anonymously published, it was introduced by a poem to the author's wife. Finally, for a first effort, the book possesses an unusual range. The verse drama with which the volume opens is not repeated, and soon a reader is given a collection of songs and a group of sonnets. Characters are widely separated in time and place. David Livingstone (1813–1873), Immanuel Kant (1724–1804), and St. Benedict (480–543) are made subjects of separate poems. Geographically the volume ranges from Table Mountain to Compass Berg to Namaqualand. One of the best poems presents the almost extinct Bushmen and others the very much not extinct Bantu. A number of the poems would be classified as pure lyrics. There is all of this and more.

Though the title work itself is not a success, one can certainly admire the author's courageous attempt. Among the various shipwrecks along the South African shores, the loss of the *Grosvenor* seemed to affect the general imagination more than any of the others. The vessel struck a rock on the coast of Pondoland, June 13, 1782, and a hundred and thirty-six of the passengers and crew reached shore. Four months later, six sailors arrived at Algoa Bay. A rescue expedition was able to find three sailors, seven lascars (East Indian native sailors), and two black female servants. The fate of the remaining hundred and eighteen was never determined, beyond the normal possibilities of destruction by wild animals, native tribes, or starvation. Using this material, together with the discovery of three unknown white women living among the natives near the Umzimvubu River, Scully attempted to write a verse play. The wonder is not that he failed, but that he was able to complete a composition of this kind with any success at all. The problem that he did not solve was the union of verse and dialogue. Spoken, the effect is distinctly unsuccessful. This is not any surprise because in English no great dramatist has been without experience of the stage. Other forms of literature have been written with success though the author lacked technical knowledge of the medium, but drama requires that the writer know what it is he is trying to control. It is of considerable interest to note that Scully did not again attempt anything of this kind. Obviously he understood a failure.

Six years after the publication of *The Wreck of the Grosvenor*, Scully acknowledged his poetic authorship in a volume of two hundred and forty-seven pages published in London by T. Fisher Unwin. Some thirty-odd of the titles from his 1886 book were retained. The most conspicuous single addition was a sequence of twenty-one sonnets and a number of translations from the German, Heine being the most generously represented. With the appearance in 1895 of *Kafir Stories*, Scully abandoned verse for prose—except an occasional piece through the years.

Despite obvious weaknesses, perhaps nothing in the early attempts shows more quickly than the simple lyricism of the songs that

Scully was trying to be an artist and not merely a South African reporter. Each of the following stanzas is taken from one of his many songs.

> As water flowing,
> And deeper growing,
> Your lives are going
>   From springs that be
> The teeming sources
> Wherefrom Fate's forces
> Fill, through life-courses,
>   Eternity.

> We stood at dawn and watched the fight
>   Between the light and darkness waged;
> The wooded hill, the mountain height,
> Flung off the fetters of spent night,
>   And shook their plumes like birds uncaged.[2]

Lyricism of this kind could also be maintained throughout an entire song—as in the following example, the three stanzas employing only one sentence.

> O when the white and ebon notes,
>   Obedient to my love's lithe fingers,
> Call music from the cave wherein
>   She darkly dreams and mutely lingers—
>
> Obedient to the high command,
>   She mounts the air on throbbing wings,
> And from some zone above the world
>   Returns with sweet, unearthly things
>
> That tell of light, and love, and joy,
>   And conquered death, and hopes that cheer,
> And many a golden-glowing sun,
>   And many a silver planet-sphere.[3]

Transition from the songs to more realistic efforts was effected with seeming ease. A poem such as "Traditur Dies Die"[4] is essentially timeless and placeless. Yet a reader who knows South Africa is likely to feel that the author employs a Cape Town setting. Slipped into the lines is the sound of waves passing through pines and on towards the grey sides of Table Mountain, with its frequently present white cloud covering. During his first period in Cape Town, Scully climbed Table Mountain seventeen times. In *Further Reminiscences* he said that the image "most wonderful of all . . . was the sapphire ocean with its faint border of gleaming foam flung like a mantle round the sleeping peninsula. Then it seemed as though Peace brooded over all. . . ."[5] This peace appears in the second stanza, after the sea and mountain have been introduced in the first.

> I saw a little child at play
>   Alone amid the mounded graves,—
> Hard by, her mother sleeping lay.
>   The soothing sound of distant waves
>   Stole up between the silent pines,
>   And murmured through the leafless vines,
> And died against the mountain grey.
>
> The mountain grey,—Its head was set
>   Around with snowy swathes of cloud,
> Far o'er the jars of stress and fret
>   That wear the ways where walk the crowd.
>   The mountain was a thing of peace,
>   Around the gravestone discords cease,—
> Death smooths the way and pays the debt.
>
> The sunflecks on her yellow head
>   Lay bright; her eyes were grey and deep—
> Kind love was as her daily bread,
>   Love smoothed the pillow for her sleep;
>   She knew not what her life had cost,
>   She knew not whose dear feet had crost
> For her, the ferry of the dead.[6]

Following this poem, no reader will be surprised to find among Scully's sonnets one called "Prayer."

> Talk not of prayers that fail, the prayers unheard
> Are not the askings Paul meant when he said;
> "Pray without ceasing." Be thou well assured,
> The true petition, not of barren word,
> But plumed of deed, scales Heaven overhead,
> Where souls and suns from God's high throne are shed.
> Pray without ceasing, let good deeds unfold

> Like petals of a rose, until, complete
> The flower of asking, full and fair and sweet,
> Is fit for God's right hand to take and hold.
> False prayers are barren breath, like vapour rolled
> Between men and the stars; they hide the feet
> Of angels, but the true prayer, wise and meet,
> From chiming sphere to sphere on high is told.[7]

Here, quite simply, is an almost perfect statement of the code by which men should live, Scully felt. What a man says is meaningless except in direct relation to what he does. A human being disperses himself throughout his environment and projects himself into the infinite only through his deeds. In English literature, the concept is certainly as old as *Everyman* (c. 1500), when it most definitely was not new.

The idea presented in the sonnet "Good and Evil" is more unusual than in the poem on prayer. Here the author imagines Good and Evil engaged in deadly conflict over the "dreadful issues" of civilization. There is, however, an interested spectator, for the sextet suggests,

> . . . as the calm-eyed ruler of each sphere
> Bore slowly past the battle-riven world,
> Firm in his mighty hand he held a spear
> Poised o'er his head, and ready to be hurled—
> To dash this globe to fragments as it whirled,
> Should Evil's brow the wreath of victory wear.[8]

Though as a botanist Scully certainly might be expected to write poems about flora in which he was interested, what he did in his sonnet on ferns is the result of imagination, not information. The floral world, of course, emerges from the earth, where no light exists, only a region of darkness. Linking this fact with the concept of prenatal existence, Scully, in "The Home of the Ferns," has written an explanation of why ferns love the world of shade.

> A wood-elf told me that, of greenwood things,
> The ferns alone remember whence they come,
> And each frond, fresh uncoiling, fondly clings
> To what is like its ante-natal home;
> That home is set in darkness, whence each springs
> To dwell in exile on the earth; and gloom,
> The dark's soft sister, unto each one brings
> Best solace, so from shade they never roam.[9]

Writing about the development of the sonnet in South African poetry, E. H. Crouch (1911) lamented the absence of serious attention to the form until William Charles Scully published his first book in 1886. Here Crouch felt were examples that merited high praise. In his essay he selected for special comment "Good and Evil," which he suggested was "unique in its conception and true in form." Among the sonnets presenting South African scenes, he states that "Namaqualand" offers the reader "powerful bits of local colour." The critic felt, however, that it was in his next volume, 1892, that Scully's "poetic instinct showed itself more completely in the publication of a sequence which he called 'Sonnets from the German.' " Crouch compares the collection with that of Mrs. Browning, so much admired during this particular period of literature. He observes that while "Mrs. Browning's [sonnets] are strong in the passion of self-abandonment, in Scully's the theme is rather the mirror or medium through which the metaphysical mind shows the potential influence and workings of this attribute [love]."[10] Sonnet seven in the sequence adopts the question and answer method. Though Mrs. Browning did use this approach, the result was very much unlike the following.

>   Is Love, then, happiness? Ah, yes, the best!
>   Is he not pain? Oh, bitter! Doth he smile?
>   As smiles the morning! Doth he weep? Yea, lest
>   His smile might lose its savour! Hath he guile?
>   As hath the red rose that beguiles the bee!
>   What doth his voice discourse of? Lo! herein
>   Lieth Love's potency; his keen eyes see
>   And smite upon each secret-hoarded sin,
>   And then he saith: Whilst this with thee doth dwell,
>   Must thou and I for ever be at strife,
>   And in thine ear my tongue must hourly tell
>   Dispraise, till thou dost cast it from thy life?
>   And most he raileth at the darling vice
>   That doth each soul so cunningly entice.

Using the ancient personifications of Time, Fate, and Hope, sonnet ten dramatizes an action which becomes quite specific.

>   I played a match with Time, and won, then Fate
>   Took up the dice, and smiled, and with one throw
>   Gained all my winnings. At the grave's dark gate
>   I sit in poverty, and count the slow
>   Beats of my heart that hungers. In the east

> Rises a small star, circling slowly near,
> And shining promise of a rich love-feast,
> And waning now, and waxing. Bitter fear
> That this may fade before my longing eyes,
> Or live to set in sorrow, fills my breast.
> But Hope oft whispers words of sweet surprise,
> That in mine anguish almost make me blest.
> O Hope, if that thy words are false, thy face
> Is foul, and weareth but a mask of grace.

Sonnet fifteen shows a gentleness revealing thought processes very different from the kind of world in which the author lived from day to day.

> The night is still, the silent frost hangs thick
> On leaf and grass the jewels coming day
> Will light to softened splendour. Bright and quick
> The starbeams through the crisp air thrill. Away
> Swifter than these a thought has southward sped,
> And back returned on faithful, homing wing,
> Bearing the picture of a golden head
> Pressed on a snowy pillow. Slumbering
> My darling lies; each eyelid, silken-fringed,
> Droops like a dove's breast-feather, tremulously—
> The lips, a petalled casket half unhinged,
> Show pearls more bright than holds the silver sea.
> For now a stray dream-spirit, at her ear
> Tells to the child some tale she smiles to hear.

In closing his sequence, for poetic observation Scully brings together the earthy and the ethereal.

> Love bound to earth is earthy, when he goes
> Above through ether spaces, he doth leave
> All earthly dross behind, and as the rose
> In dying frees her perfume, but doth weave
> Unseen within the stem, a web to capture
> The scent anew from spring's o'erflowing heart;
> As music dead, the ear doth yet enrapture,
> Even thus hath Love's most sure abiding part
> Returned all purified; my rosebud holdeth
> All sweetness and still music, that will be,—
> When in the years her petalled heart unfoldeth,
> A priceless heritage of love to me;

Of love with naught of earth within its grain,
And Fate will find his worst device was vain.[11]

Recalling that these sonnets were written in the period which saw South Africa start upon a feverish development of the gold mines of the Witwatersrand, and that during that time the author officially represented the government of the Cape in one of the least known of its areas, one may have some concept of the profoundly complex life being lived by William Charles Scully.

What a poet can do with blank verse is at least a useful measure of his technical skill. In the title poem of his first volume and in several of his longer efforts, Scully essayed the use of this meter which often serves to reveal the weaknesses of an author. Only the greatest of English poets have survived this examination with complete success. A selection of the lines from "St. Benedict" will show that Scully was far from defeated by the requirements of blank verse.

> [Here is my home.] [Henceforth no speech of man
> Nor smile of woman smite on ear or eye,]
> [Nor fan in my weak heart the flame of sin.]
> [O rocks and darkness,] [gather up my words,]
> [And send aloft the speakings of my soul:]
> [That I,] [a boy,] [am weary of the world,]
> [And deafened by the roarings from vast deeps
> Of hate and horror,] [and the whispers low,]
> [And faint,] [and sweet,] [and subtle,] [yet more dread
> Than fang of snake or lightning stroke—] [the voice
> Of the sense-devil.][12]

Here flexibility is achieved by playing the length of grammatical units against the metrical span of the blank verse line. The period in the first line breaks the five feet into units of two and three. The second line is five and the third five. Yet, because the first is a run-on line, the grammatical unit of the combination is eight followed by five. Thus a reader's breathing reaction for the first three lines is two, eight, five. Line four is split two and a half, two and a half. The split, however, does not create total balance because the iambic movement gives three shorts and two longs in the first half and two shorts and three longs in the second half.

Another danger in using blank verse is that the author may find himself writing no more than metrical prose. If he wishes to achieve strength, he must look to his images, and phrasing, and sequences.

Poems Came First 55

The following will display something of what Scully could do. "These grey stones/ Are furrowed by my knees . . ./ My mind the field of battle, and my soul/ The prize of victory."[13] Written almost totally with monosyllables, the passage with twenty words has imaged the physical result of extended prayer, the mental conflict through which man passes, and the spiritual nature of the outcome.

II Poems Relating to South Africa

Nothing in the South African section of *Poems* suggests that Scully was trying to present a systematic study of the country. He merely wrote about what he knew best and what interested him most. The area that left the deepest impression upon him was Namaqualand; the single place was probably Table Mountain. In considering both, he united his interest and knowledge to effect a satisfying balance. Namaqualand he celebrated in a sonnet, though later he was to use the area extensively in prose. Table Mountain has been commemorated in a poem of five sections, each different in form and intent. Later the mountain was employed effectively in one of his best novels. (See Chapter 5.)

Only readers who know Namaqualand from experience or study can judge the accuracy and condensation of Scully's poem. Even for uninitiated readers, however, the poem creates a feeling of authenticity.

> A land of deathful sleep, where fitful dreams
>   Of hurrying spring scarce wake swift-fading flowers;
> A land of fleckless sky, and sheer-shed beams
>   Of sun and stars through day's and dark's slow hours,
> A land where sand has choked once fluent streams—
>   Where grassless plains lie girt by granite towers
> That fright the swift and heaven-nurtured teams
>   Of winds that bear afar the sea-gleaned showers.
> The wild Atlantic, fretted by the breath
>   Of fiery gales o'er leagues of desert sped,
> Rolls back, and wrecks in surf its thunderous wrath
>   On rocks that down the wan, wide shore are spread;
> The waves for ever roar a song of death,
>   The shore they roar to is for ever dead.[14]

Whereas few people in the world have heard of Namaqualand, millions have known Table Mountain, an acquaintance covering four centuries. This difference is distinctly reflected in the two poems. To write about Table Mountain was much more difficult than about Namaqualand. Scully accepted the challenge. Part one presents not a view of the "Table" itself, which all know, but what is seen from the mountain, which comparatively few know.

> On my right a demon stands,
>   On my left a lion couches;
>   Year by year he, watching, crouches
>   Where the foam-lipped sea expands.
>
> At my back, the Cape of Storms,
>   'Neath my face, the busy town;—
>   Far beyond, the mountains brown,
>   And the cornfields round the farms.

Centuries vanish when part two begins. Here is not accepted history but the "wild tales" that came from sailors trying to round the Cape.

> When first the rover stepped ashore,
> And gazed upon my bastions hoar,
> And marked the vapour-legions pour
>
> In eddying whirl and monstrous shape,
> And saw the tempest-garments drape
> The guardian of the fabled cape;—
>
> My demon-haunted cliffs he scanned—
> Fit rampart for some dark, dread land—
> And crossed himself with pious hand;
>
> Then homeward passed, and told wild tales
> Of guardian giants—horrid gales—
> Perils to him who southward sails.[15]

In the notes added to the South African poems, Scully explained the scientific basis for the early stories. "The meteorological phenomena are very remarkable—the sea-wind being liable, on a slight lowering of the temperature, to condense into an impervious cloud, which completely hides the upper portion of the mountain for days together. This cloud sometimes takes strange shapes, and the early voyagers, terrified by the storms, the legends current, and the mysteries of unknown seas, firmly believed the crags to be haunted by demons, who at will called up the cloud to hide their unholy revels. Camoens, in the fifth book of the "Lusiad," impersonates in the mountain the Titan Adamastor, exiled by Jove for the misdemeanour of paying rough addresses to the sea-nymph, Thetis."[16] More than a quarter of a century after Scully's poem, Roy Campbell used Adamastor to supply the title of one of his volumes and with effectiveness in one of his poems ("Rounding the Cape"). In the third. section, Scully has written the meditations of a modern mind surveying the area before the explorations of Bartholomew Diaz and Vasco da Gama or any European who became a part of the history of the Cape. The fourth section offers the flora of the mountain, a close-up view of the visual beauties available, not the panoramic photographic shots usually seen.

After depicting the mountain in its gentle mood, the author uses the final section to make clear that climbers can lose even life when on the cliffs during a storm. Knowledge of weather and Table Mountain itself are the only protection against dangers of the natural world when man is not heedful. Thus, in its totality, Scully has written a comprehensive poem concerning one of the most famous rock masses in the world.

Special qualities of Compass Berg aroused the imagination of the author as he viewed another mountain. Highest peak in the Cape, the name explains the nature of the pinnacle which can simultaneously look north, south, east, and west. Isolated and abrupt, it offers a special kind of image to those who view it from a distance, but the poet imagines himself on the summit and from there presents the compass views.

>   Thou seest the last of the sun at even,
>   And Hesper greets thee the last of earth,
>   And Phosphor tells, from the wan east heaven,
>   Thee, first, the tale of the new day's birth. . . .
>
>   The rival storms in exultation
>   Clasp round thy crest in a dread embrace,
>   And ask the award of thy arbitration
>   In tempest-tones at thy steadfast face. . . .
>
>   The dying day from thy flaming altar
>   Is westward borne in an amber shroud,
>   And the failing night on thy brow may falter
>   'Neath the sunlit surface of clinging cloud.[17]

Among the best of Scully's poems are those concerned with the African natives, some as individuals and others as representatives of important groups. There are two poems under the title "Zulu Pictures," one about a man called 'Nkongane and the other the best known of all the Zulu chieftains, Tshaka (also spelled Chaka). Other poems deal with the witch doctor and the cattle thief. Finally, there is a poem about the Bushmen.

Imaginative projection of the Bushman is necessary because so few were left that Scully (nor anyone else) had little direct information, though in the Bushmanland desert he was about as close to their civilization as one of his generation was likely to get, unless making an expedition into specific regions for the purpose of making a scientific study of the few still living. Two stanzas from a poem of nine will give some feeling for what the author was trying to say.

> 'Tis here the vanished bushman dwelt—
>   He, with his brood, long years ago—
> Beneath this ledge; and deftly spelt,
>   In pictures that still freshly glow,
> The wild-wood creatures, not more wild
>   Than he, who, hiding thus apart,
> His idle days and hours beguiled
>   At his strange, harmless, limning art. . . .
>
> There, in yon cleft, is still the mark
>   Of bygone fires whose flames are dead
> As those who lit them—life's strange spark
>   And glowing ember, each has sped.
> And by the south wind's gentle sigh
>   The flickering, sunlit leaves are turned,
> And from the cliffs the brown hawks cry
>   To-day, as when each brightly burned.[18]

According to Scully "The Kafirs are probably the most expert stock-lifters in the world. They have a strange influence over cattle, and by means of a peculiar low whistle can induce these animals to follow, when no white man would ever be able to drive them."[19] "The Cattle Thief" presents a young man who wishes very much to marry a girl whose father has established the bride-payment as five heifers and five oxen. To secure the girl, the young man decides to "lift" the necessary cattle. Though in the end the poem is a serious one, the tone of the whole is light and cheerful. The author, understanding both sides, admitted that the farmers of the area did not appreciate the romantic aspects of the situation. The farmers see only the loss of cattle; the young man sees the acquisition of a bride. In the poem the girl he has chosen is identified in the following lines.

> Of all the maids
> That hoe in our glades,
> Noniese is the trimmest one,
> She's lithe as a snake,
> As a partridge brown,
> And I crouch in the brake
> E'er the sun goes down,
> Till she pass when her work is done.[20]

The reader can decide whether or not he feels Noniese is worth five heifers and five oxen and the risk of being caught and convicted of theft.

Though Scully felt there was a certain kind of humor in a young man's whistling cattle to consummate his love, he became deeply serious in writing about the witch doctor. The author's experiences had convinced him that the practice of the witch doctors was the most destructive and tragic element in the civilization developed by the Bantu. The action in "The Witch-Doctor" is horrifying to a reader, and it represents what was often repeated in life. Fusi, who had become rich in cattle, goats, and maize, is a cousin of the chief, who is about to die. When an important person was ill or nearing death, it was believed that a curse had been placed upon him. The witch doctor was called to find the guilty person. A statistical study would reveal that the "evil character" is usually wealthy, a rival, or one who has given offence to the chief or the important person. An understanding between the chief and the witch doctor will make the process an easy one. The person designated is accused of being a wizard and is then executed or tortured to death. His possessions revert to the chief, or, as in this instance, to his successor. Naturally the witch doctor gets his part. Fusi went the route of torture, tied in the sun by pegging down his toes and thumbs. Black ants were heaped around him and heated stones placed at his feet. Not only in this poem but more than once in his prose, Scully returned to the various ways in which these practices constituted a major evil imposed upon the Kaffirs.

Undoubtedly one of the greatest general curses which descended upon the Bantu tribes of South Africa was the rise of Tshaka (1783–

1828) to power as the chief of the Zulus. Early in the nineteenth century, he developed the largest, best equipped, and most disciplined fighting force South Africa had ever seen. For almost a quarter of a century he made war until the tribes of the whole area were either absorbed, destroyed, disorganized, and demoralized, or had fled to other regions and attempted a new life. As Scully brings to a close his poem that has depicted Tshaka's actions and attitudes, he presents the chieftain as a supreme ego, one man in relief against the universe.

> When men would speak my name, they sink
>   Their words to whispers,—when they hear
> My voice they tremble on the brink
>   Of death, their limbs are bowed with fear.
> The sun I am that lords the shy!
>   The stars put forth their feeble light:
> I dawn, they shrink—I come, they die—
>   I reign alone in terror's might![21]

Left over from the days when Tshaka and Dingaan dominated the Zulu world, 'Nkongane symbolizes the universal tragedy of having lived beyond the time in which one feels at ease—whether the ease is good or bad. The lines at times display humor, but finally the old man is left pathetically alone.

> Old—some eighty, or thereabouts;
>   Sly as a badger alert for honey;
> Honest perhaps—but I have my doubts— . . . .
>
> When your lips unlock to the taste of rum,
>   The tongue runs on with its cackle of clicks
> That like bubbles break as their consonants come,
>   For your speech is a brook full of frisky tricks. . . .
>
> Strange old man—like a lonely hawk
>   In a leafless forest that falls to the axe,
> You linger on; and you love to talk,
>   Yet your tongue full often a listener lacks;
> Truth and fiction, like chaff and grain
>   You mix together, and often I try
> To sift the one from the other, and gain
>   The fact from its shell of garrulous lie.
>
> You were young when Chaka, the scourge of man,
>   Swept over the land like the Angel of Death;

> You marched in the rear when the veteran van
>   Mowed down the armies—reapers of wrath!
> You sat on the ground in the crescent, and laid
>   Your shield down flat when Dingaan spake loud—
> His vitals pierced by the murderer's blade—
>   To his warriors fierce, in dread anguish bowed.[22]

Long after Scully had turned to the writing of prose, he published a sonnet motivated by the coming of airplanes and war above the clouds.

> Like Icarus he soared; the thinning wind
>   Pressed, kisslike, on his lips; young Life's devotion—
> Love, duty, fame; like blossoms intertwined
>   Shone on his path, made rich the sky's wide ocean.
> He marked cloud-pastures 'neath his feet empearled;
>   He skirted thunder-turrents robed in gloom;
> He braved the banners hurricanes unfurled
>   And mocked them, smiling in the face of Doom.
> Fate winged the dart that smote him. Uncontrolled
>   His falcon-steed checked, faltered, swerved and fell.
> His gallant heart its last swift throb had told.
>   No requiem needed he, nor passing bell—
> For as his unsensed flesh sped down to earth
>   His spirit soared to that which gave it birth.[23]

Early in his twenties, Scully had read Shakespeare's sonnets until he carried them in his memory rather than in a book. There is something satisfyingly appropriate about ending a discussion of his poetic career with a Shakespearean sonnet—brought up to the twentieth century by its subject matter.

CHAPTER 4

Prose Stories

REGARDLESS of any favor with which the poems of William Charles Scully may have been considered, there is no reason to believe that, in verse, he could reach the audience interested in short stories and novels. Few people ever touch a book of poems unless already interested in poetry itself as a literary form. Prose fiction is read for various reasons. Narratives about the natives of South Africa are of interest because they tell of things far away and often strange for many readers. Then, too, by the time Scully published his first volume of short stories, people all over the world had relatives or friends in South Africa because of the discovery of diamonds and gold. This was one way of learning of the land to which they had gone. Other readers might be very serious in following the actions and ideas of the country. A very wide variety of readers must be put into this group, for, to begin with, controversial questions usually have two or more sides. There were religious groups, political parties, and business organizations wishing to know of the attitudes and implementations in the land of diamonds and gold. Several of Scully's stories and books received publication in the United States, as well as South Africa and England.

There is, of course, no reason to believe that the author examined the situation as suggested here. Everything about his work indicates that he wrote because he felt there were ideas that should be presented, actions that ought to be reported, history that had to be recorded. According to Mrs. Betty Gray, "The first short story he ever wrote was *The Eumenides in Kafirland*. It was based on a case brought before him. One evening he shut himself into his study. He woke Mother up at four A.M. to read her what he had written—and that was the beginning of his fiction work. (He always read aloud to Mother what he wrote, and valued her criticism.)"[1] Mrs. Gray believes this first story was written at Peddie. If this is correct (and the sequence of events suggests that it is), he shifted from verse to

Prose Stories

prose fiction during 1893–94. Other titles followed: "The Quest of the Copper," "Umtagati," "Ghamba," "The Fundamental Axiom," "Ukushwama," and "Kellson's Nemesis." These are the stories that made up his first collection, showing in every way the maturity of an author who was now approaching forty. Even technically these narratives are not the work of a beginner in the literary area.

I *In Kaffirland*

Beautifully published in T. Fisher Unwin's Autonym Library, *Kafir Stories* (1895) introduced Scully the fictionist. Some of the seven stories are in the present time and others in the past. Settings vary; both good and evil characters create the action. In general the raw material for these narratives has emerged from Scully's own experiences with the people and the history and geography of the country.

Though Tshaka had been dead almost forty years before Scully came to South Africa as a boy, there were current numerous stories about the Zulu king. In addition to hearing stories, any government official in the Cape, especially in the Native Territories, would naturally encounter the results of Tshaka's actions. A fictionist employing this type of material will often be tempted to use too much biography, too much history, and too much personal comment. All of these temptations Scully appears to have resisted. In his presentation of Tshaka, he has created a carefully selected, skillfully organized, and effectively narrated story. Tshaka himself is not the central character, but one of his indunas (generals), Kondwana. The action is not that of war. As the title indicates, "The Quest of the Copper," this story employs actions not normally associated with Tshaka. The title statement is to be taken quite literally. The King has sent a regiment north, ostensibly in search of copper. This is not, however, to be one of the typical quest stories of Africa—for gold, diamonds, the source of a river, or the location of a lake. With absolute thoroughness Scully has revealed an aspect of Tshaka's character by the assignment given to Kondwana and the treatment of this commander after he returned. The King himself appears only at the beginning and end—thus in the position of an enveloping character. All else is an account of the expedition. There are, however, a few details that must be given before Kondwana can be sent on his quest.

Kondwana was called before the King during the month of March (beginning of the autumn season). An induna of the Abambo tribe, he had fought against Tshaka, but the tribe had submitted and been absorbed into the Zulu nation. Since that time, he had served faithfully and with zeal, perhaps too well. Here, thought the King, was a former enemy much too close to the throne. Thus the commander of the 'Nyatele regiment was in the King's mind placed on a list of those to be eliminated. First, he was sent on an expedition through the fever country south of Delagoa Bay, between the sea and the Lebomba Mountains. The regiment had been reduced to four hundred and fifty men able to undertake the new assignment, instead of the two thousand that a unit frequently carried. Though not even that many men would be needed to dig for copper, if ever found, all might be required to fight from Zululand to the unknown destination and return. Tshaka, however, was unconcerned about such a fact. His order was quite simple.

"You will take," said Tshaka, "what remains of the 'Nyatele regiment . . . and go to the country beyond the mountains of the Amaswazi, where the green and yellow stones from which the red metal (copper) is smelted, are dug out of the ground. You will bring back so much of these stones as will cover, when heaped up, the skins of three large oxen. You will return before the Summer rains have fallen. Go."[2]

Immediately the reduced regiment moved north, skirting the country of the Amaswazi because Kondwana did not wish to be drawn from his actual mission by serious combat. The unavoidable route, then, passed through high mountains, and the men suffered from severe cold. Those who were still weak from the fever sickened and had to be put to death mercifully. When the regiment dropped to the plains beyond the Drakensberg, they entered the tsetse fly country. Cattle they were carrying for food died. Game was plentiful, but equipped as they were they found wild animals difficult to capture. As rapidly as possible they moved towards the Limpopo. So far no one they met had any information about the source of copper. Lions became a menace in several areas. More serious, a number of the men had lost their spears in the game hunts. The ikempe (Zulu spear) was the source of much of a warrior's success as a fighting man, and the regiment was now approaching the country of the Makalakas, where opposition was certain.

Ultimately, Kondwana found that his depleted force was opposed by the assembled armies of two nations. Now the skill of command, discipline, loyalty, and courage which created the reputation of the Zulu fighting units may be seen. In the present situation, however,

Scully has effected a complete reversal of the usual sympathy. Readers will find themselves on the side of Kondwana and his men. Because the Zulu general had sent word to the Makalaka Chief (after having crushed the first Makalaka force which opposed him) that he did not come as an enemy, the Chief offered safe passage and guides through his country. Actually, as soon as the pitifully small size of the Zulu group had been observed, the Makalaka Chief laid a plan to destroy the already decimated regiment. It was important that no man be allowed to live and tell Tshaka what had happened. His plan was a simple one. Messengers were sent ahead to warn the Balotsis of an enemy's approach and to ask that they be met in the mountain pass through which his guides were leading them. He would move up from the rear with his army. Meanwhile, the Makalaka guides, according to plan, deserted just before the two armies were to close in on the Zulus.

The Zulus had one night of peace before the final agony began. Late in the afternoon, they found the bones of forty or fifty men, and scattered among these remains they discovered "copper stones" for which, theoretically, their quest was ordered. Each man was able to find at least a small sample, which he deposited in his skin wallet. Obviously this was the Makalaka expedition which never returned. Of the search the Zulus had been told, and here was evidence not merely of the effort but of the fact that somewhere in the north there was copper. It was now May, and the weather in the mountains was cold. That night, however, there was a little fuel; the warriors were warm and their spirits rose. The period of comfort was brief. At daybreak the sentries gave the signal, and the regiment rose to find itself surrounded by a Balotsi impi, (a body of warriors). The Zulus defence was so courageous that a whole army fell back to a safe distance. There was no hope, though, that Kondwana could lead his tiny group through the fighting men of an entire tribe. No choice existed. The order to retreat was given. The Balotsi followed at a respectful distance. Even their harrying attempts failed. When they threw assegais (spears) the Zulus deflected them with their heavy shields, picked them up and returned them with deadly effect. Despite months of every variety of hardship and lack of food and rest, the Zulu retreat was managed with such control and revealed so great a reserve stamina that they distanced the Balotsi by a full day's march before reaching the saddle over the mountains. On the northwestern side of the pass, Kondwana halted with his men and then went forward to determine the situation beyond. When the valley came into view, he beheld massed before him the advance division of the Makalaka army. Beyond, as far as he could see, smoke rose from unnumbered fires.

Because the Zulus noted that the guide had brought them into the mountains by a circuitous route, they now determined to seek another way which might, hopefully, bring them into the vicinity of a more direct passage to the Limpopo. They succeeded in this attempt. When a day later the Balotsi army reached the saddle, where they expected to learn of the annihilation of Kondwana's men, they learned that the Zulus had not been seen. Desperate with fear, the Makalaka Chief guessed what had happened. Quickly the trail was discovered. The Balotsi were told to pursue and tell by their fires the location of the Zulus before them. Now the Makalaka army accepted the role of the interceptor. Soon after starting on their assignment in pursuit, the Balotsi, who had seen quite enough of the Zulu spears, turned and went home. However, this was really unimportant, for when the Zulus were again confronted by the Makalaka forces, Kondwana sent ten volunteers to light the signal fires (supposed to be set by the Balotsi) to indicate their presence. The Limpopo was now two days march before them. They had had no food, and their feet were in terrible condition from the rocks of the mountains. Leaving the fires to tell where they were not, the regiment, now only two hundred, moved on through the night. By morning they had outflanked the Makalakas and were marching towards the Limpopo. When their trail was discovered, a picked group of Makalaka warriors was sent in pursuit. Finally, a detachment of the Makalaka impi succeeded in getting between the Zulus and the river. Kondwana ordered a halt. The men dropped down to rest as the enemy advanced upon them. They were outnumbered ten to one, counting only the men in the immediate vicinity.

At a signal from Kondwana, the men sprang to their feet and formed themselves into a ring, two deep, the men on the outer ring holding their shields outwards, those on the inner ring, sloping their shields inwards. More and more the enemy massed between the Zulus and the river. Keeping his men to a passive resistance for the moment, Kondwana moved the ring slowly towards the Limpopo.

... All at once they stopped in their slow, silent progress, and the Makalakas moved in closer, thinking that the time for finishing them off had arrived. Then the war-cry rang out, and with one splendid dash the Zulus were amongst the densest mass of their foes. Nothing could withstand the fury of their onslaught, and the Makalakas fell under their spears like corn to the sickle.

The sun was just sinking. The Zulus had broken almost completely through the thickest portion of the ring formed by their foes. Only a few yards before them was the dense river-forest, offering sanctuary. But escape was not to be. Having been unable to re-form after the charge, they were practically defenceless against a tremendous attack on their rear led by the Makalaka Chief in person, whilst hundreds of assegais were hurled in with deadly effect from both sides. About twenty bleeding men managed to reach the forest, but their pursuers reached it at the same time, and one by one the Zulus died in desperate hand to hand encounters amidst the twilight of the trees.[3]

Assuming that the last Zulu was dead, the Makalakas withdrew secure in the belief that Tshaka would never learn the fate of his regiment and come to wreck vengeance upon those who had destroyed his veterans. Three men, however, lived. In the final dash into the forest, they had been claimed by an old elephant pit. Darkness and confusion had kept alive Kondwana, Senzanga, and one other, who subsequently died in their attempt to cross the Limpopo.

On a morning in November, two men who were assumed to be strangers appeared at the royal kraal and requested an audience with Tshaka. The older man seemed not entirely in his proper wits. Because such persons were believed to be wizards and thus dangerous to offend, the King signified that the strangers might approach.

Two men were then led before Tshaka. They were both fearfully emaciated and gaunt, and were scarred from head to foot. The elder man could not walk alone, but leant upon the shoulder of the younger as he hobbled along, using the remains of a broken spear, the blade of which was worn down to a knob, and the shattered handle of which was bound together with little thongs—as a walking stick. This man (the elder) had the appearance of great age. His form was bent, and the little hair which he still retained was quite white. His battered head-ring, being attached only by one side, shook as if it would fall off on account of the motion caused by his walking. He appeared to be nearly blind. . . . He carried a small skin wallet slung to his waist.

The younger man looked old with the oldness that comes not of time but of suffering. His very flesh seemed to have disappeared, and his eyes had sunk deep into his head. . . .

When they, with difficulty, arose after the obeisance, a change seemed to have come over Kondwana's face. The presence of the King, and the sound of his voice seemed to act as a stimulant upon the old man's torpid mind. In fact, they brought the farther past into stronger relief than the more recent, and then reality dawned up through the mists of fantasy that had clouded his brain for so long. His eyes brightened. He remembered the past. He knew clearly where he was, and why he was there.

Gazing fixedly at the King, Kondwana let the broken spear fall to the ground, and then with his shaking right hand began fumbling at the skin wallet. After some little delay, he succeeded in opening this, and then he drew from it a lump of bright copper ore, about the size of a hen's egg. This he silently held out to Tshaka.[4]

Suddenly Tshaka understood that this old man was not a wizard to be feared but his induna, Kondwana, who had committed the sin for which there was no pardon: he had returned unsuccessful from an expedition. The order for death was given instantly.

The executioners approached, but Kondwana drew himself up with ineffable dignity, signed to them with his hand to pause, and spake in a firm voice.

"O King, for my own death I thank you, for why should I longer live? But this man is still young, and has done no evil deed. Let him wash his spear once in the blood of your enemies, and die at the tip of your battle-horn."[5]

Thrown into a rage by the request, Tshaka made "Those who beheld him thus, [feel] that they were before the very face of Death, embodied and visible. . . . He glared speechlessly at Kondwana and Senzanga, who, having gone far beyond the limit of experience where Fear dwells, looked back quietly at his face."[6]

Finally Tshaka confronted a human being who had attained a serenity which hate, anger, or force could not reach. In telling the story of Kondwana and his regiment, Scully has given the reader an understanding of Tshaka's weakness but also his strength. Early in the narrative, the author remarks that the King had the ability to inspire loyalty but did not know this. As a result, he often destroyed those who were utterly true to him. Thus one of his greatest strengths became his ultimate weakness. Certainly Tshaka's ability to get the best out of men was a strength, but that he did not know how to use this best was a weakness. Again and again, Kondwana and his men display the value of their training as compared with that of their adversaries. The most important quality of all is their self-reliance. Once in the field, they looked to no one but themselves to care for themselves. Finally, the induna was expected to lead mentally as well as physically. Repeatedly it is Kondwana's judgment (and that of his nephew Senzanga) that makes it possible for a group of several hundred to hold off and almost defeat two armies. That Kondwana led physically is revealed by the condition of his spear—"the blade of which was worn down to a knob, and the shattered handle of which was bound together with little thongs. . . ." There can be no question as to where Kondwana was when the Zulus made their charge against the massed Makalaka impi on the edge of the forest beside the Limpopo.

Both Kondwana and Senzanga are dead within a minute after they are carried from the presence of the King. With that action the story ends. There is no comment from the author. None is needed. What the characters say and do presents them self-revealed. Tshaka and Kondwana live within the same time and human frame of reference, but as men they assume a position which establishes them as opposites. Tshaka was a destroyer. He obliterated Kondwana and everyone associated with him. In the story, what he did to one man and one regiment is a symbol of what he did to the native tribes of South Africa. Tshaka came to power by spilling the blood of others; his successor came to power by spilling his blood. This, however, is not the point of the story. An understanding of those who give and those who take emerges from the action. Men who take are often the ones who rule. At the end of the story, the sympathy of readers will be with those who give.

Jim Gubo, a native policeman in a story called "The Eumenides in Kafirland" practiced destruction of a lesser kind than that of Tshaka. To Kalaza, who has just returned from prison, Jim explains that so few sheep thieves are being caught that his officer tells the police that they are no good and that Government is convinced they are not performing their duties. Jim evolves a plot in which Kalaza will be used as the detective to catch someone stealing sheep. A victim has already been selected. Kalaza visits the man who has been chosen, whose name is Maliwe, and with despicable skill tricks him into stealing a sheep. Immediately he turns and gives evidence to convict him. The details have been arranged in such a way that Maliwe has no chance before the magistrate. Kalaza receives his fee as the detective; then he and Jim Gubo spend every shilling for brandy at the local canteen. Maliwe receives twenty-five lashes and pays a fine that uses all his resources. The "lobola" cattle, marriage payment, he had made for his intended bride are seized. When he attempts to communicate with the girl, her enraged father has his sons beat Maliwe until he lies senseless for a long time before he can drag himself away. The Eumenides live on far from the borders of ancient Greece, now performing a special task.

That Scully was not taking the side of Kaffirs as against Government and the native police is demonstrated by another story, "Umtagati," (magic) in which Vooda, a constable, in upholding that which is right wins a victory over one of the Pondo chiefs who defends that which is wrong. Though the principles with which the story is concerned are serious and important, the action and method of handling the material creates one of Scully's lighter narratives, at times delightfully comic.

For thoroughly grim humor, nothing that Scully wrote quite equals "Ghamba," a fictional presentation of a remnant of cannibalism reaching into the nineteenth century. The basis for the story is historical, and in a note the author gives the necessary details.

> Many people have heard or read of the cannibals of Natal, who turned large tracts of country into a shambles in the early part of this century, after Tshaka's impis had swept off all the cattle, and then kept the miserable people continually on the move, so that they were unable to cultivate. One Umdava originated the practice of eating human flesh. Gathering together the fragments of four scattered tribes, he trained them to hunt human beings as others hunted game. This gang was a greater scourge to the country surrounding the present site of Pietermaritzburg than even Tshaka's murdering hordes. It was broken up in or about the year 1824 when the Europeans first came to the country, and the remnants of many scattered tribes returned and settled under their protection.
>
> All this is history with which most people in South Africa are familiar, but many do not know that some of the cannibals fled to Basutoland where, amongst almost inaccessible mountains, they carried on their horrible practices for many years.[7]

Scully creates a sharp focus using only one family of the Basutoland cannibals. The father of this family, Ghamba, has selected as the next candidate for his table Trooper George Langley, of the Natal Mounted Police, stationed on the Upper Tugela. Langley was the most boyish looking member of the force. His face was smooth and ruddy, and he was inclined to stoutness. The aspect of his character which created his reputation was his passion for talking. Langley would talk to anyone who would listen. One day he noticed an old native man sitting on an anthill, just outside the camp. He approached and started a conversation. With delight he realized he had discovered one who would gladly converse with him. There was about the old man, however, a fact Langley should not have ignored: his teeth. "The incisor teeth were very large and white, but it was the development of the eye-teeth that was most startling. These, besides being very massive, were produced below the level of the incisors to a depth of nearly a quarter of an inch."[8]

Having established a bond which drew Langley to him, Ghamba one day revealed that he knew where Chief Umhlonhlo was hiding, for whose capture the Government had offered £500, dead or alive. Wanting the reward but afraid to undertake the action alone, Langley bargains with Ghamba to add to the expedition his friend Trooper Hiram Whitson, a combat veteran known to be the most accurate pistol shot in the unit. All three will share the reward. Whitson is one of the few Americans to appear in Scully's fiction. A "down-East" Yankee, he is Langley's opposite in every way. He is suspicious while Langley is trusting, strong as compared to weak, courageous to fearful. It is, of course, Whitson who destroys the cannibal family and saves the life of his friend, as well as his own. Just before he returns to camp, he gives Langley a lecture on keeping his mouth shut, especially about what has happend to them. This is surely the longest speech of Whitson's life—and effective. There is no difficulty in understanding the sacrifice Langley will have to make in suppressing the marvelous stories that could be told about this particular adventure. What happened would have provided him with conversation for the rest of his life.

The confession that Ghamba makes at the end of the story is amazing to the point of having a comic aspect. Yes, he says, the family had eaten their fellow troopers, Francis Dollond and James Franks. He commented, concerning a girl who had strayed from her family wagon and been taken, "She was very young and plump, and I have never eaten anything that I enjoyed so much. . . . His flesh (glancing again at Langley) looks something like hers did, and I am sure it would taste just as nice."[9] He freely admitted that he accepted the presence of Whitson on the expedition because he so wished to taste Langley. One suspects that he might have passed Whitson to his sons, whose taste was perhaps as yet not so highly cultivated as his own.

Problems that arise from discrepancies between theory and practice becomes the reason for a story called "The Fundamental Axiom." Missionaries proclaimed to the natives the brotherhood of man, but many had no belief in equality and certainly did not practice it. There is no general condemnation in the story, for within the action the author develops a distinct contrast between characters. Some believe and follow the faith; some proclaim but do not follow the announced position. Unlike any of the other stories of the collection is "Kellson's

Nemesis," about a magistrate who returns to a district many years after he had been there as a young clerk. Here a forgotten indiscretion is revealed in all of its tragic consequences. The story is a study in the strengths and weaknesses of human nature, not merely in South Africa but wherever man may be.

Accepting witchcraft is very different from accepting the witch doctor, whose power over the natives Scully deplored with every aspect of his being. In a story which he callsd "Ukushwama," he frames an action with a discussion of witchcraft (or belief in the supernatural) and supplies the events from the carrying out of a custom still followed by the Bacas and some other Bantu tribes. The custom is that of Ukushwama, feast of the first fruits.

> Each chief sends away by night, and has a pumpkin, a mealie-cob, and a stick of "imfe" (sweet-reed) stolen from the territory of some chief belonging to another tribe. These are mixed with medicines by the witch-doctor, and partaken of by the Chief and his family, in the calf-kraal before dawn on the morning of the day of the new moon. You have no doubt also heard that when a chief confers the honours of chieftainship upon his "great son," who is to succeed him, a special Shwama is held, and that on such an occasion the stolen first-fruits have to be mixed by the witch-doctor in the skull of a man who has been killed for the purpose. Many Europeans refuse to believe that this kind of thing still happens; nevertheless it does, and it will happen in spite of all the Government may do, so long as the Baca tribe is in existence.[10]

The skull used should be that of a person of high rank. On the particular occasion narrated in this story, the person killed by the witch doctor was the young and promising husband of the narrator's first and favorite daughter, Nomalie. This daughter the chief, Lukwazi, had desired as one of his wives. The custom, therefore, was used by the Chief to eliminate the one who had opposed him. Nomalie led her father to the place of the murder, under a large "umgwenya" (Kaffir plum) in the Ghoda bush, a well known landmark. A spear had been thrust from behind through the left shoulder-blade of the husband, Xolilizwe. When he was discovered, his head was missing. Here he was buried under the umgwenya tree. Nomalie, who committed suicide, was laid beside him. The anniversary of the tragedy was the feast of the Ukushwama, the new moon in February.

What had happened to Xolilizwe and Nomalie at the Ghoda became the basis for the discussion with which the story begins. The narrator, a government official, had stopped by the kraal of Numjala,

Headman of a section of the Baca tribe. Numjala urged the visitor to remain for the night, but the invitation was declined. The traveller had assured his wife he would be home by midnight, and he did not wish to cause her anxiety by his failure to return when anticipated. If he used the footpaths, he was sure he could reach home on schedule. Numjala warned that since his friend expected to take the path leading past the Ghoda bush he would never be able to ride by that point because it was the night of the new moon. Severely upbraided for such a superstitious belief, Numjala withstands the attack with great poise.

"You told me the other day that you believed in witchcraft. Surely you did not mean that?"

"Why not? Did not your great Prophet—every one of whose sayings all you white people believe so thoroughly and follow so carefully"—it will be seen that Numjala can be sarcastic—"believe in evil spirits, and even drive them forth? Is it not this that the witch-doctor claims to do? Did not the Prophet of the Wesleyans believe in witchcraft? Now, if you believe the words of your Prophets about some things, why not about others?" . . .

"But, surely, Numjala, your experience must have taught you that witchcraft is all humbug (imfeketu), and that before the English rule, the witch-doctor was simply the instrument of the chief for suppressing people who became too rich or too powerful."

"The witch-doctor may often be a humbug (kohlisi), and yet it is possible that there may be such a thing as witchcraft. A missionary, to whom I pointed out that some who preached the gospel had been since proved evil men, once said much the same thing to me about religion. I am an old man, and I have learnt many things, and one is this: He who always says of the thing he does not understand, 'This cannot be,' is in danger of being put to shame."

"Well, Numjala, tell me the story about the Ghoda bush, for I am sure there is a story."

"I will tell it if you will stay here to-night."

"But I must go home."

"Well then, I will make a bargain with you. You have already passed the Ghoda, and therefore you know the footpath leading to the drift."

"Yes, I know it well. I travelled it only the day before yesterday."

"Very well. You will take the pathway to-night, and if you can ride your horse past the Ghoda, well and good—you will go home to your wife. If not, you will return and sleep here. The kid will be roasted, and you shall hear the story. Do you agree?"

"Certainly I do."[11]

Riding away, he heard Numjala giving orders for the meal to be prepared. As he proceeded, all went well. His horse was good, and he went along briskly as he approached the Ghoda. The rider prepared himself and assumed that in a few moments he would be beyond the fateful spot and its ghost. Suddenly the horse gave a loud snort and wheeled to the right, unseating the rider. Another attempt was made, with similar results. A return to the kraal was the only course left. Numjala showed no surprise, nor did he ridicule the visitor. After an excellent meal, he told the story of the Ukushwama, with its tragic end for Xolilizwe and Nomalie. Next morning the departing guest stopped at the Ghoda and found the umgwenya and the two graves. As he stood watching, "A large bush-buck leaped up and crashed through the undergrowth. His doe followed immediately afterwards, passing so close that (he) could see the dew-drops glistening on her red, dappled flank."[12] After viewing the symbol of the tragic pair, the traveller went on his way. No difficulty was experienced in riding his horse past the Ghoda on the day after the new moon.

II *More Stories*

Once he started writing prose fiction, Scully continued and soon had another volume ready for publication, *The White Hecatomb and Other Stories*, 1897. Here were thirteen more stories, giving him a total of twenty published within two years. The subject matter used still represented what the author had experienced, heard, or read of South African history and legend.

Initiating his poetic career with the tragic outcome of an early shipwreck, Scully used another shipwreck in this volume of short stories; but this time he treats his reader to a happy account of the one person saved from the havoc wrought by the destructive storm. The only human being who reached shore alive was a little girl whose mother had tied her in what today would be called a life preserver. This child became queen of the Tshomanè Clan, immediately northeast of the mouth of the Umtati River, in what is now Pondoland. During her life, Fortune was good to the clan, and upon her death misfortune descended upon them. This was all early in the eighteenth century, but the remnant of the clan continued to honor her memory. Here Scully was working with native tradition which had persisted for almost two centuries.

Witch doctors and soothsayers of the clan announced that the ship was one of the creatures of the sea sent to bring the white maiden to the Tshomanè. When old enough, she was to become the "great wife" of 'Ndepa, the chief's "great son." She was, they said, a daughter of the mighty beings of the sea. Her nature was clearly shown by her hair, which was long and yellow as sea weed, and her eyes were blue as the sky. She fullfilled all that was said to be a part of her mission; and when she died, she was with proper ceremony returned to the sea.

Obviously this child was for the Tshomanè and subsequently for Scully a symbol of that force, whatever it is or from whence it comes, which guides man to the good. The little girl of the sea appears to be the original of Elsie, in a novel to be published a year later than this collection of short stories. In the longer work the development is much fuller than in the short.

Another story with a calmly happy conclusion is "The Return of Sobèdè." Convicted of a crime which he did not commit, he was sentenced to three years in prison at hard labor. He left behind a young wife, a son two months old, and his elderly father. Hardship of almost every possible kind made miserable the little family left behind. Before Sobèdè's release, 'Mbopè, the father, died. The wife, Mampitizili, and small son, Kungayè, were taken to the kraal of Manciya, a brother. This, however, did not make life easy for them. In fact, as Manciya more and more forced his attentions upon Mampitizili, she in desperation fled back to her old kraal. When she reached her home on the rocky ledge, she saw a fire in the hut and beside it a man was sleeping. She cried out in despair, for it seemed that even this refuge had been taken from her. No! for the man who rose from his sleep was the exhausted Sobèdè, who to reach home had walked long and hard after his release from prison. His return was eighteen weeks before he was expected because the family knew nothing of the time dropped from the three years because of his good behavior record. "Soon the three were sitting together in the hut, where the fire was now again blazing cheerfully;—the man and the woman with hearts too full for speech, and the child looking with wonder at the big stranger who did not treat him unkindly."[13] Despite the fact that Sobèdè had been in prison with criminal characters, he did not become one himself. When he emerged after his sentence, he was probably a better man than the day he entered. Under the burden of a punishment he did not deserve, he developed a healthy philosophy for use upon his return to the world. Unto the three around the home fire a soothing peace had come.

Peace of a different kind comes at the end of "The Seed of the Church." The title of the story is found in a passage from Tertullian,

"The blood of the martyrs is the seed of the Church." The narrative is concerned with the Christian conversion of Matshaka and his rejection by the tribe and even his family. Denounced by the witch doctor as an enemy of the chief, Matshaka found himself host to some thirty men of a killing party. Surrounded by the delegation, he knelt down and offered a silent prayer. Then he rose and announced his readiness. All was finished quickly. The whole proceeding was in sight of the church. Male members and the minister carried the body into the sanctuary and laid it before the communion table. "And every one there knew it to be an acceptable offering."[14]

How firm a grip certain ideas have upon the collective mind of the natives is illustrated again and again by details of various stories. In "The Imishologu," however, Scully has dramatized explicitly this tenacious hold. A little girl of six has strayed from home and fallen into a mountain crevice from which she cannot extricate herself. Her father is absent. A careful and wide search by mother, friends, and neighbors has been in vain. Meanwhile, a beer drink was in progress where four famous witch doctors have gathered to cure a girl who has epilepsy but is said to have had an attack of "umdhlemnyana" (love frenzy) caused by a young man who has cast a spell upon her. Into this gathering rushed a boy who had been herding cattle on the mountain side. Having entered a steep gorge seeking honey, he had noticed the cries of a child seeming to rise from under a flat rock. The locality was close, and to the spot the feasters went. The faint cries of a child could distinctly be heard from the stone indicated by the boy. The assembled witch doctors were asked for their ideas. The most celebrated spoke first. He did not suggest an opinion but gave a positive explanation. Certainly there was a child under the stone, but placed there by the "imishologu," spirits of the earth. No one should interfere with their actions. They might be asked in some orthodox way to return the child, but any violation of their domain would surely bring punishment. The other witch doctors claimed to have arrived at the same conclusion by an independent route. Asked for an orthodox method of obtaining the child's release, the most celebrated witch doctor advised that the trampling hoofs and clashing horns of cattle were pleasing to earth spirits. Cattle were collected, and the area well trampled. The "imishologu" did not respond. During the night one of the witch doctors had a vision that goats could achieve what the cattle had failed to do. This effort was not successful either. Nor could the child's cries now be heard. After what appeared as an epileptic fit, the most celebrated witch doctor revealed that the earth spirits had taken the child, who would never again suffer hunger, thirst, or pain. True!

When all of these proceedings were reported to Nomayeshè, the mother, she rushed to 'Ndondo's kraal, arriving about two hours after the trial by goats had failed. Starting with 'Ndondo and then to each man present, she asked to be shown the spot from which the sounds had come. 'Ndondo declared he knew nothing of the matter; then, fearful of the displeasure of the witch doctors, each man maintained complete silence. The needed information was obtained from some of the women at the kraal. Into the crevice under the rock the mother descended, and in a few minutes she emerged with the dead body of her child. A mother's love is more powerful than expediency.

Paternal love was likewise willing to oppose the system. In "The Vengeance of Dogolwana," the chieftain, with the intention of burning alive a family whom he considers to be blocking his desires, is tricked into burning the hut which houses his great wife, two sons, and a half-brother. The story ends with this episode; yet before the climax is reached, the reader has received a rich presentation of some of the conflicts found in native affairs. Here was material that Scully knew intimately from his experiences as a representative of government in those areas which were moving from a tribal civilization in the direction of something approaching an attitude present in what is usually called Western civilization.

Having served his chief long and faithfully, Dogolwana inherits a very difficult situation at the time of his leader's death. Umsoala had been a good head of his tribe; but his great son, Songoza, had not inherited the father's abilities and attitudes. Umsoala had asked the Government to accept this son in his place because the tribe would expect it, in fact would accept no other. The magistrate had been called, and in his presence and that of Dogolwana the dying chief gives his last will and testament. Again he admits his lack of the desired qualities. Once more the magistrate agrees to this choice. Now Umsoala turns to little Gqomisa, his youngest son, whom he loves, and wills to him his herd of black cattle. The herd is left in charge of Gqomisa's mother, Notemba (a daughter of Dogolwana), of Dogolwana himself and of his son Kèlè. Explaining that Songoza has already been given his cattle, the old chief requests the magistrate to support his bequest to Gqomisa. The magistrate affirms that he will give his support. The old chief dies early the next morning.

Succeeding to the chieftainship as planned, Songoza soon begins to reveal all of the characteristics predicted. His first act is to take possession by force of the herd of black cattle inherited by Gqomisa. Using great pressure, the magistrate compelled Songoza to return the herd. Next Songoza pretends great friendship for Kèlè. Then he decides that he wishes a wife from across the border in an independent native state. Along with three others, Kèlè is sent across the border with the lobola cattle. Meanwhile, Songoza's mother has become ill, or it is said that she is ill. A witch doctor is called to identify the person who has caused the illness. The answer, as might be predicted, is Kèlè. Now a messenger is sent to the three men on the road with Kèlè, instructing them to kill Kèlè before they return across the border, which will put them under the power of Government. The murder is performed.

Almost certainly the next move will be against little Gqomisa, who is being guarded carefully by his mother and grandfather. As they watch, Dogolwana and Notemba realize that a plot is being developed. Philip, the old chief's "educated" son, a perfect example of the evil councilor, becomes a resident in Songoza's kraal. When a son of Songoza's great wife becomes ill and then the mother, the witch doctor declares that spirits who oppose the great house are causing the illnesses. The remedy is for the chief to move his great wife and her children to the home of his late father. A black bull from "the herd" is to be sacrificed. This will please the ancestral spirits, who then will drive away the inimical spirits. Mahlokoza and her sons are assigned a hut beside the one occupied by little Gqomisa. Philip is a frequent visitor, and Songoza calls in passing. Clearly the plot is maturing rapidly. Kèlè's widow, announcing that she is going to the forest for medicinal roots, hides in the hut occupied by Mahlokoza. When Philip and Songoza drop by for a consultation, she hears the whole plan. On the next night, after all are sleep in the hut containing little Gqomisa, his mother, and grandfather, Philip is to fasten the door firmly from the outside, then Songoza is to set fire to the hut.

Immediately Dogolwana determines to use the plot they have created against Philip and Songoza. During the day Philip is made quite drunk, then bound and gagged. Mahlokosa is treated in the same way. Finally, the two boys are secured. All are safely deposited in Dogolwana's hut and the door fastened from the outside with copper wire. When night comes, Dogolwana and his family retire to Mahlokosa's hut and fasten the door from the inside. During the night hours, Songoza sets fire to the hut which now contains his great wife, two sons, and half-brother. When he thinks to awaken Philip, he hears the voice of Dogolwana saying, "My chief, Philip with your wife and children, is sleeping in the next hut on the left."[15] With a shriek, Songoza rushes forth as if pursued by fiends.

Surely what interested Scully was the power of profound traditional influences and the superficial effect of Western influences. What he knew as a magistrate, he employed as a fictionist. In this situation, the representative of Government realizes that his success with the old chief was not going to be transmitted to the next generation. Essentially, this meant that a new start had to be made. What is perhaps even more important is that the sympathy of the old chief for Western modes of thought was not followed by the people. They objected to and turned away from what they could not understand. Scully believed that time was needed to solve the problems created by the impingement upon each other of two very different civilizations.

Admittedly and inevitably, Scully wished to use the actions, attitudes, and ideas of the Bantu as raw material for his stories; yet this interest was not exclusive, for he did write about other races and situations. The principal character of "The Tramp's Tragedy" is an Englishman who works, when he works, for the Dutch farmers of South Africa. He had been in the gold rush at Pilgrim's Rest, but at the time of the narrative he is a brick mason, wandering about the Transvaal. One of the most skillfully articulated stories of the volume is "Aiāla." Scully has revealed here his love for Cape Town and Table Mountain, but more importantly his interest in Islam. Most of the action is set in a house of the Malay section of the city. The two characters around whom the narrative is developed are Lourens Brand, Dutch, and Aiāla, Malay. Now residents of Cape Town, they had shared a Java childhood without knowing each other. Aiāla belonged to an important Malay family, though her father, now dead, had been English. Brand's great-grandfather had married the daughter of a Singapore rajah. Drawn together twice by accident, the two were finally separated by smallpox, which at the time was devastating the city. Thus ended a very passionate love relationship.

Turning to South African history for the title story of this volume, Scully revealed again his interest in the extensions of wars waged by Tshaka. The immediate precipitating event of this story was the defeat of the Amangwanè tribe by Cape forces under Colonel Somerset at Imbulumpini, August 27, 1828. Three bodies of fugitives escaped from the battlefield. One group was pursued almost to the source of the Orange River, and there in a valley of tall grass burned to death. A second went northeast and was cut to pieces by the Amabaca, at the base of Intsiza Mountain. The annihilation of the third is told in "The White Hecatomb." As the final remnant struggled towards Basutoland to find protection under Moshesh, they perished in a snow storm on the top of a mountain. There had been no rain during their entire flight. As they ascended to the heights, the weather turned warm; but then black clouds rolled up. Suddenly the wind became cold, and snow began to fall. Clothing had been thrown away in flight. Nothing was possible except to huddle into circles. Women and children were placed in the center, and the men tried to hold their shields like the walls and roof of a hut. Nothing prevailed, however, against the storm driving fine snow. When morning came, the entire group (save one) lay frozen under a white canopy. The traditional *one* had to be left to tell the world what had happened.

Pondering the stories of these two volumes, one understands that never again can he feel the same about South Africa. Not only will he know more but he will also comprehend much more than previously about assembled facts. A more complete grasp of the nature of life among the natives will be possible because the reader has seen ideas and attitudes lived, not merely stated.

CHAPTER 5

Reaction to Experiences in the Desert

DURING the first fifteen years of his work with the Civil Service of the Cape Province, William Charles Scully was twice assigned to an area adjacent to the Bushmanland desert. Two aspects of this little-known world moved him as few things in his life did. The physical characteristics of the region impinged upon him with a force which penetrated to the very center of his imaginative faculties. Simultaneously, the conglomerate human and animal population appealed to both his mind and his emotions. When still very close to his period of residence there, Scully wrote two novels which offer readers, as perhaps never before recorded on the printed page, a feeling for the environment and the people of Bushmanland and those to its south. Years later, engaged upon the *Reminiscences*, he gave very special attention to the periods spent in the area. Finally, he wrote a nonfictional work as a valedictory in honor of the place and the people of that part of the earth in which he had spent some of his best days.

I Man Is Always Man

Locked in a vise between the seldom avoidable sun and the intimately associated sand, life in Bushmanland is depicted in *Between Sun and Sand*, 1898. All actions and reactions are made in relation to the presiding pair. Man soon learns that life itself depends upon complete respect for what surrounds him. In the first chapter of his novel, the author makes very specific the nature of the setting into which he expects to introduce the action of his story. It should be understood that the environment presented is an actual and not a fictional one. People called Trek-Boers have come to this area—according to Scully, human beings "unlike any others in South Africa, or possibly in the world."[1] Now the dominant group in the land, the Trek-Boers (Trek, to journey by wagon; Boer, a farmer) had replaced the diminutive Bush people, at the time of the novel almost extinct.

81

The Trek-Boer is a being *sui generis*.² He is usually ignorant to a degree unknown among men called civilized. He is untruthful, prejudiced, superstitious, cunning, lazy, and dirty. On the other hand he is extremely hospitable. Simple as a child in many things, and as trusting where his confidence has once been given, he cannot be known without being loved, for all his peculiarities. The desert life, which has filled the Arab with poetry and a sense of the higher mysteries, has sapped the last remnant of idealism from the Trek-Boer's nature, and left him without an aspiration or a dream. The usual lack of fresh meat and the absence of green vegetables as an item in his diet, has reacted upon his physique and made him listless and slouching in gait and deportment, as well as anaemic and prone to disease. This is especially true of his womankind, who, besides being extremely short-lived have, as a rule, lost nearly all pretensions to beauty of face or form.³

Despite the preponderance of Trek-Boers in the population of this area, Scully has not made his novel a study of these descendants of the Dutch blood in South Africa. Actually, the person who gives the novel its special character is an elderly Koranna Hottentot named Gert Gemsbok, though all natives were called Bushmen. Also indispensible are Nathan Steinmetz and his younger brother Max, German Jews, who as orphans had been raised by an uncle in London's East End. Oom Schulpad ("Uncle Tortoise"), was closely associated in the plot development with Gert and Max; he was a violinist and a character essentially beyond classification by local inhabitants. Of necessity the novel contains an assortment of Trek-Boers, the most prominent being Old Schalk Hattingh, whose grandniece Susannah is beloved of Max Steinmetz. The most important of the Trek-Boers in the development of the plot is Koos Bester, who lives at some distance from the only thing resembling a settlement in the whole region.

Among the characters created for a special purpose are Max and Susannah. "Max had a face which, had Raphael seen it through the bars of the Ghetto gate at Rome, would have made him take pains to secure the young Jew as a model."⁴ Susannah, too, was in contrast to her associates, "a well-favoured squirrel among a family of moles."⁵ Though Max, Susannah, and Gert are idealized characters, the first two are subject in various ways to human change as the story progresses. Gert Gemsbok, however, undergoes no change. The reason for this is simple. Although Max was twenty-one and Susannah nineteen, Gert was already old at the beginning of the action—which is of very short duration for him. In addition, Gert loses his position in the territory and finally his life because he tells the truth before the district magistrate. Obviously since Gert is to be among other things the symbol of truth, he cannot change. It is, of course, his other qualities that individualize him, the most important being his musical genius.

Developed for its own sake, Gert Gemsbok's life would have made an interesting narrative. Gert had taken part in the Koranna-Griqua rebellion on the northern border of the Cape Province during 1879. Having been captured and identified, he was sentenced to a severe flogging and long imprisonment. The first part of his sentence was served in the Breakwater Convict Station, Cape Town. Then he was moved to Kimberley. Upon discharge, he secured work in the mines, with the hope of saving enough money to return to his beloved desert and make a search for his family. His intentions were fulfilled, but upon his return he found only his mother and wife, in misery and want. With his help, existence for them became more bearable. Then fate chose him as an object to torture and destroy. Because he had witnessed the action which was the basis for serious criminal charges against Willem Bester (a Trek-Boer), Gert Gemsbok was called before the Special Magistrate for the Northern Border. Instead of lying and thus exonerating the accused, he told the truth and brought a long prison sentence upon one who was related to his master. Gert was immediately dismissed from his employment and boycotted throughout the territory. For six years he supported his mother, wife, and himself on bulbs, leaves, tubers, snakes, lizards, an occasional jackal, and at long intervals a klipspringer, of the antelope family. Each year when the Orange River was in flood because of heavy rains in far-away Basutoland, Gert journeyed to its banks in the hope that he could salvage from its waters something of use. The sixth year brought a miraculous bounty. As a raft swept towards the shore, Gert noted upon it a man dressed in European clothing. The man was obviously dead, but closer inspection revealed that he had been lashed to the raft while still alive. The prize which Gert desired was the man's shoes; which he managed to secure. As he examined them he discovered that the layers of leather which formed the sole of one shoe seemed to be coming apart. Probing disclosed a scrap of cloth in which had been wrapped a diamond about the size of a hazelnut. Altogether the boots yielded six stones, pure white and of the type found on the banks of the Vaal River, in contrast to those coming from the "dry diggings" at Kimberley. Because he had worked in the diamond fields, Gert knew very well what he had in his possession. He also understood thoroughly the near impossibility of disposing of the gems or convincing anyone that he had actually found and not stolen them. In this mass of material there is definitely the basis for a full novel, but this was not a book that Scully wished to write. To all of the above, he devoted a few pages; but nevertheless he did use Gert Gemsbok for a crucial part in the novel he actually wrote.

Characteristics of Bushmanland itself create the environment in which the action of the book moves.

Its bounds begin immediately to the eastward of the rugged mountain chain which runs parallel with the coast-line, about eighty miles inland, and it stretches on for hundreds of miles until merged with the central Karoo plains. These also form its indefinite boundary to the southward. It is, for the most part, almost absolutely level. To the northward, however, a chain of mountains, occasionally very lofty, arises. For stern, uncompromising aridity, for stark, grotesque, naked horror, these mountains stand probably unsurpassed on the face of the globe.[6]

Despite its harsh dangers, Scully insists that the desert possesses "For some natures . . . a deep and abiding charm. The fresh, crisp air of early morning; the peace which sinks like a benediction upon the wearied earth when the scorching sun has fallen from the sky, and the sand gives off its heat in rapid radiation; the sense of immensity made manifest in the wide, wide plains by day, and in the almost supernaturally bright skies at night. . . ."[7]

Reactions of this kind, however, emerge from sensibilities such as those possessed by men of the Scully type, not the Trek-Boers who lived in the area. These men were represented by such a character as claimed the only camp at Namies (pronounced "Namees").

The camp consisted of a wagon with a fore-and-aft canvas hood, or, as it is called in South Africa, a "tent." On either side of it stood, respectively, a mat-house and a square tent. The particular Trek-Boer who was the owner of this establishment was a somewhat distinguished specimen of his class. Old Schalk Hattingh had, like his father before him, lived his life upon the fringes of the Bushmanland Desert. . . . Namies was his headquarters, and had been so for nearly forty years. His well was the best there. Even that, however, ran dry during the early part of summer about once in three years, and he would then shift his camp to some more fortunate spot. . . . Old Schalk was a well-known character, and was looked upon as a patriarch and an oracle by the Trek-Boers for hundreds of miles around. He had been a famous man in his day, and could tell interesting, semi-veracious anecdotes of adventures with Bushmen, lions, and other things—predatory or preyed upon. He had never seen a village in his life, excepting the adventitious assemblages of

Reaction to Experiences in the Desert

the Trek-Boers. . . . He held the appointment under Government of Assistant Field Cornet. It was his duty in this capacity to report all crimes to the Special Magistrate, to arrest criminals, and to hold inquests in cases of deaths by violence in regard to which there was no suspicion of foul play. . . . Old Schalk's wife was only a few years younger than himself, but, as is especially the case with Boer women, she looked much older. His special grievance against Providence was that Mrs. Hattingh had lived so long, and thus kept him out of the enjoyment of the charms of younger women.[8]

Most of the action of the novel emanates from Namies and the persons associated in one way or another with this locality. From his brother's shop, Max Steinmetz could see the Hattingh camp, which for him meant Susannah. The plot begins with Max and Susannah, and the story terminates with the two married, starting a family, and looking to the future. Scully framed the narrative with their life and hopes.

Rain had come to the Bushmanland desert for one of its extremely rare visits, and Susannah felt within herself stirrings such as water had made in the natural world. She acted upon her impulse and soon was making for a kopje (small hill) upon which grew an ancient koekerboom, a large arboreal aloe.

As she ascended the kopje the breeze freshened, and the stiff, awkward branches of the archaic tree seemed to be seized with excitement unfitting its age and experience; it beckoned violently, and until Max, who was standing at the door of the shop, saw not alone its signal, but the flutter of the delicately flowered print dress which at that moment was rippling against its gnarled knees.

Max hurriedly locked the shop and sped up the side of the kopje toward the antiquated tree. . . .

Susannah heard the nearing footsteps. She had now taken off her cappie, and was lying back between two of the shapeless roots which were continuations of flanking buttresses thrown out by the tree towards the north-east, from whence the storms had been trying to uproot it—probably ever since the days when the galleys of Pharaoh passed down the Red Sea and returned to Egypt through the Pillars of Hercules. The girl arose into a sitting posture and turned towards the boy a face flushed with exercise and eyes liquid with delight. Max put out his hand in mute greeting, and she clasped it silently. Then he threw himself on the ground at her feet.

These two had for some time attracted each other. On Max's side the attraction had lately begun to ripen into something very like love. But of this as yet he was unaware. . . .

Spring, in a graciously capricious moment, resolved to crown her holiday with an idyll. Max arose and held out his hand to the girl. She took it, and he drew her gently to her feet. They wandered on together with scanty, broken speech and averted eyes, through lately arid nooks and hollows made sweet and full of the promise of verdure by yesterday's rain. . . .

They came to a flowering mass of gethyllis—that strange plant the curled leaves of which wind out their spirals in winter to catch the dewdrops and conduct them down their tube-like channels to the deep-underground bulb, which waits until the fiercest sun of summer shines before it sends up its lovely, tulip-like cup of snowy white or vivid crimson. The luscious scent filled the air and caused a faint, delicious intoxication. They bent over the blossoms and began gathering them. In doing this their hands met by accident and they started apart suddenly, thrilling with unknown confusion.

Their faltering speech died away altogether, and they more than ever avoided each other's gaze. After retracing their steps for a short distance they again paused. The vague horizon seemed to become of absorbing interest. . . .

Careless Nature, to bring them together, sacrificed a life. She sent a message down through a cleft in the rock against which Susannah was dejectedly leaning, and called from the depths where it had long been sleeping a poisonous red centipede. The creature crawled down over the girl's shoulder and endeavoured to enter her sleeve at the wrist. Then Max saw it. He sprang forward in a spasm of terror, brushed the centipede aside with his hand; not, however, before it had given him a venomous nip. In an instant he had crushed the life out of the creature with his foot; then, with an exclamation of pain, he turned towards the girl. His hand was already beginning to swell. Susannah tore a piece off the curtain of her cappie and began to bind up the injury. As she did so she came so close that she leant slightly against Max. Then the opportunity triumphed over the pain—he passed his arm around her, drew her to him, and kissed her on the quivering lips.

The centipede and its sting were soon forgotten. Nature held them, embraced and embracing, for a blissful eternity. . . .

As they paced away, hand in hand, a small army of fierce desert ants were dragging away the still writhing body of the centipede to their underground storehouse. Nature, so very lavish in large matters, is extremely economical in trifles.[9]

Conflict immediately developed from this relationship between Max and Susannah because it brought others into an area where opposition was inevitable. Normal objection came at once from Old Schalk when Susannah revealed that Max had declared his love and she intended to marry him. Old Schalk exploded with, "You promised to marry *him*—a Jew—one of those who denied the Lord Jesus and crucified him?"[10] Mrs. Hattingh gave it as her opinion that the minister would refuse her the sacrament if she married Max. None of this made the least impression upon Susannah in her resolve to join her life to the man she desired. Despite their youth, Max and Susannah display determination and strength.

Though the love story has about it much that creates interest, it is soon absorbed into a broader action. Max had called upon Old Schalk to discuss his wish to marry Susannah. Just as he had vowed his intention of becoming a Christian if that was required, he was interrupted by the arrival of Gert Gemsbok begging work from Old Schalk. As might be expected, Gert was crudely repulsed because his testimony, though true, had convicted a Trek-Boer. Max was revolted by what he heard and saw. He followed Gert and engaged him because at the moment he needed a herd to care for sheep received as barter. That night Gert told his story in the shop and next day went to work for Max. Had Nathan, his brother and owner of the business, been present, this would never have happened. Though the hiring was in good faith, the firing might be expected to take place immediately upon Nathan's return. The engaging of Gert, along with other things, brought Max and Nathan into violent conflict as soon as the older brother reached Namies.

Scully introduced harmony of two kinds into the discord present, as Oom Schulpad and Gert Gemsbok joined in human companionship in a meeting place provided by Max Steinmetz. Oom Schulpad was accepted throughout the whole area as a musician unexcelled. He and his violin were welcome everywhere. Now he not only found his equal, but, as he himself generously acknowledges, his superior in Gert Gemsbok and his "ramkee." Of Gert, the author explained that within his being he carried a quality identified as genuis, "which might be called the flower that bears the pollen which fertilises the human mind, and without which the soul of man would not exist."[11] Together the two musicians filled the shop with instrumental as well as human harmony. Soon Oom Schulpad found that if he played an air upon his violin, Gert could accompany him after hearing it once. Not unnaturally, the concord of their music was followed by a significant human sympathy each for the other. Max and Oom Schulpad bestowed upon Gert Gemsbok the only acceptance he had ever received outside of the Hottentot world. Though the number of days remaining to him was few, he came to his tragic death having known the most important thing in human existence.

Now the very essence of materialism and physicality returns to Namies, in the person of Nathan Steinmetz. Nathan takes no breath or step except for physical and material reasons. He follows the customs of the Jewish religion but had no beliefs; he is a regular attendant at Nachtmaal[12] but only to make money from those present; he treats the natives in the same manner as the Trek-Boers treat them because it is good for his business with the Trek-Boers. Nathan, however, has a limited understanding of human nature, and soon he will have to exchange his life for this lack of understanding.

While in Cape Town, Nathan had signed a contract to supply a firm of butchers with slaughter oxen. On his return he had called upon Koos Bester at his camp and purchased from him a number of cattle running half-wild in Bushmanland. Nathan was now planning to ride with Koos, who was at Namies, to his camp and collect the cattle, which could then be sent to Cape Town. When Koos visits him in the shop, Nathan suggests that the young Trek-Boer give Gert Gemsbok "a good licking" because he had presented evidence against Willem Bester. Koos agrees that he would welcome revenge, but as the days pass he does not avail himself of the opportunity. A reader begins to understand that an important conflict is developing within Koos Bester. Human good in him says "Hold thy hand"; evil says "Seek vengeance." For the present, good prevails.

However, evil never rests, as Koos was soon to learn. As he and Nathan drove out of Namies, the tempter, in the form of this "friend" beside him, pointed to Gert Gemsbok tending the sheep entrusted to him by Max. At the suggestion that here was another chance, Koos excused himself by saying that he had no sjambok (a heavy leather whip, often of rhinoceros hide) and thus would not secure sufficient revenge. A second time Nathan pressed Koos by saying that a stomping with his feet would be great punishment. Again Koos resisted. Once more Nathan tried, insisting that before he returned Max should have acted upon his order to dismiss Gert, making it impossible that he would ever get revenge. A third time Koos withstood the tempter. Finally, Nathan reminded him of Willem's death as a prisoner and taunted Koos with a lack of manhood. Under this attack, Koos yielded and started out after his supposed enemy. Even now Gert, who saw him coming, might have escaped and Koos been saved had not Nathan, from the elevation of the cart, directed him to the Hottentot's hiding place.

> The sorry deed did not take long to accomplish. With his powerful hand Koos seized Gemsbok by the skinny arm and hurled him to the bottom of the gully. . . . The old Hottentot was like a paper doll in the hands of the heavy, muscular Boer, and he fell with a thud upon the soft sand. Then Koos . . .

stamped upon the shrunken body with his heavy feet, and kicked it until his toes, badly protected by the thin and supple-soled veldschoens, began to hurt him severely.[13]

Excruciating pain in the great toe of his right foot forced Koos to retreat from the realm of vengeance into the practical world of his own body. Actually his toe was completely dislocated, turned in the opposite direction from the normal. At the next camp, two strong young men were needed to pull it into place again, and Koos fainted from the pain. Yet the physical pain was trivial compared to the torture that was developing in his mind. Had he killed Gert Gemsbok? Would the sand hold his tracks as evidence? Would the family accept the invented story of his injury? What place would Nathan hold in the event? Almost immediately Koos began to see Nathan as the Satanic character that he was and to hate him in a way he could never have directed against Gert Gemsbok.

Because Gert's little dog returned in fright and distress to the shop, Max knew something had happened. He closed the shop and, interpreting the dog's strange actions, worked his way to the spot where Gert lay close to death. The old man lived long enough to permit Max to understand what had brought him to his end. (Gert's diamonds were given to Max.) Following Max's report of the death, Old Schalk, as Assistant Field Cornet, gave it as his official opinion that Gert had been thrown from a horse. Twice Max protested and was quickly silenced. Before he could resist further, he felt an arm slipped within his, and he was in the friendly custody of Oom Schulpad. Soon they shifted their attention to the necessary funeral arrangements. Together they prepared the body and made Gert Gemsbok's grave beside that of his wife. As they did all they could do at the moment, Oom Schulpad made clear to Max that he had plans to care for Koos in a special way.

Without any pressure from the violinist as yet, Koos begins the life of the sensitive guilty. Returning to Namies, he seeks to learn if Gert is dead. Yes! Then he has committed a murder. Next he hears of the verdict—"accidental death," thrown by a horse. This means he is free. Then he discovers that Gert lived long enough to speak to Max of the event. What Gert had told he does not know. Now he makes a serious error. He goes to Nathan for information. Nathan uses the situation to force Koos into business deals that are entirely to Nathan's advantage—in fact he begins to assume he can drive Koos to do anything he asks, even offer him the attentions of his wife. Initial success causes Nathan to ignore the dangers of the couse of action he has planned. Having "purchased" another group of oxen from Koos, he insists that the young Trek-Boer drive him to the Bester camp, taking the exceedingly dangerous short cut through the dunes. The night before they leave Koos is given the special treatment Oom Schulpad had promised Max to administer. The old musician, knowing Koos would sleep beside his cart and horses, had arranged a performance certain to attain a much desired effect. After all lights were out and Koos felt he could get some rest, Oom Schulpad caused a flame to burst up from the locality which had been Gert Gemsbok's home. This was followed by a tune which Koos would be sure to associate with Gert. Thinking he is pursued by Gert's ghost, Koos flees to Nathan's shop and begs to spend the night. At dawn the two men start across the forbidding dunes. As they advance into the infernal sand, Nathan's sadistic nature leads him into insinuations, liberties, and proddings which sink deeper and deeper into the almost crazed mental state of the man beside him. Naturally Nathan had not read the title of this chapter, "Whoso diggeth a pit . . ." If he had examined the statement, he would not have known the conclusion, ". . . shall fall into it." He was not a student of the *Bible*, nor did he take any notice of the reactions of Koos to all that was being said. Midway through the dunes, just as they have reached the highest point of the most difficult assent to be made, Koos stops to give the horses a chance to recover after the strenuous effort they have made. Before starting again, he asks Nathan to stand up and permit an adjustment to the seat. As Nathan rises, Koos grasps him before he can anticipate the move and hurls him down the dune. Then Koos lashes the horses into a gallop. After two hundred yards, he stops and turns to see Nathan stumbling down the dune and falling every few steps. When he comes near, Koos puts the horses into a walk. Again as he draws close, Koos sends the horses into a trot. When last he looks back, he sees a prostrate form on the sand. With a wild laugh, he urges the horses into a gallop.

Because the annual Namies Nachtmaal occurred at this time, everyone was puzzled by the absence of Nathan Steinmetz and Koos Bester. Investigation was swift and thorough. A young Boer from the east had learned that Koos was at home but very ill, also that he had killed two of his horses on the trip through the dunes. Someone who had seen him driving into his camp reported that Nathan was not with him. Of course, everyone knew that Nathan had left Namies with Koos. A party of six men was formed to start immediately for the dunes. At Inkruip they rested, filled their water bottles, and at dawn moved through the dunes, following the clearly defined spoor. Soon they noticed that the ordinary course was not being pursued, but tended towards Bantom Berg, and passed through an area never before crossed by a vehicle. "Suddenly the spoor curved towards a gap in the right-hand dune. In climbing to this the men, with one accord, dismounted from their horses. When they reached the middle of the gap they stood still to recover breath."[14] Several hundred yards beyond, they found the remains of Nathan Steinmetz—keys, papers, watch—all there, except life.

What of Koos Bester? He had reached home in a state of wild excitement. Illness descended upon him, an illness of the mind. His wife was helpless before such a force. She moved the children a slight distance away from their father and did the best she could with the situation. One night Koos stole from his bed and into the open to free himself from the burning guilt of his actions. The Hottentot servants were sitting beside their fire a short distance away. His confused mind changed this fire into the one Oom Schulpad had "arranged" at Gert Gemsbok's home. Suddenly he heard a "ramkee" playing Gert's special tune—performed beside this fire in his own camp, played by an old Hottentot who had heard the original Gemsbok version. Though natural and actual, to Koos both fire and melody created the ghost of Gert Gemsbok, and he fled into the night and towards the dunes. Nothing could stop him. On and on and on he went until he descended into that "darkness which men call death."[15] The next day Mrs. Bester and the servants tracked him and returned to the camp with a now quiet, cold, and rigid body. Soon "two constables came with a warrant for Koos Bester's arrest, but he had gone before a higher tribunal than that of the Special Magistrate."[16]

Packed into this simple final statement of the novel are a number of meanings. Obviously the constables are left holding a warrant they cannot deliver. The magistrate will be unable to administer "justice." Characters within *Between Sun and Sand* may react in various ways, depending on their knowledge of the action and individual grasp of what they know. The story, however, tells all, and shows what it means for Koss Bester to stand "before a higher tribunal" than that of the Special Magistrate. As constituted, the magistrate's court can try Koos for murder, nothing more. If he has committed a murder, he can be declared guilty. He has indeed committed two murders. The case is a simple one. Koos, however, is seemingly oblivious of the practical criminal situation. The problem is not that a man has committed a crime but that a human being is guilty of sin, in fact two sins, and they are quite different. This suggestion is not intended to imply that Koos had rationally considered his predicament. He definitely has not. One can understand what has happened. In taking vengeance against Gert Gemsbok, he has become guilty of a sin perpetrated because of weakness. Not complete weakness, however, for of his own volition he had abandoned an opportunity to deliver a beating to Gert Gemsbok. In addition, he resisted Nathan the Tempter once, twice, three times. Thus, though he had displayed admirable powers of resistance, he finally allowed himself to be taunted into attacking the frail old Hottentot. Now his hatred, this time carefully meditated, planned, and executed, turns against the Tempter, who had maneuvered him into a crime he did not intend to commit. On that tragic dawn he approached Nathan as prosecuting attorney, judge, and executioner. Though Nathan was burning with guilt, Koos was committing the sin of usurping God's place. "Vengeance is mine, I will repay, saith the Lord." (Romans 12:19.) As the action moves swiftly to a conclusion, a reader witnesses a Koos who is tortured by his sin against Gert Gemsbok and seems not even to remember what he has done to Nathan Steinmetz. None of this is intended to suggest that Koos will be declared not guilty—of either action—as he comes before the higher tribunal. Nor does it imply he will be found guilty of both. Nor does it direct attention to a split verdict. What Scully has done is force one to accept the fact of a tribunal higher than human institutions, to decisions the meaning of which man may not be able to grasp. At the moment of death, man enters a realm of mystery, in the original meaning of the word. Koos now stands before the highest of all courts, and beyond this tribunal there is no appeal.

II *A Tragedy of the Rinderpest*

Few if any of William Charles Scully's narratives show a more carefully articulated progression of events than "Noquala's Cattle."[17] The composition is an excellent test of the author's fictional skill because the rinderpest epidemic, which is the basis for the story, was an occasion which demanded all of Scully's strength, endurance, courage, ability to handle people of many kinds, and desperate faith in the possible assistance science could bring to the tragic situation. An account of the work that was done is given in *Further Reminiscences of a South African Pioneer.* (See Chapter 2.) Nothing in the nonfictional record is taken from the historical setting and related as if it were fiction. "Noquala's Cattle" is an artistic creation, with attention focused upon a single man and the tragedy which develops from his individual loss of cattle. Though a reader is aware that the disease exists in other areas and is moving across the entire country, the story concentrates upon the specific and not the general. Human emotion reacts to the particular, not the all-inclusive. After being moved by a single tragic event, one can universalize the experience, but the first person singular initiates the chain of reaction.

Despite the effectiveness with which Scully depicts the physical reality of what is happening, indeed bringing the reader into complete sympathy with Noquala (whose mind is destroyed by the total loss of what he loved most), ultimately the author has written a story which presents a significant idea in relation to Noquala and thousands around him. The idea, the problem created by the impingement of western civilization upon that of the Bantu, is implied rather than stated, but it is clearly intended from the very beginning of the narrative.

Scully has presented the necessary characters systematically and revealed the growth of individual conflicts. Chief among the persons of the story is Noquala, about fifty, of the Hlubi tribe, and owner of the finest herd of cattle in the neighborhood. Through intelligent selection and careful attention to their needs, Noquala had developed a herd which numbered more than a hundred. There were sheep and goats, but he gave his love to the cattle—a very general attitude among the native tribes. In strange contrast to Noquala's love for his cattle was a love of money by his wife, Makalipa. Contrast between husband and wife is symbolized by the fact that one is heathen and the other Christian. Because Makalipa had become a Christian, she refused to marry Noquala until he promised to take only one wife. This he agreed to and kept the promise—which very likely surprised even Makalipa. As a pagan, Noquala loved the physical, above all his cattle, his noble dun-colored bull and the herd around him. Makalipa had adopted the Christian practice, if not theory, of bestowing her love on money.

Following the division of the parents, one son, Elijah, was being educated for the ministry. It was his mother's dream and appeared to be his own sincere wish. The second son, Zingelagahle, was happy with the care of the cattle and was likely to continue what his father had started. When the action of the story begins, Elijah was on the way home for a vacation break from school. While there, he became ill with typhoid fever. Thoroughly alarmed, his mother sent for a European doctor, the District Surgeon. This doctor, not making adequate allowance for the various limitations of the native mind, honestly believed that in serious cases such as the present, his medicines and his advice were of no avail. His journey to Noquala's kraal was a long one, and he arrived at the end of the day. Fear of being lost in the dark as he started back caused him to hurry his attention to the patient and the situation. What he saw and what he received as answers to his questions convinced him that he could do nothing for Elijah, who seemed destined to die before another sun set. The doctor mounted his horse and rode away, leaving the mother in despair. At this moment Noquala arrived. He had been absent while inspecting some of his cattle located at distant points. He immediately proposed sending for 'Ndakana, a native "gqira," or doctor. What superficially appears to be a contest between the doctors of two civilizations is no contest at all because the European doctor has already refused to compete. The gqira wins because Elijah had passed the crisis before his arrival and would have been one of the few cases to recover with normal attention and nourishment. The parents are, of course, profoundly thankful for what seems to be the saving of their son from certain death. Elijah himself, a candidate for the Christian ministry, was not at all grateful for being practiced upon by a witch doctor, the greatest obstacle to the development of Christianity. Since his convalescence was quite real, however, he could do nothing about what had happened to him. Thus he returned to school for the beginning of the new term.

Victory is often a transient gift, slipping from one's grasp as it comes into that grasp. Thus the native doctor will soon have to compete again, and this time the contest will be real. As the rinderpest approaches, he convinces Noquala that it is he, the gqira, who can protect the cattle. Reports have reached the area saying the government has discovered that by injecting a certain medicine into the blood of the cattle they can be made immune from the infection. The European doctor, however, had failed to cure Elijah, and 'Ndakana had restored him to health. The gqira was told to use whatever means might be needed to save Noquala's herd. A reader follows the "doctor's" action, which obviously can have nothing to do with preventing the spread of infection. If 'Ndakana had understood the law of averages, he would have found it convenient to arrange a long

Reaction to Experiences in the Desert 95

trip just at the time Noquala required his services. A conceivable turn in the progress of the infection which had attacked Elijah restored him to health. Without having to be tested again, 'Ndakana could claim complete success for his methods. In the new situation, one of the infected cattle might get well, or be immune naturally in the first place, but the second, third . . . eighth, twentieth might die. His first error, showing a lack of understanding of how infection is spread, was to demand that Noquala gather all his cattle, even those from distant points. Thus it happened that the infection, which was not present in the "home kraal" herd, was brought from a distant point among the Drakensberg. Soon this group began to sicken. The gqira insisted that the Drakensberg cattle had eaten a poisonous plant on their way down to Noquala's kraal. He administered a "medicine," but it had no effect. Death followed quickly after the appearance of the disease. The entire Drakensberg group was destroyed, and the formerly healthy cattle began to contract the disease. It was then that in the middle of the night the gqira decided to start on a long journey in search of a more powerful medicine to treat the situation. Noquala was left alone to watch as hour by hour his magnificent herd was taken in death. The last to die was the great dun-colored bull. At the break of day, Noquala, who had kept watch to the end, was found so stiff and cold that he had to be carried to his hut. When he finally emerged into the sunlight again, he was a cripple. His memory was dormant. Makalipa now cared for him as a small child. Boys brought him clay cattle which they had molded, and he sat playing with them in the sun, waiting for the return of 'Ndakana, the "great doctor," who went in search of medicinal roots.

Though Scully does not here make it a part of the story, the government fight against the rinderpest ended in great success. Science did not save all of the cattle treated, but where one was lost, hundreds were saved. This information was available to Noquala, but it was rejected. In Scully's story, however, he is not condemned. The purpose of the narrative is to show how a man of intelligence, practical sense, and detailed experience can make an error of this kind. Scully has shown the reader a double tragedy. First, there is the crushing loss of the cattle, an event which destroys Noquala physically and mentally. The other tragedy is the revelation that it is impossible to reach the native mind quickly or along any easy route. As the author suggests, the first effect of western education upon the native is, frequently, to make of him a prig. This is at least in part what has happened to Elijah. Only careful instruction and time will produce the desired results, with the next generation, and then the next, and into the future.

III *Love Is Stronger Than Hate*

Certainly the title *A Vendetta of the Desert* (1898) is accurate in the sense that this novel presents a story of revenge, with all of the hatred that can be generated when brother opposes brother. Added to the revenge emerging from blood opposition is the emotional tension created by the belief of one brother that his twin has taken the girl he loves and should have possessed. To complicate the situation, the girl actually loves the brother she did not marry—though she reveals this fact only a few minutes before her death. Here indeed is enough conflict to create a very powerful novel, and Scully has not failed in the use of his materials. Yet *A Vendetta of the Desert* is more than a story of action or lost love. What the author has undertaken to dramatize is his belief that love which emanates from a divine source is stronger than hate which arises from Satanic impulses.

For this novel the author has selected true Boers as characters. The brothers who dominate the action descended from Tyardt van der Walt, good Netherlands stock, whose grandfather emigrated from Holland in the mid-eighteenth century. The first van der Walt became a wine farmer in the Stellenbosch district of the Cape. Already this area was producing excellent wines, and here close to Cape Town the family settled down to life in a new country. There were several daughters, but a lone son, Cornelius. The boy elected to continue the life his father had chosen. The third generation produced another Tyardt. It was this Tyardt who turned away from the fruitful fields of Stellenbosch and trekked into the unknown lands beyond his peaceful fields. He passed further than the last sign of civilization and finally halted in a high valley where the Tanqua River gorge cuts the southern side of the Roggeveld Mountains. Here he built a homestead and claimed as his own the land for miles around. He named his new home "Elandsfontein" because of the preponderance in the vicinity of elands, one of the large antelopes. For many years his solitude was complete, though finally neighbors settled within fifteen or twenty miles of Elandsfontein. If the neighbors came too close, Tyardt was comforted by the vast uninhabited desert beyond the mountains on the north.

Leaving at his death half of the homestead to each of his twin sons, Tyardt unintentionally created the foundation for the family feud. In normal times, there was sufficient water on each half. Drought, however, drove both sides to a spring on the land bequeathed to Stephanus. According to the terms of the will the spring was designated as common property between the brothers. Under usual conditions, this clause would have preserved the peace; yet there came a year of drought when the spring was not sufficient for the use of both families. The case was finally carried to the Supreme Court of Cape Town, but without resolution because of a clumsily-drawn will and the refusal of either son to make any of the needed concessions. Conditions finally reached a point at which Stephanus and Gideon were called before the court of elders of the Dutch Reformed Church at Stellenbosch. So recalcitrant were the brothers that the conference ended in an unseemly brawl and both were excommunicated.

While water rights could openly be contested, the tragedy of unfulfilled love moved silently beneath the day to day lives of each of the persons involved. It all had started in Stellenbosch. Stephanus and Gideon had carried a wagon load of skins and produce for sale. Here they met Marta Venter, a cousin, with whom both boys fell in love. Stephanus, more quick and easy in speech than his brother, left Stellenbosch engaged to be married to Marta. The wedding ceremony was performed at the next Nachtmaal, but Gideon found a pretext to account for his absence. It was some time before he married Aletta du Val, daughter of a farmer in the neighborhood.

Intense hatred of the kind which had developed between Stephanus and Gideon could not continue very long without some kind of desperate action bringing one or both to a point of decision. As might be expected, the event occurred at the spring. One morning in early summer, Gideon saddled his horse, took his rifle and belt of bullets, and started for a ride along the western edge of his farm, his intention being to check on a flock of sheep kraaled at some distance from the homestead. The weather had been dry, and the herd had to be watered every morning at the stream which flowed from the spring. When he reached the kraal, he found that the sheep had been turned out sooner than usual. Next he rode to the spring and could easily see that the flock had already been watered. He lit his pipe and stood for a moment. A sound caused him to turn, and then he saw his herder, Gert Dragoonder, who assured him that the flock was grazing safely, some distance from the dividing line. He gave Gert the horse to take to the kraal and then settled down to finish his pipe and wait for the air to cool, as he planned to go on foot up the mountain side, where perhaps he would have a shot at a rhebok. Quiet rest soon became sleep. A noise awakened him, and on the other side of the spring he saw Stephanus dismounting. Allowed to graze, the horse moved towards the boundary line and then across it. Gideon grasped his gun and went swiftly in the direction of the animal, with the intention of seizing the trespasser. Seeing his brother making this move, Stephanus ran forward. A violent stuggle followed, from which Stephanus emerged with the gun. Gideon stood in impotent fury. Stephanus, seemingly in control of the situation, held his anger within more rational limits. Then a vicious taunt from his brother caused him to fling the gun into the scrub and rush to meet Gideon in a fair fight, man to man. As the gun crashed through the branches, it fired. Gideon fell, the bullet having torn open his shoulder. As quickly as possible, Stephanus began to administer first aid to Gideon and succeeded in reviving him. Seeing his Hottentot herder near, Gideon gasped, "Gert—come here—you are my witness—the man, there—my brother—he shot me.—There lies my gun in the bush—he threw it there to hide it.—I shall die of this.—Go to the Field Cornet.—He tried to murder me—I am already a dead man.—He must hang—"[18] Here Gideon lost consciousness again, and Stephanus sent Gert to the homestead to tell his mistress of the accident and to ask for men and poles to make a litter. He explained to Gert that after delivering these instructions he was to ride swiftly for Uncle Diederick, the most famous bone setter and herbalist in the whole area. Soon help arrived from the homestead, and Gideon was placed on a litter. All attempts of Stephanus to accompany him were repulsed, and Gideon insisted that the gun be recovered before he would permit himself to be moved from the spot. As the injured brother was carried away, the whole one fell to his knees.

. . . The crisis of his life had come upon him; he stood upon that spiritual eminence from which men see good and evil and must distinguish one from another. . . . The tangled sophistry which his mixed motives weave to blind the wrong-doer . . . was cut by the sword to which the Apostle of the Gentiles likened the Word of God. . . .[19]

When Stephanus van der Walt arose from his knees he felt that his sins had fallen from him. . . . His heart was burning with a deep and fearful joy,—his brain was braced with giants' strength to a sublime resolve.

In the exaltation of his newly acquired faith Stephanus knew for a certainty that Gideon would not die of the accidentally inflicted wound, and he thanked God for the agony that would purge his brother's soul of its share in the mutual sin.[20]

Reaction to Experiences in the Desert

When the author sends Stephanus out from the accident in the state of mind indicated above, he has written only sixteen and a half pages. Obviously, Scully intends to move his characters towards life rather than death. Physical conflict between the brothers ends with the accident at the spring, for Stephanus is charged with criminal action, convicted, and sentenced to ten years in prison at hard labor. During the trial at Cape Town, Gideon repeated the false testimony he had given the Field Cornet on the day of the accident; Stephanus had pleaded "not guilty" to the charges but had made no defense. When sentenced, he left the room with a spring in his step and a brightness in his eyes logically associated with moving to embrace that which will bring satisfaction, joy, or whatever may be most desired. Indeed he is moving towards what he most wishes—purification.

Only one wild moment of exultation was granted Gideon as he saw his brother led away. In the crowd passing out of the courtroom, Gideon found himself looking into the face of his brother's wife, the girl he had loved and desired. In her eyes he did not find reproach, as he expected, but love and an appeal that he forgive the wrong done him. Now the lie he had told to convict Stephanus fell upon him with an accusing force he felt he could not endure. "So the long-looked-forward-to triumph of Gideon van der Walt sank foully smouldering upon its own ashes, and he entered into that hell out of which there is seldom redemption."[21]

Having sentenced Stephanus to Robben Island for ten years and burdened Gideon with the guilt of his perjury, Scully turned to the presentation of three very special individuals, persons who possess rare human characteristics and are extremely important in the plot of the novel. The first of these to be introduced is Blind Elsie, the younger daughter of Stephanus, eight years old when her father is convicted of attempting to murder Gideon.

> The soul of this blind child, with the sweet inscrutable face, expressed itself in a passionate love for her father, and from the day upon which it came home to the strong, dour, hate-preoccupied man that this being who seemed the very incarnation of sunlight was doomed to walk in darkness all her days, he had wrapped her in a protecting love which was almost the only influence that kept him human, and which was the salvation of his better nature.
> Her touch . . . would cool, for the time being, his hottest resentment; the renewed hatred born of an encounter with his brother would sink abashed before the unconscious glance of her deep, sightless eyes. . . .

Elsie possessed intelligence far in advance of her age and circumstances. It seemed as though she never forgot anything that befel her or that she had heard. With a strange, uncanny intuition she would piece together with extraordinary correctness such fragments of disjointed information as she acquired, and thus gain an understanding of matters almost as soon as she became aware of their existence. . . .[22]

Only to Elsie did Stephanus reveal what had occurred to him on the day of the accident at the spring. That night, alone under the stars, Elsie questioned and her father answered.

"Father—you are not angry—but what has happened? I cannot read your face."
"Angry—no, my child; I shall never more be angry."
"Strange—you seemed to have changed to-day; your voice has got so soft and your hand throbs. Your face . . . feels happy—although you are not smiling."
"My child—one does not smile when one is happiest. Yes I am happy, for God has forgiven me my sins and whitened my heart."
"Do you no longer hate Uncle Gideon?"
"No, my child—all that is past."[23]

During the first half of the novel Kanu, her diminutive Bushman guide is inseparable from Elsie. Captured when a child, Kanu had grown up in the van der Walt household, had learned some Dutch, though he never abandoned his own language, and came literally to worship the blind child with the long, golden hair. With Kanu, Elsie was safe anywhere at any time. Because of compelling circumstances, it becomes necessary for Kanu to return to the desert, where he again joins his own people. Here he displays a very high quality of leadership.

Though early in the novel Uncle Diederick is summoned for his skill as a surgeon, he is later seen to be one of the best of Scully's comic creations. He and his daughter Jacomina are a delightful relief from the intense hate that pervades much of the narrative. Uncle Diederick would have been considered remarkable whatever the place or time. His ability, interest, and industry might be expected to create a successful physician and perhaps an eminent one had he ever been offered medical training. The author remarks that he cared for Gideon's wound with as much success as if he had been a member of the Royal College of Surgeons. Here all is profoundly serious. The manner with which he handles a patient such as Aunt Emerencia is very different, when she visits him requesting treatment for her *benauheid* (indigestion) and perhaps also having matrimonial hopes. In this situation, however, Jacomina keeps careful watch over her father. As Uncle Diederick knew quite well, Aunt Emerencia exercised too little, and ate, and drank too much. Thus her illness was always and only indigestion. To the doctor she explained, "Last night I dreamt that Nimrod built the Tower of Babel on my chest."[24] For these cases Uncle Diederick had his cures, and he delivered to the patient a large bottle of "medicine" in return for two pumpkins, honey, and a new pair of veldschoens for Jacomina, who pronounced them to be a good fit—before Uncle Diederick examined the patient and prescribed.

Even without her father's presence, Jacomina provides some of the best comedy of the book. Jacomina had her eyes upon Adrian van der Walt for a husband, and he had long been very much in love with her. His extreme shyness, however, made it impossible for him to tell her of his feelings. Jacomina understood the situation quite thoroughly, yet all of her skill fails here as it never did in her father's medical practice. Again and again, Jacomina brings Adrian to the point of proposing, only to have his courage fail. Finally a turn of fate, or more precisely a turn in the events of the novel, gives the young lady her chance. Thus Jacomina's pursuit of Adrian until he catches her is a delightful bit of fun spread through the serious events of the story.

Following the trial in Cape Town, Gideon quickly discovered that he was living in a world from which peace had disappeared. Life with Aletta and Adrian was one of misery for him, and his moods and outbursts made their existence horrible. Then, as Marta lay dying, she sent for him that at least in death their love might be confessed. Instead of love, Gideon confessed his guilt and made her final moment on earth one of agony. He fled from her room in terror. Yet, honoring Marta's final wish, Gideon accepted the children, Sara and Elsie, into his home, and Aletta gave a motherly welcome to them. Uncle Diederick and Jacomina were brought to the vacant house of Stephanus, to care for the place until the owner's release from prison. All went well, except with Gideon, who could find no peace.

Now, when his load of unrecognised remorse hung heavily upon him, he sighed his tired soul towards the vast and vague unknown which lay, rich in the glamour of the unknown and the mysterious, beyond the frowning mountain rampart. There, he had come to think, Peace must surely have her habitation; into that solitude the ghosts of men and things could not follow.

He put his wagon in order, loaded it with provisions and ammunition enough to last for several months, and went forth into the wilderness.[25]

After four months Gideon returned with all of his cattle and horses, together with much game. He did not, however, return with peace. Some time after this first journey, a group of hunters, strangers to Gideon, passed the homestead, and he decided to join them on their adventure into the wilderness, seeking large game. Nearly a year passed before he returned from this expedition. He had left his companions and reached a point beyond which no European had gone, yet he found no peace, for "the boundless desert had proved to be as close a prison to his guilty soul as the valley where stood his home."[26] Almost immediately after his return, he began to plan another penetration of the wilderness, alone, this to be the ultimate quest for the land of peace. During his periods at home, he had developed the habit of visiting the spring, a common enough action under the circumstances. One day when he came to the spot, he fell upon his knees and struggled and argued with the Almighty over his relationship to Stephanus. Resting in the shade close by were Elsie and Kanu, following a walk on the mountainside. Though his words were often incoherent, Elsie understood one simple fact very clearly—her father was innocent. The next morning she and Kanu had disappeared. Search parties and word went out in every direction for many miles, but not the slightest trace was found. Only Gideon guessed. Secretly he examined the ground near the spring and found the feared evidence. Again he turned towards the burning northern deserts.

While Gideon fled in vain from himself, Elsie and Kanu were cautiously stealing across veld, through valleys, and over mountains in a desperate effort to reach Cape Town and report to the Governor what they had heard. It would be foolish indeed to judge Elsie's resolve and its subsequent execution by realistic tests. Elsie is more nearly a pure symbol than any other character Scully created. Yet at the same time the author is successful in establishing verisimilitude as Elsie and Kanu proceed in their quest of the Governor and the release from prison of Stephanus van der Walt.

Initially, it should be observed that had Elsie searched the entire globe, she could not have produced a more perfect guide and guardian than a Bushman. Without Kanu, Elsie would have been found during the first hour of the search after she left the homestead. With such a guide she was able to travel by night and hide during the day. Kanu provided food—more easily for himself, it is true, than Elsie. For her he often had to steal and cook, both risks. As they approached Cape Town, their troubles increased. In his native area, Kanu could survive on the land, but as he moved south the flora and minor fauna became unknown and thus to be avoided. Finally, however, Table Mountain appeared in the distance, and towards this they pressed with new hope. Suddenly Kanu gasped in exclamation. There below them lay Cape Town. Passing into the city, they selected a large house at which to inquire for the Governor. Seemingly an inn, here they met an English captain who, though drunk, fed them but was suddenly called away on business and abandoned them to their quest. Next they were physically thrown from a large business establishment to which they had been falsely directed as the Governor's residence. In the streets Kanu again and again asked for information as to the location of the Governor's home. Most of the questions went unheeded. Some answered him with jibes. Few would take his question seriously. Late in the day, as they stood before a small shop, they were noticed by a kindly-disposed woman and taken into her home. Here they were fed and cared for, but the woman could not tell them how to find the Governor. Next morning the wanderers moved on in their search, having been begged to return at the end of the day. Helplessly the strange pair wandered through the streets: "Kanu, clad in a few tattered skins,—gaunt with famine, his body and limbs scarred by brambles and his quaking soul glaring out through his eyes,—his questions clothed in badly-broken Dutch. . . ."[27] And Elsie, ". . . pale with the hue born of that fatigue and starvation against which her frail body had been braced by a great resolve and a transcendent hope,—but staring through this pallor was the bitter agony of disappointment and fear. . . . Her face had taken on a terrible beauty that seemed to radiate calamity and despair."[28] Late in the afternoon the two were surrounded by a crowd of tormenting street boys. The one thing that seemed to protect them was Elsie's hair. When any boy came close enough to tug at the long golden masses of her hair, he drew away instantly and slunk to the outer edge of the crowd. Ultimately the youthful mob was dispersed by three British soldiers who, unable to understand Kanu's Dutch, passed on. Now Kanu, though unerringly he might have found his way in the desert, even in the darkness, was completely baffled by the maze presented by the streets of Cape Town as he attempted to return to the kind woman who had taken them in the previous night. Finally and instinctively, he turned towards Table Mountain and led

Elsie to a place of safety. Now it was decided that on the next day Kanu would go alone on the quest for the Governor. From a blind Hottentot beggar he learned the location of the Governor's residence and was told of its appearance.

With this joyful news he returned to Elsie, also carrying two small chickens which his extremely skillful "hunting" abilities had secured for the evening meal. Since Elsie's feet were still so much inflamed that she could hardly touch them to the earth, she remained in their retreat upon the mountain side and Kanu set out for Rondebosch in the hope of finding that elusive object, the Governor's residence. This time the little Bushman had no difficulty. He started back to Elsie, with only one task remaining. Securing food in the city was not, however, the same as from the countryside. Kanu was unsuccessful in his attempt, was brought into court, given the lash and a week in jail. When he was released, he went swiftly to Elsie's hiding place, but there was no Elsie and no evidence of what had happened. All he found was "a yellow thread,—bright as materialised sunlight. It hung from the bough of a shrub. . . . Kanu carefully disentangled the precious filament, rolled it up into a minute coil and put it into a little bag. . . ."[29] Again he made a careful examination of the area but found nothing to direct him to the one he had served so unselfishly. "Then his eyes began to swim with what in the case of a European would certainly have been called tears, and his throat tightened once more with the same sensation he had a few minutes previously experienced."[30] A third time he covered the area, lest he had left a small spot unsearched or failed to read some sign correctly. No trace had been left, and then once more there was a recurrence of the unaccountable sensation in the throat. No choice seemed left to him. Kanu turned north and "went forth for ever from the shadow of the dwelling-places of civilized men."[31]

During the day when Kanu had gone to Rondebosch, Elsie sat in the sunlight and doctored her feet in the cool stream which ran close to their place of hiding. She waited until night with composure. Then, though naturally concerned and puzzled, no panic appeared in her reactions. It was cold and she wished for a fire, but she could neither control the weather or build a fire. She was also hungry, and there was no food. Despite conditions, she did whatever she could for herself. Moving to the lee side of a rock for protection against the wind, she drew her knees up to her body for warmth and spread her heavy hair over herself as a tent. Soon she fell asleep.

Suddenly Elsie awoke to shrieks and roarings from the cliffs above, and down upon her came stones dislodged by a troop of baboons having a scuffle. In terror the child started on a descent of the mountain. Soon she lost her footing and fell over a ledge and was knocked unconscious. When she was somewhat revived, she attempted to continue down the mountain. Now she began to realize that the baboons were making one of their raids upon the gardens and orchards of the city's outskirts, and she was caught in the line of advance. One of the animals found Elsie and gave her a slap to her face. She rose and ran down the steep slope. A thorny shrub caught and held her dress. Thinking that one of the baboons had her in his paws, Elsie fainted.

Having experienced previous baboon raids upon their orchard, the du Plessis family had prepared themselves carefully for these attacks. Not only the servants but Mr. du Plessis and even the two daughters, who looked upon these occasions as sport, were up immediately when the alarm was sounded. This morning the enemy was soon driven back, but now there was excitement when the group came upon the prostrate form of Elsie. Immediately she was moved to the du Plessis home, given every possible preliminary attention, and very soon the family doctor was beside her. For many days there was no assurance that she would live, but finally her body began to regain normal functions. Her mind, however, had lost all consciousness of the past.

Immediately an interesting reversal occurred. "The strange story of the finding of the blind girl with the wonderful hair . . . spread abroad. . . . Many now recalled having seen the strange pair wandering up and down the streets upon their hopeless quest, and regretted, too late, that they had not rendered assistance. . . . Many were the visitors at the cottage on the mountain slope during Elsie's illness. When the child grew better a favoured few were allowed to take a peep into the dimly-lighted room where . . . tragic suffering lay."[32] Slowly Elsie was absorbed into the du Plessis home and assumed an identity which extended back in time only to the morning of her discovery. Four years passed, and "the blind girl who dwelt in darkness was the sunshine of the household."[33] The du Plessis daughters were now grown, and Gertrude had become engaged to a young minister who after being graduated from Leyden came out to the Cape. One aspect of his work which meant much to him was his visitation of prisoners on Robben Island. Just at this time, he explains to Gertrude that recently he has met there a very remarkable man who makes him say to himself, "That man is a better Christian than you."[34] The Reverend Mr. Brand explains enough of the prisoner's history for the reader to know that he has met Elsie's father.

Because Elsie never failed to react with fear when she heard the bark of the baboons from the mountain side, the family doctor had insisted that some day she would recover her memory. That day came in early spring, when the family had gone to the shore. Elsie, comfortably situated, had fallen off to sleep. Suddenly she sat upright, her face drawn, her breath coming in gasps. The initial word she spoke was "Kanu." When Helena replied, she asked, "Where is Kanu?" Both girls understood what had happened. When they called her by the name used for four years, she said, "My name is not Agatha,—my name is Elsie,—Elsie van der Walt."[35] The girls turned to each other knowingly. This was the name of the prisoner about whom Mr. Brand had spoken. Now they ask her father's name. When she says "Stephanus," Mr. Brand assures the du Plessis family that he will take her to Robben Island the next morning. Word that her father is near and well brings to Elsie a happiness which cancels all previous hardship and pain.

Without delay father and daughter are brought together. He explains to Elsie that he must finish his sentence, not for legal reasons but because it is God's will. Elsie is asked to return home and say nothing of what she knows. Everything proceeds as planned. Uncle Diederick comes for Elsie who, when she returns, convinces Aletta that Stephanus will not come home seeking vengeance. Gideon, however, believes only what is in his own mind. Yet no one has long to wait. Though Stephanus did not know it when he met with Elsie, his pardon was already being considered because of his exceptional behavior. Soon a letter reaches the homestead announcing the imminent arrival of Stephanus. In frantic haste, Gideon prepares to leave before his brother comes home.

During the hours preceding the arrival of Stephanus, Aletta passes through a period of desperate fear. All of Elsie's past and present efforts are in vain as she attempts to assure Aletta that Stephanus will not come in anger. Yet when his wagon arrives and Aletta hears him say "We both [Stephanus and Gideon] need the mercy of God," she finally believes.

> A great happiness welled up in Aletta's heart and seemed to transfigure her. . . . She felt that her dark hour had indeed been the prelude to a day brighter than her starved soul had known for many years. With feverish haste she completed the preparations for departure, and when the wagon rolled

Reaction to Experiences in the Desert

away up the steep kloof-track . . . she watched it until her sight grew dim with happy tears. Then she and Stephanus knelt down and he breathed forth a prayer as humbly exultant as ever the rapt singer of Israel uttered like trumpet blast whose sound still fills the centuries.

Afterwards, Stephanus followed the wagon on horseback, and Aletta turned to the joyful task of garnishing the dismal, unkempt house in preparation for her husband's return.[36]

Unhesitatingly Stephanus took Elsie with him as he started out to fight against Satan for his brother Gideon's soul. The moment towards which both had been moving for many years arrived. Unarmed Stephanus approached his brother. Though armed himself, Gideon's nerve failed and he retreated. Finally he stood with a cliff behind him and Stephanus before him.

"Keep back—keep back—" he shouted hoarsely, "or I will shoot you dead and follow you to Hell over the krantz."

"You cannot do it, my brother," called out Stephanus; "the shield of the Lord would turn the bullet aside and His hand would bear you up from the depths."[37]

Crazed with the fear of seeing into his brother's eyes, Gideon raised his gun and fired. The powder flashed in the pan. Stephanus moved composedly towards his brother, who dropped in nervous exhaustion before him. When Gideon regained consciousness and looked into his brother's eyes, he saw not the hate and passion for revenge he had feared but instead love and pity. Along with anguish and terror slipped away his sin. One sentence said all that was necessary: "It was as though the unveiled souls looked at each other, revealing all and wholly revealed."[38] As the two brothers returned to Elsie awaiting them in the wagon, "it seemed to them as though the Spirit of Peace inhabited her and looked out from the unfathomable depths of her sightless eyes."[39] This is the last sentence of the novel.

In this discussion the action taken by one character in the resolution of the plot has been very carefully omitted. In pursuit of his brother, Stephanus had driven his wagon into a desert which had seen no rain for two years. Finally his oxen, not as the very carefully selected and trained as those of Gideon, had fallen, never to rise unless water could be found. Stephanus went down on his knees and sent his heart up to the God he had trusted. As Elsie came out of the wagon, her father rose and stood beside her. A few yards away a startled Bushman called, "Baas Stephanus—Miss Elsie—here is

Kanu."[40] Kanu it was indeed. Knowing where to find water, Kanu soon changed what would have been death into life. Then privately Elsie asked Kanu if he would steal the oxen and horses of her Uncle Gideon. This he agreed to do. Next morning Gideon's camp awoke to the horrifying news that they had no means of transport. All of their animals were in the camp of Stephanus. It was this maneuver that brought Stephanus and Gideon together.

Where had Kanu been during the past four years? Obviously he had lived in the desert. Having succeeded in getting into a family, instead of being killed upon his approach, as he might have been, Kanu became in the passage of the years the leader of the Bushman unit he had joined—eight men, seven women, and fourteen children. One night his investigations had been rewarded by the discovery of a permanent spring of pure water, extremely well hidden and seemingly unknown to others. Here the group established residence, and it was from this spring and another near it and more open that Kanu was able to supply the water which saved Elsie and her father.

Discovery of the spring deep in an inaccessible cave had more than ever convinced Kanu's followers of his supernatural powers. Under his leadership they prospered as never before. Then, too, he gave them things other than water. Bushmen are well known as actors, and often Kanu entertained the group with stories of his experiences in the world beyond their desert. The old magistrate of Cape Town, who had sentenced him to be whipped, would have seen his dignity seriously diminished if he had witnessed the diminutive victim perched on a rock and mimicking his every word and gesture and orating gibberish to his audience. Then, too, there were serious moments of important decisions. One of these was his resolve to keep the Bushman's traditional method of preserving fire. Usually an older woman was designated to carry the fire when the group traveled. Kanu had learned the use of the tinder box, and once in an emergency had employed it. His action was looked upon as miraculous, but he very wisely saved the use of flint for unusual occasions. Had he made it commonplace, he would have lost the credit for performing miracles. Also he would have taken an important duty from an elderly person, who would then have been given harder but less important work. She and her relatives would have been made unhappy. No, Kanu was wise enough not to force change too rapidly upon his people. At this point Scully paused in his narrative and commented that Kanu had shown "a very sound political instinct, and his example might be profitably followed by many reformers whose impatience to put the whole world straight all at once, often defeats its own ends."⁴¹

Concluding his account of Kanu as leader of his clan, the author had the following to say.

... Kanu was venerated by his subjects as a powerful but beneficent magician, who had gone to some wonderful "other" world and returned laden with gifts of useful knowledge. Ksoa, Delilah-like, tried to get him to reveal to her the secret of his power, so he told her that he had been taken captive once by a monstrous being which was about to eat him,—when a blind lioness of wonderful size, strength and beauty had set him free and destroyed his enemy. This lioness had given him as a charm a hair out of her own splendid mane. So long, he said, as this hair were not stolen from him, or lost, all would go well with him and his. If, however, the hair were to be stolen,—not alone would good fortune depart from Kanu and his clan, but dire disaster would fall upon the stealer.

One day, after much persuasion, Kanu consented to show his wife the talisman. It had been carefully rolled around a dry leaf; Ksoa marvelled greatly as she saw its length uncoiled and saw how it glinted in the sun. She did not dare to touch it, but begged her lord to put the precious thing safely away at once, lest anything should happen to it.

"What a great and wonderful lioness that must have been.—And a lioness with a mane—" she commented in an awed whisper.

"Yes," answered Kanu, with a sigh.⁴²

Long before this point, it should be quite clear that Kanu does not appear in the novel as a servant, nor as a representative of an interesting native race. Even in the earliest days at the van der Walt homestead, he was Elsie's eyes. As soon as they started for Cape Town, he became everything she could not be. At the end, Kanu supplies water—ancient symbol of life, and in this situation life in a literal sense. Without Kanu Elsie, as she appears in the story, could not have existed. The converse is also true. Kanu could not have been as he is unless Elsie had been present to elicit his actions and reactions. Only Elsie and Kanu hear Gideon confess. When her father sends her back home after she visits him in prison, he tells her to say nothing of what she knows. This applies to all the world except Gideon (and Kanu had he been present). When Gideon asks why she "ran away" from home, she calmly inquires if he really wants her to answer this question. He recoils from the words. At all times Elsie is in possession of the truth. Elsie's attempt, with Kanu's devoted help, to reach Cape Town and her father reveals the hardships and agony through which love and truth are willing to pass in an effort to be heard. All of the particulars of the quest change the tame abstract into pulsing life.

Similarly, Stephanus and Gideon are far more than typical Dutch inhabitants of the Cape, though they do have the characteristics of the Boers during that era and in that locality. They exist in the novel, however, for the purpose of depicting a story as old as civilization—conflict between brothers. In an Old Testament civilization, such as the Boers felt they had created, this suggests the Cain and Abel story. At an extremely crucial point in the narrative, Gideon feels that he cannot allow himself to receive the curse of Cain, though in certain ways he has dramatized that curse.

Despite the fact that the story of hate between brothers is a universal one, Scully has done what all good fictionists are supposed to do. He has effected a union of the abstract and the particular. The concept of sin, repentance, and forgiveness is normally without excitement. Likewise, a narrative concerned merely with purgation is likely to prove very dull. All of this Scully has avoided in various ways. For nine years, Stephanus is withdrawn from everything that happens while he "pays for" his sin. It is Gideon who is presented as he clings to hate yet seeks above all else peace. Brought up, as he was, in the rigid doctrine of the Dutch church, he feared the judgment of God. Yet this judgment was perhaps far away. What he feared most was the eyes of his brother, something near and very particular. Well he knew that this brother was the one human being who had seen what had happened at the spring. Into those eyes that knew the truth he dared not look. (Later it is Elsie and Kanu who possess this truth from his own lips.) He was wrong, of course, in what he was sure would be found in his brother's eyes; yet no one could tell him what rests in those eyes. He must see it for himself.

What place does Elsie have in the novel once her father has been sent to prison? As an infant and child she had brought love into his life. After he has left home, she becomes the first to invite her Uncle Gideon to visit her mother, who is near death. Then she and her sister are taken into Gideon's family. "Insensibly Elsie became the centre of the household."[43] It is Elsie who knows her father's spiritual state, even before he is arrested. In her mind and out through her eyes this knowledge is directed towards her Uncle Gideon, and he trembles before it.

Perhaps nowhere does Scully show his skill as a novelist more completely than in the setting of the story and the people of that world as Gideon attempts to find relief from the guilt that refuses him peace. For a specific reason the author turns to the Boer's passion for isolation. "The Boer has ever been intolerant of near neighbors; he likes to feel that the utmost expanse his glance can sweep over is his, to use or neglect as suits him. He has a great objection to any habitation being within sight of his homestead."[44] Then, concerning the kind of man the Boer became in general, Scully offered the following brief summary: "Steadfast in his narrow faith, tenacious as steel to his limited purpose, valiant as any crusader that charged the Saracens on the plains of Palestine, the primitive Boer was of the texture of the strongest of the sons of the earth."[45] Immediately he continues by saying that "Such a typical Boer was Tyardt van der Walt. . . ."[46] Then he explains that when Gideon was old enough he accompanied his father on some of his trips into the wilderness beyond the mountains to the north. Thus, by inheritance and experience, Gideon looked to the wilderness when he needed to avoid a world pressing upon him. One is made aware of the increasing tension as a second trip follows the first, then a third being necessary after the second. Each is longer in duration than the preceding, and the penetration into the wilderness is greater each time. The last journey, naturally, is to have no return. Fate in the form of Stephanus interfered at this moment.

Ending a feud always requires the breaking of a chain. Up to the day of the accident at the spring, each brother felt that he must retaliate for every wrong or imagined wrong inflicted upon him. When Stephanus accepted the sentence and entered the prison at Robben Island, he ended a sequence of actions and reactions which had been in progress for twenty years. Whether he wished it or not, now during a period of ten years he would be unable to act against Gideon. Nor would it be possible for Gideon to reach him in any way. Though lack of action is negative, it was a necessary beginning. The first affirmative move which Stephanus makes is to see that his own conduct in prison is entirely exemplary. Next he begins to do good for others. Nothing that he undertakes is abandoned because it is difficult. In all that he starts he is steadfast. Naturally he thinks of Gideon, but not with hate and hope of revenge. Hate and any desire for vengeance had ended even before the trial at Cape Town. The reader learned this from his conversation with Elsie the night of the accident at the spring. Because he himself has secured peace, he understands Gideon's need. Gideon is thoroughly aware of the absence of peace, but he does not know where to seek what he desperately desires because he refuses to contemplate the attitude and conduct that will achieve release from his sin. Stephanus knew that though Gideon went away from the trial free and he himself entered a prison, in spirit he was free and Gideon was a prisoner. It was Gideon who suffered, not Stephanus who had admitted his transgression and accepted his ten years of purification. Stephanus assumes that Gideon does not have to follow the course he himself has pursued. At the end of the novel, Stephanus and Gideon stand together as equals, that is to say, they are truly brothers.

IV Across South Africa

Within the decade preceding the Anglo-Boer War, Scully had published a volume of poems, two collections of short stories, and two novels. Only one book represents the decade following. The problems and dislocations caused by the conflict were clearly reflected in this publication record. A novel concerned with a particular situation coming at the end of the war period was written but withheld from publication for almost two decades. Scully returned to the world as an author with *By Veld and Kopje*, 1907. The volume was prefaced by a poem which he called "Voices of Africa," from ancient days to the present. Thirteen stories fill the body of the book, one nonfictional, and the whole concludes with an essay on "Kaffir Music." That Scully's reputation had grown is attested by the fact that the materials of this volume had already appeared in widely scattered magazines.

No less than five of the stories in *By Veld and Kopje* have been written with some interest in the comic. The five display a wide variety of subject matter and characters. Two of the stories use native life, two the affairs of the missions, and one a pool room in the hotel of a small town—which could be in any country.

Already it has been made clear that Scully deplored beliefs among the natives which led to the "smelling out" that ended in ritualistic murder. His stories approach this problem from many directions. In "The Wisdom of the Serpent," he employs the methods of the humorist in his attack upon these practices. At the very beginning of the story, a reader is alerted to his intention by the tone of the language.

In the good old days in Southern Africa distinction of any kind on the part of a Kaffir was a decided subjective disadvantage. Any man among the southern Bantu tribes possessing to a remarkable degree such attributes as strength, valour in war, or skill in the hunting field, or who distinguished himself by any especially notable deed, was liable to be waylaid by the myrmidons of his chief and expeditiously killed. His skull would then be taken to the principal of the Royal College of Witch-doctors, who would fill it with a potion and give the gruesome cup to be quaffed by the head of the tribe just before dawn next morning at the gate of the calf-pen. It was held that the chief would thus acquire in a simple, easy, and expeditious manner the much envied qualities of the distinguished deceased. . . .

When the late Kreli, chief of the Gcaleka tribe, was a young man, he was thought to be somewhat dull and lacking in power of initiative, so a great council of the tribe was held to decide as to what should be done to improve the chief's understanding and sharpen his wits generally. After long and anxious deliberation the council decided that the best way to endow Kreli with the missing qualities was to cause him to drink a potion out of the skull of one of the councillors—an old man of great parts who had been an ornament to the tribal senate since long before the death of Hintza, Kreli's father. The proposition was carried by acclamation, there being only one dissentient. Certain rites had, however, to precede the killing, and during the celebration of these the distinguished possessor of the coveted skull managed to make his escape across the colonial boundary.

The elders, no doubt shocked at the want of patriotism displayed by their colleague, once more met, and it was then decided as an alternative to remove the first phalanx of the little finger of the young chief's left hand. That the operation had the desired effect there can be no doubt, for Kreli became astute in peace and valiant in war—facts which the British and Colonial Governments ascertained to their joint cost on several subsequent occasions.[47]

Regardless of how much any one or all qualities a chief had poured into him, he seemed always ready for more. One of the most effective potions was the gall of a python drunk from the skull of the mighty serpent. In that part of South Africa with which this story is concerned, a certain trader named John Flood had made what seemed to be a very secure place for himself by foresight, astuteness in business affairs, and hard work. One day he had the fortune (or misfortune as it turned out) to kill a giant python. The news spread swiftly through the area, and soon a witchdoctor of the young chief of the Bomvana waited upon John Flood and demanded the python. Flood refused to surrender the snake. Finally a compromise was reached. For his purpose, the witchdoctor needed only the head and gall. Flood valued only the skin. With his treasures now in his possession, the witchdoctor and his deputation hurried home and before daybreak was ready to serve the gall of the python in its own skull to his chief. "History does not record whether the potion acted as an emetic or not, but it may be safely assumed that the chief made an exceedingly wry face."[48]

When Kreli heard of the events, he (and the head of the Royal College of Gcaleka witchdoctors) went into a rage at what was considered an infringement of Kreli's prerogatives. A great council was called, but three days of deliberation failed to solve the problem. It was naturally the witchdoctor who revealed a way out of the dilemma. To the council he announced, ". . . it is my duty to reveal what was told to me in a vision. Know, then, that 'Munyu,' which was slain by Folodi, the European, was a messenger sent by the 'Imishologu' (ancestral spirits) to convey tokens of their favour to Kreli, and that if the qualities of the serpent be wholly lost to our chief, the 'Imishologu' will turn their faces from us in the hour of danger." . . ."What, then, must be done?" he continued. "Why, this: If the chief cannot obtain the skull and gall of 'Munyu,' there is nothing to prevent him getting the skull and gall of 'Munyu's' slayer. The European has vanquished the snake, therefore is he greater than the snake. Bring unto me this man's head and gall, and I will prepare a draught for Kreli which will make him so wise and subtle that you will all be as children before him, and so fierce that the warriors of Umtirara will flee from before his face."[49] The council adopted the proposal and began organizing a group to kill John Flood for his skull and gall.

Fortunately for John Flood, there was at the council a man he had treated and cured after the native doctors had pronounced his case hopeless. He hurried through the night to warn his friend, who was wise enough to select his best pony, most trusted gun, and to start for the Colonial boundary without bidding farewell to anyone at his trading post. John Flood lived to an advanced age without ever learning to love pythons.

Though "rainmaking" was a profitable pursuit in South Africa at the time of Scully's story, it required genius to remain in the profession for a long period of years. His story "Rainmaking" presents a character who secured honors, wealth, and lived to old age. The achievement, however, demanded certain specific qualities.

Severe drought had covered Pondoland and a deputation had called upon Umquikela, paramount chief, and requested that he summon Umgwadhla, the great tribal "inyanga ya'mvula," and order him to make rain. As soon as the chief could be sobered up enough to issue the order, the "rain doctor" was called. Since the last great drought ten years before had destroyed his predecessor and brought him to power, he had prospered with the rains that had come each year. Having studied both the weather and the situation, he understood what was happening. It is normal for rain to fall in various areas of the earth; yet at intervals a drought is certain to occur. It is then that the current "rainmaker" will be deposed. Though droughts are inevitable, so is the end of any particular dry spell. When rain finally comes, there will always be a new "rainmaker" ready to claim the credit. Thus the cycle continues.

Forced to predict that rain will come after he has performed the proper rituals, Umgwadhla announces that rain will fall on the fifth day after the "making" process was completed. No rain comes. When the inevitable delegation visits the great "doctor," he is far away from home. A week later abundant rain falls in exactly the manner originally predicted. Now Umgwadhla displays his genius. He immediately returns to Pondoland and accompained by influential friends appears before the chief and delivers his "explanation."

"On the night before the day on which I declared that rain should fall, the 'imishologu' revealed to me in a vision a dreadful secret. There dwells, I was told, a powerful wizard in the land of the Ambaca, who, by means of his medicines, drives back the rain-clouds when these are called up by the spells of your servant. This is done in revenge for that your illustrious father Faku slew Ncapayi, the Great Chief of the Ambaca, in battle. Seek, said the 'imishologu,' the root of a certain plant that grows in the depths of the forest; eat of it, and then go forth without fear to the Baca country. Find there the hut of the wizard; before it stands a high milkwood-tree and bound in the branches thereof is the skull of a baboon with the dried tail of a fish in its teeth, facing the land that is ruled by 'the young locust' [the meaning of the Pondo chief's name]. 'Remove the skull, and within a day the rivers of Umquikela [the Pondo Chief's name] will be roaring to the sea."⁵⁰

From beneath his kaross (rug made of skins, used also as a garment) he produced the baboon's skull, warning all to beware of touching it or the fish's tail. His maneuver worked. He was returned to his position, and many honors were bestowed upon him. Along with a knowledge of wind and weather, an understanding of how to make native beliefs work for rather than against you is a requirement. The reader chuckles with Umgwadhla as he adjusts the mantle of the new honors to his old shoulders.

Inevitable tensions and petty jealousies which develop in institutions such as a mission school, where some persons have more power than they know how to handle, are treated with delightful humor instead of oppressive seriousness, in "Chicken Wings." The existence or nonexistence of the supernatural offers the ultimate focus in "A Case for Psychical Research." The substance of the story is provided by the life and death of Isaac (whose surname the town never learned) as the billiard marker in a town hotel. Obsessively in love with his billiard table, Isaac comes back as a spirit to haunt those who were the regular players. Or did he come back? Perhaps research is needed.

Everything about "Mr. Bloxam's Choice" hints that the author enjoyed writing this story. He is simply having good fun with a very human situation. Three ministers sent out to South Africa have requested that the Mission Board which had sponsored them now select three ladies willing to become wives in a foreign country. The ladies have reached Port Elizabeth, and the men have been told to come to the parsonage of the Reverend Josiah Wiseman and his wife Louisa for the introductions, selections, and marriages—all of which will cover only a few days. The Reverend Peter Bloxam, in his middle forties, as the senior member of the "fortunate three," will have the first choice. He speaks much of Providence guiding his selection, but he is clearly rejoicing because the three ministers have been told that one of the ladies available is quite young and very pretty. The Reverend Mark Wardley, who is young, having no choice at all, is likely to receive a bride much his senior. Louisa Wiseman has determined, however, to place her ample proportions between Providence and the decisions being made by the ministers who have come for their brides. Actually this means maneuvering Mr. Bloxam away from the choice he intends to make.

When the ladies arrive, they conform to advance reports. The two older ones are propriety and rectitude itself mounted on a splinter. Their much younger companion reveals vitality ready to blossom but restrained by official frost. Mrs. Wiseman makes a rapid and accurate analysis of the situation and determines that the youthful Stella Mason must not be captured by Mr. Bloxam. The Reverend Samuel Winterton, knowing that he must accept the second choice, immediately associates himself with the lady seeming to be the more desirable of the two older arrivals, Miss Matilda Whitmore. The lady appears much more willing to engage in a love relation than initial stiffness had suggested; therefore, Mrs. Wiseman's problem is slightly simplified. In her conversations with Stella, she conceives the idea of a way to get Mr. Bloxam to reject that young lady. On the ship coming down one of the officers, Donald Ramsay, had confided in Stella about his engagement to a girl in Scotland. Mrs. Wiseman had requested that Stella invite him to luncheon. Then she has Stella drop a compromising note, signed with Donald Ramsay's initials, beside Mr. Bloxam just as she is called away from his side by Mrs. Wiseman. Mr. Bloxam picks up the note and telling himself that she is already the same as if his wife proceeds to open and read it. Deeply distressed by what he finds, he turns to Miss Lavinia Simpson, the oldest of the "brides to be" and asks her to become his wife, since the second choice has already been taken. She accepts. Then he goes with the damaging note to the Reverend Josiah Wiseman. Soon Mrs. Wiseman is summoned to a solemn conference in the parsonage study. She is told of the evidence supplied by the note, presumably to Stella, which her husband now holds. With one look at the evidence, she announces that she picked it up in the street and must have dropped it in the summer house when she went there for Stella. Now she produces Donald Ramsay's reply to the luncheon invitation, which in no way corresponds to the handwriting of the note found in the street. Mr. Bloxam is given great pleasure by hearing of Stella's innocence, then subsides in misery when he remembers that Lavinia has already accepted him to be her husband. To close the conference, Mrs. Wiseman reminds the men that the very least they can do for Stella after making the false accusation is to say not a word to anyone of what has happened. Then she announces that luncheon is ready.

Reluctantly, at the end of the day, Mrs. Wiseman retired to her bedroom. She had given her husband more than ample time to be sleeping soundly. Yet he was very much awake, and the inquisition began. Among other things, Mr. Wiseman was disturbed by the suspicion that his wife had lied to him. This uncertainty he felt he must resolve by asking a direct question.

"Louisa, you said you picked up that letter in the street. Was that statement true?"

"Of course it was." She answered him with indignant asperity. "May I inquire if you suspect me of telling a lie?"

"Louisa, do you know how the letter came to be in the street before you picked it up?"

"Of course I do. I dropped it there myself."

Mr. Wiseman groaned heavily in body and turned his face to the wall. . . . he recognized the hopelessness of further discussion.[51]

Indeed he was correct. About affairs of this kind, Louisa was probably the superior Wiseman.

Soon after Scully went to Tarkastad as his first assignment in the

Cape Civil Service, he discovered that his seven years at Kimberley and Pilgrim's Rest had introduced him to a life at a very much more elemental level than he was likely to find in the villages, towns, and cities of South Africa. (See Chapter 2.) Now entering his fifties, he was writing stories which recorded how human beings *qua* human beings reacted to elemental situations in which decisions had to be made. In "The Lepers" a Government order announced that all persons with leprosy must leave their homes and be transported to a designated place. Word is sent out to the headmen from the magistrate requesting that all those listed by the medical officer as lepers be assembled on a designated day for the journey to Emjanyana. Among those who have been identified is a young man named Mangèlè, who physically appeared to be one of the very superior men of the area. Yet leprosy had already attacked a hand and knee. Mangèlè's first action was to lead a group to the magistrate and ask that he shoot each one of them that they might die looking out upon the scenes they had always known. Deeply grieved by the situation, the magistrate explains that the law will not permit him to do as requested. Next, Mangèlè proposes, and the others agree, that they will meet upon a well known cliff at sunset, and there they will end this life still in view of the fields and cattle and homes they love. Though all keep the appointment, only one can perform the final act: Mangèlè. Despite pain and absence of hope, all except Mangèlè cling to life regardless of what it might bring them. To him death is to be preferred to deterioration into nothingness. He decides without hesitation.

Glorying in his own strength, neither fearing God nor regarding man, Sarel van der Merwe loved hunting to a point at which he almost deserted the society of man, including his own family. As he tells his story to a visitor, in "The Writing on the Rock," Old Sarel reveals the reason for the inscription his guest has discovered, "HIER WORDT EEN ZONDENAAR BEKEERD" (Here a sinner became converted). Sarel, then young, was on a hunt in the mountains.

"One day in summer, about forty years ago, I was riding across the head of the kloof where the stone stands whereon you read those words to-day. A thunderstorm was sweeping down from the north-west, but I took no heed, for I had never known fear of lightning nor anything else. The Bushmen were driving on a troop of elands, and I expected them to cross the saddle at the head of the kloof; so I left the horse concealed in a hollow and took my stand, with the rifle on my arm, at the foot of the rock.

"Soon the elands appeared; they ran for a short distance down the kloof, then halted just opposite where I was standing. One great bull stood apart

Reaction to Experiences in the Desert

from the others. As I lifted my rifle to take aim a flash leaped out of the cloud and struck the ground close to where the bull was standing, igniting the grass. . . . I fired—and it rolled over, dead.

"Then I laughed aloud and shouted that my aim was more true than that of the Almighty. An instant afterwards the heavens opened and flame enveloped me like a sheet. I fell, senseless, to the ground."[52]

No image of man, animal, or the natural world had been seen by Sarel van der Merwe since that moment. At the time, he cried out against God. He sought his gun to end his life, but the gun had been twisted as a handful of straw. Days, months, and years spread out in darkness before him, and in them he had to make several ultimate decisions. What he decided is revealed in the reaction of the visitor to the home of this old man. "Here was one who had solved the Great Enigma, who was at peace with himself, who apparently thought strongly and with originality, and who, although stricken with a misfortune that might well bring despair, was probably happier than nineteen-twentieths of his fellow-creatures. There was no trace of self-righteousness about the man. The unmistakeable seal of peace was upon him."[53] Through Sarel van der Merwe, Scully is identifying several of what he considered the ultimate goals of human life.

Withdrawal toward an elemental environment and existence is depicted in "Afar in the Desert" and "By the Waters of Marah." The first story seems definitely connected with the author's years at Pilgrim's Rest, in the gold fields. Before starting the narrative, he writes an introductory summary of what he intends to do.

> This is the story of a boy and a girl who met in a South African wilderness under strange circumstances more than thirty years ago. [Thirty years takes the story back to the time of Scully's life at Pilgrim's Rest.] The girl was desert-bred; her feet had never trodden those paths of convention which, in the aggregate, are called civilization. A chance medley of unusual happenings drove the boy forth from the haunts of men, but the absorbing spell of the wild fell upon him. . . .
>
> It is a love story; but Love revealed the shining wonder of his face to these two for less than one fleeting day, the while Death hid close behind him.
>
> Some of that which is here related is true.[54]

Because of a good deed done for Dan the Reefer, the camp's most celebrated prospector, the boy was taken into partnership on the next venture. The Reefer made it quite definite that he would do the prospecting and the boy was to carry the gun and supply the meat.

The arrangement was entirely satisfactory. Everyone knew the Reefer's habits. It was not love of gold but a passion for discovery that had driven him to the far parts of the earth—California, Alaska, South America. Now here he was at Pilgrim's Rest. Having come to an agreement on Sunday, the two assembled necessary supplies and on Thursday started. Some days later, after reaching the Olifant's River valley, they heard the sound of a violin coming from one of the gorges. Soon the wagon of a Boer hunter, Dirk Fourie, came into view. As they approached, he jumped down and came to welcome the strangers, at the same time calling to his daughter, Anna, to bring coffee. After introductions and some conversation, the Reefer slipped away to explore the area. Upon his return, he announced that they would remain for further explorations. He found gold and then became engrossed in efforts to trace what he had discovered to the main reef. Meanwhile the boy hunted with Dirk Fourie and slowly felt himself drawn to Anna. Fourie was a superb hunter. Killing lions was an obsession with him. A lion killed his father, and already Dirk had avenged the death thirty-one times.

Dick Fourie killed his last lion after the night when the boy made known to Anna his feelings toward her. When the mother fled, she left behind two very small cubs. Anna begged her father not to kill them; so they were taken with the group back to camp. After supper, the boy went down to the river for water. As he returned, his hunter's ears detected trouble beside the camp fire. Dropping the water, he rushed forward with rifle ready. A great, tawny lioness was violently pawing the cubs in an effort to release them. The boy's movement drew from her a charge, and his bullet went to the heart. Now the boy and the fire were the only living things inhabiting the circle of light.

Whereas no evil touched the world inhabited by Dirk, Anna, the boy, and the Reefer, the opposite is true in "By the Waters of Marah." The narrator of this tragic story was moving north towards the Orange River. One day he approached the home of a Boer, now blind, and his three sons. A niece of the blind old man completed the family. These boys mocked their helpless father, persecuted the girl, and ill-treated the guest in various ways. Soon the visitor found himself naturally drawn to the father and the girl, Alida, against the sons. At the moment of the father's death, the visitor was absent from the farm. So were the two older brothers. In a struggle with the youngest son, Alida had killed him. Upon the visitor's return to the farm, he did what was possible for the dead and took Alida away with him for protection. As expected, they were pursued. In defending them-

Reaction to Experiences in the Desert

selves, the man found it necessary to kill the two older sons. Now for a period, he and Alida possessed the peace of the desert. They even made friends with the Bushmen. Then severe drought came. All of the normal sources of water disappeared. Both they and the Bushmen were driven to depend, as in *Exodus*, upon the bitter waters of Marah. As long as possible the Bushmen kept Alida alive from their reserve stores, but finally even these sources failed. Drinking the bitter water sickened and finally killed Alida. Afterwards her one love and protector decides to remain beside the grave. At the time of the story, he has been faithful for twenty years. Not only have the Bushmen remained his friends but the wild animals respect him and do him no harm. He has made his peace with what the forces of destiny have willed him.

Loneliness pressed upon Tommy Winwood, aged eight, until he disobeyed his parents' most solemn order not to play with Danster, who was a mixture of Hottentot and Bushman, and according to father and mother "Tommy's Evil Genius." After prolonged obedience to his parents' demands, Tommy finally succumbed to temptation and followed Danster, who was as lonely as he, into the wonderland of the natural world. On that day Fate threw a fire in the thick and tall Tambookie grass between home and the explorers. Without hesitation, Danster slipped from his kaross, wrapped it around Tommy and ran, completely naked, with all the speed and force he could command from his body. He was able to save Tommy. His own burns were fatal.

Though his life did not have to be sacrificed, Dumani saved little Lucy Westbrook from a terrible death. Dumani had been accused of stealing, and Lucy was able to establish his innocence. The story reveals "The Gratitude of a Savage." Through an accident, Nolala, the daughter of Nomandewu, had been killed. Lucy's mother was held responsible by Nolala's mother. Without being able to say why, Dumani is sure that Nomandewu is planning revenge. He endures floggings and threats of dismissal for neglect of his duties as cattle herder because nothing can turn him from trailing Nomandewu in her strange activities. On a day that he is sent from the farm to deliver some cattle to a distant point, he is sure that what is to happen will happen. Starting very early, he is able to deliver his cattle just before sundown. Without rest he starts back and at dawn reaches the cave in which he had learned through following her that Nomandewu had constructed a rustic seat of the kind in which Lucy always sat as she played with Nolala, on the ground before her. Dumani was certain this was to be the scene of the revenge. What he finds at the mouth of the cave is a silent Nomandewu, hanging from the limb of a tree. In the cave, Lucy, alive, has been tied securely to the rustic seat. The little mound before her is Nolala's grave. Dumani has arrived in time; Lucy is released from the "death chair" and carried to her parents, who with friends and neighbors are searching the whole area for their daughter. Having delivered Lucy, Dumani goes into a sleep of exhaustion, for two days. To him the desired reward was Lucy's life.

While at Pilgrim's Rest, Scully "joined an expedition to Delagoa Bay organized by Pres. T. F. Burgers to transport materials for war against the Bapedi chief, Sekhukhune." Under the title of "A Forgotten Expedition," he inserted in his book an account of this undertaking. The trip was commanded by Major M'Donald (formerly of the United States Army), whose civil office was Gold Commissioner. From the mountain heights beyond Pilgrim's Rest, Scully had gazed longingly towards the Low Country. When a chance presented itself, he became part of the group making the attempt—now at the advanced age of nineteen. At last he was to cross the Crocodile and Komati, visit Lourenço Marques, and live through many new experiences. All of this was stored in his mind for this future use.

During the mid nineties, Makaula sent his brother Diko from the Matatiele border to Mount Frere with a group of carefully selected singers to present their tribal songs. Scully's wife recorded the words and gave musical notation for the lines. From the material, Scully developed an essay on "Kaffir Music." Whenever possible, the event which was the reason for composing the words and music has been given the reader. This material was orginally published in *Pall Mall Magazine*. The essay is not to be taken as a study of Bantu music but an account of what Scully and his wife had experienced.

With the publication of *By Veld and Kopje*, 1907, Scully terminated the first half of his literary life. More than a hundred poems, thirty-three short stories, and two novels had been published. The material already in print would have been sufficient to establish a reputation, but fortunately there was still much to come.

CHAPTER 6

Autobiographical Writing

HAVING lived in South Africa more than forty years and knowing that soon he would retire from the Civil Service, William Charles Scully began to write and publish accounts of what he had experienced between 1867 and the end of the nineteenth century. In the Union Number of *The State of South Africa,* June 1910, he offered the first installment of what he called *Unconventional Reminiscences.* The magazine was issued on the day of Union, an appropriate date for the beginning of a serious attempt by at least one individual to preserve a record of what had happened in South Africa during an important period in its life. That the author was interested in writing about South Africa and not himself is revealed in his "Foreward," when he explains that his account "must to some considerable extent be diluted with autobiography."[1] Scully had kept no diary, journal, or notebook; thus the material is almost completely devoid of the various kinds of biographical facts one might wish to have. For example, no mention is made of marriage, nor are there any details about his children. Often he is equally reticent in supplying information concerning himself. Few dates are given. However, much can be learned about South Africa, the physical aspects of the land itself and its varied people. Indirectly, of course, very significant characteristics of Scully himself emerge.

Starting in June 1910, the installments ran until December of 1912. Reaction to what Scully had written encouraged a publisher to present the whole series in two handsome volumes, 1913. The author revised the material slightly for its appearance in book form. Everything was complete and in print the year before his retirement from the Cape Civil Service.

I *Remembering the Diamond Diggings and the Gold Fields*

Though William Charles Scully did not write his autobiographical volumes until he had reached the fifties, his experiences in the diamond fields and adventures while gold mining were those of a boy—between fourteen and twenty-one, 1869–1876. It is impossible to say what he might have written if he had recorded action and thoughts at the time of occurrence, yet it seems quite likely that the mature mind determined with considerable accuracy what the youthful temperament responded to at the age of fourteen, or seventeen, or twenty. Much of the value of the first volume of the *Reminiscences of a South African Pioneer* derives from the aggregate of events because many details apply to actions performed by ordinary people. The actions themselves, however, are often not ordinary. Certainly the finding of a 90-carat diamond is not very usual. The finder was an elderly Boer who had probably hoped but never expected to change his poverty to riches. When the sought-after stone actually appeared, the discovery sent him into wild flight. Seeing what he had found, a few followed and called to others. Soon some several hundred persons were pursuing the frantic old man—who believed they were chasing him to take away the diamond. He dashed for a nearby store, climbed over the counter, and hid in a pile of sugar bags. Much persuasion was required to bring him out from under the bags and counter. He was difficult to convince that his followers were merely curious. Scully accepted this type of conduct as genuine. Quite likely the reason is simple: each person was glad to see a diamond found because he hoped to be the next one to make a discovery and was reassured to know that diamonds were there to be dug out.

Inevitably the rich returns from the fields at Kimberley brought in adventurers, and what was worse, from every part of the world. The first change resulting from their arrival was illicit diamond buying. This new element tempted the native workers to steal from the claims where they were employed. Scully explained how the workers were instructed in methods of taking and hiding diamonds. He illustrated one method, that of dropping an imitation stone in soil being sifted. One of the men picked up the stone between his toes and then casually sauntered away to hide what he had acquired. At that moment he was apprehended. This type of detection was satisfactory in one way, but it was more important to destroy the source of the trouble. The clearing houses for this illicit trade were the low canteens. Because there was no adequate law to control the practice, the reputable diggers simply "burnt down the more notorious establishments. This was done calmly, judicially, and without any unnecessary violence."[2]

Just as unusual methods were required to maintain law and order,

Autobiographical Writing

special attention often had to be administered to preserve social standards. The author's account of a wedding will illustrate what could happen. All of the workers in the area had stopped and assembled in front of the church, each with an old boot for the occasion. As the newly-married couple came out of the church, they passed down between the lines of cheering men. At a signal, all of the boots were thrown—care being taken not to hit the bride or the groom. Then one man picked up a book and deliberately threw it to hit the bride in the back.

> The bridegroom turned around, took off his coat—which he handed to the bride to hold—and rolled up his sleeves. He knew quite well who had thrown the missile. A ring was at once formed, and the fight began. . . . The bridegroom was victorious. . . . It was, however, just as well for [the offender] . . . that this was the case, otherwise we would have ducked him in the muddiest tail-race within reach. As the victor marched off with his proud mate he received an immense ovation.[3]

Seemingly everyone who writes about African adventures feels that he must say something about lions. Scully has obliged. Among other things in his effort to consider the lion is his discussion of the *roar*, the *growl*, and the *silence*.

> Leaving the brazen-toned roar, which is but seldom heard, out of the question, the lion's ordinary voice seems to be emitted by some being of incalculable immensity. It resembles a series of deep, half-smothered detonations linked together by querulous gruntle. It is difficult to realize that the sound originates from anything less huge than a mammoth.
> Three times only have I heard a lion roar wrathfully. The sound is harsh and shattering, and is pitched in a higher key than that of the growl. To me the growl was far more awe-inspiring than the roar; it carried a suggestion of stealth combined with latent ferocity and unimaginable force in reserve. The adjective "thunderous" does not fit the roar at all; the latter suggests, more than anything else, the tones of a mighty, cavernous brass trumpet. Most terrifying, however, is the suspicion that a lion is silently padding round your camp just before daybreak, debating with himself as to whether he will or will not attack.[4]

Along with others, Scully has an amusing lion story to tell. Near Pretorius Kop on a chilly night a man had wrapped his feet in a gunny-bag as protection against the cold, certainly not thinking of this as protection against lions. Just before dawn he was awakened to discover that he was being dragged from the tent by his feet. Since no weapon was available, he grasped a pot half-fiilled with cold tea. With this he succeeded in driving off the lion, who must have been very old.

Quite naturally any author writing about a new or strange country will supply physical descriptions of the region. Scully always gave careful attention to the area in which he lived or any country through which he was passing. Often it is possible to anticipate the coming of a natural setting which calls for some type of description. Late in the first volume, however, an occasion arose of which not even the author was aware. Long after dark, Scully and two bearers had made camp, in a dense mist, on a precipitous slope beside a lone tree.

> When I awoke next morning I was wet through and chilled to the bone. The mist was so dense that objects six feet away were almost invisible. . . . The light waxed; a strange and undefinable sensation thrilled me. . . . For a considerable time the air was perfectly still. Then, suddenly, a movement became noticeable; a sudden breeze sang out of the west, and the mist-shroud rolled away. . . .
> . . . I was just on the northern verge of the Great Kaap Basin. It is in extent probably thirty miles long by twenty wide, and is shaped somewhat like a pear—the larger end being scooped out of the mighty mass of the Drakensberg. . . . straight across the widest part of the valley the dark-blue mountains of Swaziland were piled in abrupt immensity, shimmering through an opaline medium which I cannot describe as haze, for the atmosphere was as clear and limped as a dew-drop. . . .[5]

Reminiscences of a South African Pioneer provides much information about William Charles Scully and the environment in which he had made his home since the age of twelve. Scully has left the historian valuable materials which he can use without having to make any effort to disentangle the author from the writing. This is true because the environment can quite easily be separated from Scully, though the man himself cannot be separated from the environment in which he lived. The literary critic, happily, receives the whole man while he is in the process of examining the documents Scully has left for posterity.

II *Meditations Upon Places and Human Conduct*

Considerable difference exists between the first and second volumes of Scully's *Reminiscences,* though there is only a week between the events at the end of the first book and the beginning of the second.

During his years at Kimberley and Pilgrim's Rest, Scully belonged to a group in the process of making history, albeit he may not have known this until he was able to look back upon the events of that period. When he entered the Cape Civil Service, slowly he became aware of the opportunity he was being given to assemble historical data before it passed beyond the point from which it might be retrieved. He comments that while at Mount Frere, "Occasionally I heard of some old Native who had been an actor in the tremendous drama of the Tshaka wars. Such men I always made a point of visiting. I have sat for hours next to such a patriarch, feeding him, as he lay on his mat, with teaspoonfuls of brandy and soup, endeavouring thus to stimulate his flagging memory. I was thus enabled to collect some valuable historical information. . . ."[6] Several of his short stories use the device of the listener who wishes to record what a speaker can tell because of his experiences.

Because of the nature of his various activities, Scully was acquainted with much more of South Africa than is normal for a person living in any country. Of all the areas with which he was familiar, he seems to have been most deeply moved by Table Mountain and Namaqualand, especially the Bushmanland desert. His longest and most detailed published reactions concern these localities. The complete contrast offered by the two is of considerable significance. Table Mountain entered into his life first and thus is discussed first.

Surely there are few lovelier or more varied land- or sea-scapes in the world than those visible from the summit of Table Mountain. . . .

And the aspects of these scenes changed with the journey of the sun, with the moving seasons, with the cloud-caprices of the sky. . . .

What a fairyland the mountain itself was! What joy it brought to discover some still, dreaming tarn ringed with great red Disa orchids, lolling, Narcissus-like, as though to kiss the loveliness of their own reflection. What a wealth of vivid colour, of rarest scent, of grace in form, was here strewn broadcast. How the scarlet Crassulas blazed in the rock-clefts; how the many-hued lilies and the sky-blue, foamed-lipped orchids glanced shyly from the moist peat-beds in which the wine-coloured rivulets were born. How the iris-plumed honey-birds dipped, seeking nectar, into the smoke-and-purple hued Protea chalices, and the ochre-tinted, blue-lunuled *Meneris* butterflies swept in swallow-strong flight from trove to trove of blossom treasures. . . .

Not least of joys connected with the mountain was to lie snug in some cave . . . listening to the howling tempest that reigned outside, or occasionally to stand at the cave's mouth and gaze on the Brocken-spectre of one's shadow flung by the camp-fire on the dense, hurtling masses of vapour.[7]

Whereas Table Mountain caused the author to look out and at, the Bushmanland desert urged him to look inward at self in particular and man in general.

> . . . the desert is a severe task-mistress, and, by the imposition of heavy toil, draws one's mind from the rag-fair of unrealities in which we spend our days. . . . For with the flaming sun above and the red-hot sand beneath, you have no time for trifling. Your environment is one of danger; the breaking of an axle might spell your death. Therefore your axle, or any other necessary gear that might possibly give way, becomes a matter of absorbing interest. You know of a place where, at a given time of the year, water may usually be obtained by digging. Yet it is possible that some nomads may have lately tented there and used up every drop. Should this prove to be the case, you would have to deal warily to avoid perishing. At night the cobra, whose bite is certain death, emerges from his deep, cool lair and glides over the surface; in the morning you will see his zigzag track close to your camp. But the sense of danger, the possible immanence of death, wakens the manhood within you from its convention-drugged sleep. Throughout the seemingly interminable hours of the day the sunlight pours on you like a fiery flood; you suffer acutely as the torrid air-waves, sped from the glinting silver-furnace-sea of the mirage, overwhelm you. But you do not lie down and gasp, as you would do in your ordinary sedentary environment when the heat is excessive. No; you want to resist, to fight with all your strength, and your latent potency wells up from deep, unsuspected sources until you almost rejoice in the torment that your new-found fortitude enables you to sustain. . . .
>
> The secret of the desert's health-giving lies, I think, in this: that it tends to lead your soul forth from the dank, dark cavern in which stifling convention, the dire inheritance of dead centuries, has pent it. At the desert's liberating word you and your soul stand forth, face to face, real and vital, naked and beautiful as God and Nature have made you. You have probably never met before; your eyes have been sealed, your tongue tied, your ears bandaged. Now you meet like the first man and the first woman in the Eden myth, and you find each other fair. . . .[8]

More and more as the years passed did Scully ponder the nature of things. Looking at the huts constructed by the various Bantu tribes caused him to probe for the reason far beneath the surface of what he saw.

> The Native hut is, I think, a form of dwelling of a very old type. From the Sudan to the Amatole Mountains, from the Congo and the Niger to Mombasa and Inhambane, the myriad millions of Bantu have adhered universally to the same architectual form—a form which probably has not varied materially for twenty thousand years. Why, one wonders, has Africa never produced a type

of building capable of lasting more than a few years? The characteristics of the people indicate permanency, their law-codes are elaborate and comprehensive, many of their customs probably date from the days of Abraham. The wooden pillows in use today among the Zulus and Swazies are identical in workmanship and design with the head-rests found in Egyptian tombs which were sealed up five thousand years ago. But the African apparently never built anything more permanent in the shape of a dwelling than the beehive-shaped structures of wattles, grass, and clay, with which all are familiar.[9]

With seeming ease, Scully moved from native huts to the European legal system which was being imposed upon the Bantu tribes.

... Next to the liquor traffic nothing has so much demoralized the Natives as the European legal system. It would have been a priceless boon had attorneys and law-agents been prevented from establishing themselves beyond the territorial border. When the Amabaca first came under British rule it was a point of honour with every native to plead guilty if he had committed the crime laid to his charge. But with the advent of the lawyer all this was changed. Thus a premium was at once placed on lying in a large number of cases, and a tribe which had been noted for its truthfulness became steeped in mendacity.[10]

Visiting London for the first time, Scully found there an object made by man in which he discovered some of the characteristics which drew him to the Bushmanland desert.

To me the most inspiring spot in London was the Temple Church. In its gracious stillness I used to take refuge from the roar of the Strand and Fleet Street. ... Here I would recall the extraordinary history of the Templars— so glorious in its morning and noon, so piteous when the stormy evening fell. The valour of these lofty-spirited warriors of the Cross, the agony of their extinction, and the hideous injustice which led to it—surely the perplexed mind of man has never had a harder task than to adjust this record to the concept of an omnipotent and omniscient Providence. ....[11]

He found the life and being of the average Londoner totally opposite to the qualities of the Temple Church—that is to say the major element of any large city.

My experience of the rank and file of Londoners gave me the impression that life in a mammoth city does not develop the human intellect to such a pitch of effectiveness as life in the veld. The individuals of whom I had sufficient experience to enable me to judge, appeared to have made themselves familiar with a few grooves and, in fact, to have become highly specialized therein, but if one endeavoured to exercise them in the vast field of the ungrooved, they stumbled badly. It may be that the constant impact of crowding impressions dulls the perceptions. There can be no doubt that the ready-made and speciously argued opinions served up in the daily papers, dealing with every imaginable subject, tend to get people out of the habit of thinking for themselves.

The average Londoner, so far as I had an opportunity of judging, appeared to read solely for amusement. The editor of one of the most important illustrated weeklies of the English-speaking world told me that year by year it was found necessary to lower the intellectual standard of his columns. I often traveled by the Underground Railway in carriages crowded with clerks. Each of the latter would usually be engaged in reading one or other of the (so-called) comic papers. . . .

The old South African Boer, who only read his Bible, has often been derided for his ignorance and his prejudices. Yet, if a man's reading be restricted to one class of literature—using that term in a most comprehensive sense—I think few will question the superiority of Isaiah to *Sketchy Bits*, or of the Psalms . . . to *Comic Cuts*. If the young men I allude to read anything else, the case would not be so hopeless, but I am certain that in the vast majority of instances they did not. . . .[12]

What Scully found in London he feared was developing rapidly, much too rapidly, in the cities of South Africa. Johannesburg, of course, was so far the most dangerous; yet one could not expect Cape Town, Durban, Port Elizabeth, Pretoria, and others not to follow the established trend. This visit was made in 1898. One can rejoice in knowing that Scully did not yet see what was to happen before his earthly sojourn would end.

CHAPTER 7

Opposite Worlds

THE period between 1910 and 1915 was for Scully feverishly busy. Serial publication of his *Reminiscences* had started in 1910, and all of this material was gathered into two volumes in 1913. Meanwhile a visit from Port Elizabeth to East London, Durban, Lourenço Marques, Pretoria, and Johannesburg became the basis for a book which he called *The Ridge of the White Waters*, 1912. This was the Witwatersrand, the great gold-bearing reef which had made the high veld famous throughout the world. Conversely, the Bushmanland desert was known to few people, yet nothing else which impinged upon Scully's imagination had influenced him quite so much. In *Lodges in the Wilderness*, 1915, he bade farewell to this region which he had loved long and deeply. Hundreds of miles separated the desert to which the Bushmen had given their name and the Witwatersrand, the Rand, to which gold had given its fame. Nothing would ever bring these extremes together.

I   *The Rule of Mammon*

Though Scully has constructed *The Ridge of the White Waters* as a travel book, his dominant purpose was to offer a study of life as it existed in Johannesburg about 1912. Leaving Port Elizabeth on the *Dover Castle*, he begins a nostalgic retracing of events thirty-six years into his past. At East London he recalls the work he performed for the Boating Company. Then at Durban he remembers that he could not find work and was completely without resources. Much attention is given to Lourenço Marques. Here he recounts in detail the difference between what he observed in 1874 and all that spreads before him a generation later. Changing now from travel by sea to train, he starts for Pretoria and Johannesburg.

Once inside the city limits of Johannesburg, the author begins to study the situation he has come to examine. He does not hesitate to condemn, but is equally willing to offer praise. His visit starts with

131

the Rand Club, where he is to stay. Though the accommodations are comfortable, he considers the "ornamentation" excessive and in poor taste. The shops of the city he compares favorably with those of London and Paris. Very high praise is given to the Johannesburg Art Collection, for the moment housed in the School of Mines. A visit to the country club brings from him the comment that the people he observes there show a lack of ease. "They are endeavouring to live up to their wardrobes and their automobiles, and the effort makes them self-conscious."[1] All of this, however, is incidental to the central purpose of the book, which is to consider the impact of the Rand gold mines upon the civilization of South Africa.

Ultimately what Scully has undertaken is to examine the conflicts which develop when various kinds of dislocations occur in the human structure of a region. Given the circumstances, the dislocations could be expected to become complex. Even before the discovery of gold, the population of South Africa presented grave complications. In his stories and the *Reminiscences,* Scully had shown much of the conflict which existed between the various Bantu tribes—in addition to the wars waged by Tshaka. Into this environment the Dutch settlers were introduced in the seventeenth century and in the early nineteenth century, the English. Then the Indian and Malay components of the population were added. Discovery of rich gold deposits on the Rand brought to the spot a heterogeneous group of human beings from all parts of the earth.

Mining on the Rand was an operation which required a large capital outlay and thousands of men. Each requirement invited abuses which created problems. Scully explains in considerable detail how capital was obtained. Though the great reef was certainly a reality, and working the various mines a legitimate undertaking, what existed in physical substance made possible fraudulent schemes—schemes intended to be frauds, indeed, from their inception. Johannesburg, Scully writes, was not built by the "Main Reef" or the rich "leaders" but "from the pockets of those who paid enormous prices for acres of scrip—in many instances not worth the ink used by the directors in signing the share certificates."[2] These shares were purchased by thousands in England, across Europe, and elsewhere—whose minds had been hypnotized by the prospect of large dividends from the Witwatersrand. All appear either to have forgotten or ignored the precept which warns that no safe investment can yield large profits. Large profits were made, it is true, but not by small investors who contributed from distant points. Profits of a certain kind were made above ground by those who operated on the stock exchange and simultaneously had control of the men who sat around the various tables as directors of the mining operations whose shares were being sold to the world. Scully describes explicitly how "moves" were made and what resulted from the actions.

Admitting that his chapter explaining how certain things were arranged would not help those who had lost their investments, he suggests one use for what he has written. To his readers he says, ". . . if once a week such of you as have families will only read this chapter to your sons after family prayers, the lesson may stand them in good stead when they reach man's estate. For just about then the next big boom will be due, and the main reef on the southern slope of Mount Erebus[3] may be convulsing the Stock Exchanges of the world."[4]

Simultaneously with his explanation of how certain stock companies were organized, Scully attempts to correct what he says is an inaccurate image of the great Rand magnates. Hoggenheimer, the stereotype, is not at all the true magnate. Hoggenheimer was drawn as

> . . . a heavy, loudly dressed person of pronounced Hebrew physiognomy; . . . a corpulent person, with a chain as thick as a cable spanned across his assertive paunch and a large cigar protruding from his coarse lips. . . .[5] Hoggenheimer was a bludgeon—a brutal thing that crushed what it smote into splinters and gore. The real magnate was like a tempered blade that seemed to kiss when it wounded. He was never a gross materialist; like Goethe, he possessed "die Lust au fabulieren" in a high degree. The medium through which his imagination worked, through which the poetry of his nature expressed itself, was the prospectus, a branch of literature which has gone out of fashion, and in fact is now hardly read at all. . . .[6] The real, genuine magnate is often a retiring, mild-mannered man with a cultivated taste for some branch of art.[7]

No one should think for a moment that any word here is written in defense of the great magnate. What Scully wishes to make very clear is that the actual magnate is far more dangerous than the caricature. Hoggenheimer signals in every direction that he is ruthless and to be avoided; the actual magnate seems gentle and harmless, thus to be cultivated with safety. It was this assurance of safety that lured thousands into the area of economic loss.

Regardless of amalgamations and of maneuvers on the stock market, there was gold on the Rand—gold which was mined. This type of mining required technical knowledge, machinery, and strong bodies. Large amounts of technical knowledge were available in small packages and could be secured as necessary from outside of the country. Machinery could also be obtained from the outside. Massive quantities of labor, however, had to live close to the mines. This created problems in the early days of the mines and has continued to create problems. (Though it might have been possible to find a labor supply from outside the country, the bringing in of such a force would have created special problems of its own.) Whatever one thinks about the situation, the vast experience of William Charles Scully in dealing with the Bantu will make valuable anything he has to say about this situation.

Initially, it should be noted that the mining engineers found available a vast and cheap supply of labor. Scully states, without qualification, "no gold-field that history tells of has ever been worked under circumstances so favourable in this respect as is the Rand. The Native labourer is cheaper, more skilled, more muscular, and more manageable than any other labourer who has ever been engaged in mining—outside China, perhaps."[8] Bantu workers were also healthier than European because after six months underground the native miner insisted on having six months at home with his family. It was this six months of life in the sun that protected him from miner's phthisis. The first stage of this trouble is a condition, not an infection. The infection signals the second stage. After six months at home, a native returned to work in a state of health identical with or close to that with which he started.

Following his investigations, Scully reported that physical living conditions created no serious problems. On this point he is very emphatic.

. . . I visited many of the compounds in which Natives are housed. In almost all of these I found a high standard of comfort maintained. The Natives had enough—and occasionally more than enough—to eat; the food was well prepared and wholesome. At many of the mines there is a weekly or bi-weekly issue of excellent Kaffir beer. Experience has shown that the more beer a Native gets the more sober he remains. This apparent paradox is easily explained. It is only occasionally that beer intoxicates a Native; even then it does not demoralise him to any appreciable extent. But as soon as the Native can get brandy, he becomes both drunken and demoralized.[9]

Throughout his entire magisterial life, Scully did everything in his power to keep brandy away from the natives of his district. Here is one of the problems which is easily understood and for which the cure is quite definite. Yet effecting the cure is very difficult. First, it is necessary to recognize the fact that the problem is not with the native but with those elements in the population who are willing to break the law if there is enough profit to be made. Second, it is also necessary to understand that frequently it is the general attitude of the community which makes it possible for breaking the law to become profitable. When it becomes necessary to work with an entire population, any reformer will discover that he has encountered a complex rather than a simple problem.

If the area of concern were restricted to the mining compounds alone, solutions might be found. Unfortunately, though, a city which had reached the size of Johannesburg, even in 1912, demanded a vast domestic and commercial labor supply. Here no planned meals, issue of Kaffir beer, or any of the other things done in the compounds helped regularize life and ease tensions. Infiltration into this mass was relatively simple for evil elements, who could prey upon their immediate surroundings and use this locality as a point from which they could attack the compounds. It was in the areas other than the compounds that Scully found every evil known to man. He expressed great admiration for the Johannesburg Chief of Police, but the conditions he described seemed beyond any skill man might possess and all the diligence at his command. No longer was the problem one of excessive numbers of blacks. Scully writes that "In one comparatively small slum-warren I found Europeans of various nationalities —Indians, Chinese, Arabs, Japanese, Kaffirs, and miscellaneous coloured people of every hue."[10] He was especially distressed by the Dutch he met, having known them under the healthy conditions of the veld.

When Scully began to probe the economic "arrangements" in the slums, he found the answer to certain questions that might be asked. Upon viewing one piece of property, he estimated that it might have a value of £100. A check on the rents indicated that it brought in for its owner perhaps £348 a year. Now he understood why a business friend had been unable to buy the slum property for desired normal expansion. Though there were exceptions, a large percentage of this type of property was under the control of foreign (mostly European) ownership.

Regardless of what else is considered, any discussion of gold from the Witwatersrand always returns to the use of natives as a source of labor. Near the end of his book, Scully focuses upon this as a major problem. What he has to say should be considered calmly and with a completely judicial attitude.

> A fact which is too often lost sight of is this: the prosperity of the Rand is based upon conditions which are abnormal and disintegrating. It has been attained through wrenching hundreds of thousands of men from their proper environment and forcing them to live a life which not alone acts as a destructive solvent upon their ethical code, but is apt to turn ordinary human emotions into explosive passions. Some people smile at the notion of the Native having any code which could be referred to as ethical, but their doing so only betrays their ignorance. In no people in the world is the aristocratic idea developed to such an extent as among the southern Bantu. It might almost be said that loyalty to their chiefs and to the great ancestral "houses" was a greater deterrent, as regards wrong-doing (according to their own code, of course), than the fear of hell or the hope of heaven ever were to the Christian.[11]

Careful note should be taken that Scully does not claim the prosperity of the Rand to be based upon the presence of native labor but that the presence of native labor has created "conditions which are abnormal and disintegrating." This is a fact and not a value judgment. It was the men who were desired for the mines, and generally they were drawn into the compounds without their families. How abnormal the situation was may perhaps be understood from the fact that it brought into existence "large brothels at Johannesburg filled with European women who catered for the Native only."[12] Though it was important for the men to return for six months of the year to the home kraal for sun and freedom of the veld to avoid miner's phthisis, the home kraal was far more important as a return to the family. This period at home also returned him to the physical presence of the chief. All tribal organization was lost in the compounds, except for a few special activities. A man was here a laborer—not a Zulu, Xhosa, Pondo, Tembu, Shangaan, Swazi, Matabele, or otherwise. Loss of tribal identity was serious because it created a vacuum, and it is imperative to remember that the building of a new sense of identity is likely to be a very slow process.

How little the Bantu understood of European civilization may be grasped by observing how little the European understood of Bantu civilization. The missionaries approached the Bantu prating of the equality of all men. In terms of his tradition, the idea was meaningless to the Bantu. "Bantu social structure knows no equals."[13] Even in an individual family, there are no equals. If a man has three wives, they are not equal. When a wife has five children, they are not equal. In this way classification continues—through the family and through the tribe. Regardless of what one thinks of the system, it has existed for generations upon generations and makes it possible for each person to know who he is and what his position is in relation to all others. The system solves the question of identity, often said to be the greatest human problem of the modern world.

Approaching the end of his book, Scully makes no attempt to solve all of the questions raised by his visit. After observing that the "spirit of haste" has been the greatest curse of South Africa, he offers one very simple piece of advice. What he has to say is so old that it could be given in the traditional Latin phrase, *festina lente*.[14] The meaning he intended has been implied in much that he had already written. Great change cannot be hastened, otherwise the shift will be destructive. That he certainly does not wish, for as he leaves the Rand from his train window he breathes this benediction,

. . . The days and nights of thy passion are many and full of woe, but again, in some cleaner future, the dross wherewith thou art defiled will disappear and thou wilt come to merit thy old name.[15]

As a young man, Scully had hunted blesbucks on the present site of Johannesburg. Then it was called Witwatersrand, the Ridge of the White Waters, and one who walked its ridge felt close to the sky. Today the university which calls Johannesburg home is named *Witwatersrand*.

II Splendid Indifference

Almost a quarter of a century intervened between the experiences which formed the substance of *Lodges in the Wilderness* and the publication of the book. At the time of Scully's residence in Namaqualand, as Special Magistrate for the Northern Border of the Cape Colony, he was thirty-five. When he published an account of his experiences, he was sixty. This book was not merely a literary farewell but a simple physical one.

My eyes have gazed their last upon the face of the desert. Although I love her still,—although the memory of her burning ardour, her splendid indifference and her wealth of illusive charm is my abiding and most valued possession, we shall meet no more. She is not a mistress to be lightly courted. As Brunhild slew Siegfried so would the Desert inevitably slay one who remained her lover after desire had outlasted strength. Her lioness-like caresses are not for those whose blood slows down as it nears the ocean of eternal silence—even as the force and fury of the Gariep sink to the tranquillity when the mighty stream nears the Atlantic—and extinction.[16]

Urgent need of his knowledge and ability had sent Scully to Namaqualand in 1890. Maps had to be made and the number and location of residents determined. In his movements throughout the area, he took careful note of all animal and plant life. The most extensive trip undertaken was at the explicit request of officials in Cape Town, who wished information about punishment administered in a particular locality and to learn whether or not gold existed where it had been reported. Scully returned with the answer to each question; but here as elsewhere he acquired far more information than Cape Town required. When, after an extremely difficult trip, he met with the Reverend Mr. Hein, Resident Missionary of Kuboos and Dictator (Scully's term) of the Richtersveld, and his Raad, he concluded that the punishment they had decreed was just and proper. Indeed he was thoroughly impressed with their handling of the business brought before them. To his readers, Scully said, "I regarded that body with deep and sincere admiration. It might be of incalculable benefit to the British Empire if the speakers of the respective parliaments of the self-governing Colonies, led by the speaker of the House of Commons, were to visit the Richtersveld and sit on that arid hill-side listening to the Raad's deliberations. I should be prepared personally to conduct the tour."[17] Along with impressions of this kind, he collected specimens of rare flora and fauna taken from an area completely withdrawn from the normal paths of men.

Hunting in the desert was almost as specialized as visiting distant missions. One shot a day, or a series at the same target, was the normal expectation. After a rifle had sounded across that vast level expanse, no game was likely to get close enough for a shot until the coming of a new day. Thus the entire emphasis was upon preparation and approach. The nature of the earth beneath and the elements above was inseparable from all hunting arrangements. To Scully the supreme hunting experience was pursuit of the oryx. In the volume discussed here, he tells of firing from a fixed position and also firing after a long chase on horseback. The first was a "chance" shot. There was no meat in camp, and he had gone out before dawn to find whatever might be available. The later hunt, which involved a chase, was premeditated and executed according to plan. In the process of

Opposite Worlds

presenting the second hunt, he discussed the special qualities of the oryx.

Though from time to time springbuck were killed for meat, Scully showed more interest in the visual images presented by these animals and also their migratory habits than in hunting them. Of the springbucks Scully says that often these "gazelles of the desert fled before us like thistledown borne on an eddying wind."[18] The springbucks were also alerted by lightning flashes at night, and followed the path of thunderstorms for the growth rain would bring wherever it fell. The great total migration in winter was to the one area of the desert which could provide food during the season when fauns were expected.

When Scully first went to the Bushmanland desert, he provided himself with books for the long silent hours. Finally, however, he used only one title for these periods—Ludwig's translation of the Vedic Hymns.

> The open volume of the desert . . . was sufficient; nevertheless those large, primordial utterances of the Vedas seemed appropriate whenever one was brought into contact with unspoilt Nature in her vaster aspects. Although they originated under conditions very dissimilar to the local ones, the Vedic Hymns are tuned to the desert's pitch. In India, as in Bushmanland, rain is the paramount necessity. When the rain-gods forget Bushmanland a few thousand fat-tailed sheep may perish; a hundred families may have to retire from its magins and live for a season by digging wild tubers among the granite hills, or by robbing the ants of their underground store of "toa" seed. But if a similar thing happen in India, perhaps ten millions of human beings die a horrible death.
>
> In the desert,—away from man and everything that suggested him, the Hebrew Scriptures seemed to be too overloaded with ethics, too exigent towards enlisting the services of the deity on the side of tribe against tribe. But the Vedic Hymnist was a worshipper who imposed no conditions upon his gods. He had passionately realized the fundamental fact that his own continued existence, as well as that of all organic life, depended upon the beneficent fury of the sky, so he offered awed and unconditioned adoration to Indra, Agni and the "golden-brested" Storm Gods through a symbolism of sincere and homely dignity. Submissive, he accepted death or life, the thunder-bolt or the Soma-flower,—the drought that slew its millions or the rain that brought a bounteous harvest.[19]

Naturally there are descriptions of the desert itself. Here Scully was more concerned with variations than with sameness. The most distinctive of all the variations was Bantom Berg, which was approached at dawn and was revealed gradually as the light grew stronger.

Irregular and convoluted ridges arose from it here and there; it appeared to be absolutely bare of vegetation. In the centre was piled a humped, bulging mass; out of this Bantom Berg lifted its clean-cut cone of granite,—a soaring sphynx still waiting for the carver's chisel. Here and there columns of dust—slender beneath but widely dilating above at an enormous height, stalked slowly over the body of the prone monster, marking each the path of a miniature whirlwind. As we drew near, the face of the dune tract once more became indefinite and complicated; for a time the eye could not follow nor appraise its details. But suddenly the thing explained itself; from the central mass, the prostrate carcass of the obscene creature, a number of league-long tentacles, consisting of sand dunes, extended. These were thick at the base, but they tapered away to nothingness. Like a crouching spider or a half-huddled cuttle-fish the monstrosity sprawled,—its talon-tentacles seeming to gather in the plains—to infest them like a malignant cancer.[20]

Later in his book the author, during a day of violent wind, identifies the desert monster.

Was he not Typhon, Lord of Evil and Autocrat of Desert Places—that monstrous deity who was cast forth from the councils of the Egyptian gods on account of his unspeakable iniquities? Yes,—it was Typhon and none other; he wandered south in search of a kingdom to usurp, and found it there. But the rain-god, whose throne is the distant Drakensberg, stretched forth his silver sword, the Gariep, and ham-strung the intruder. Otherwise the Kalihari might now be stretching forth a hand to grasp l'Agulhas, and all the African southland be a waste.[21]

During one of the days that the group camped beside Bantom Berg, Scully went on an expedition to the Kanya-veld, about ten miles away. This was an uncharted region of round stones, four to eight inches in diameter, embedded in red soil to about two-thirds of their size. Scully admitted that he had no idea what the geological explanation was for this strange formation. He was not, however, seeking scientific explanations. This was his day to be alone.

For we meant . . . to feel that we [Scully and his horse] had got close enough to the heart of Solitude to hear its beats,—to try and capture in our ears, dulled by so-called civilisation, some syllables of that lore with which the desert's murmuring undertone is so rich, but which only the great soul can fully understand. The cast of the desert's message is epic rather than lyrical. The cloud-mantled mountain and the green valley,—the forest, the stream and the foaming sea teach the poet his sweeter songs. But it is the Prophet of God, the law-giver and the warrior who listen for and learn their stern messages from the tongues of the arid wilderness.

The difference between the desert and the fertile tract is that between the ascetic and the full-fed man. The desert appeals to the intellect; the verdant, rain-nurtured valley to the emotions. The variance is as that between percipience and sensation. The stimulation with which a healthy organism responds to rigorous conditions expresses itself in an increased efficiency that is usually invincible. Thus it is that from the physically unfruitful desert all really great ideas have sprung. The wilderness has ever been the rich storehouse of spiritual things. Man gains corporeal, moral and intellectual power in the arid waste, and loses them in the land of corn and wine. Dearth is the parent and the tutor of thought, the desert is the harvest-field of wisdom. Solitude is the fruitful mother of noble resolve,—the kind nurse of the spirit.[22]

Though there is no reason to believe that Scully had any illusions concerning his own worthiness as a child of the desert, he was willing to learn. Together with the wilderness itself, he had selected as guiding forces two who displayed, in relation to the desert, a harmony which probably could not be surpassed. Leading each expedition was Field Cornet Andries Esterhuizen, "a typical Boer of the better class. . . . His blue, laughing eyes shone from a ruddy face. His brown beard was streaked with grey. His great fist could have felled an ox; the tempest of his laughter was like the neighing of war-steeds."[23] With the desert he took no liberties. Scully says he was sure that had even he, the magistrate and thus superior officer, disobeyed orders the result would have been the lash of a sjambok. The second person with whom his destiny in the wilderness was associated was a Bushman-Hottentot called Hendrick, assigned to him by Andries. Hendrick's orders were never to allow Scully to leave camp without being followed. This duty he performed with scrupulous faithfulness, but it was his other qualities that were of interest to Scully. His sense of direction (as that of Andries) could not be explained, perhaps even by himself. His eyesight seemed to equal powerful binoculars, corrected for all possible aberrations. On the back of a horse he displayed the unity of a centaur. Had either Andries or Hendrick failed in his duties or respect for the desert, Scully might not have lived to write of his experiences. Yet he did live to record events and to comment upon the places, actions, and men known during those years in Namaqualand. When farewell had to be said, his wish was that "if when the body dies the spirit still lives, this soul which was nourished by your hand until it grew to a stature sufficient to enable it to realise its own littleness, will return and merge itself in your immensity."[24]

Great joy must have come to the author as he was writing *Lodges in the Wilderness*. Everything about his experiences in the Bushmanland desert suggested satisfying memories. The most difficult and distant journeys had been successful. At both of the secluded mission stations he had found things of interest. He had received faithful assistance in his work among the lowest levels of native life and sincere appreciation for the smallest kindness. Though hunting had not been the most important part of his activities, he could take satisfaction in some of the best shooting of his life. Few hunters can hit the spinal column of a speeding ostrich at nearly three hundred yards or an oryx at almost the same distance. The human companions who shared all of this were of the proper kind. Nothing that happened had been talked to death. In fact, there was no chatter of any variety about anything. Only when the edge of the desert was reached did conversation recommence, and even then it was in subdued tones. The desert itself remained dominant in all ways and at all times. Thus ultimately what was remembered was the wind, rock, and sand; the sun, moon, and stars; the heat of the day and violent dropping of temperature at night; the desolation when there was no rain and flowering as if by magic if rain fell. Permeating all was solitude which forced one to live with oneself and perhaps discover the true nature of that self.

CHAPTER 8

The Painful Growth of a Nation

A first reaction to William Charles Scully's *A History of South Africa*, 1915, is likely to be that it is useful, very useful. Hundreds of facts are given here in a concise and consecutive order, with a table of contents sufficiently full to locate most materials and an index which supplies a student's final need for direction. The substance of the book itself represents what was known about South Africa at the time. In his preface Scully disclaims all credit as a research scholar and states that what he has written "is almost wholly founded upon the standard histories—more especially those of Dr. Theal and Professor Cory—and Leibbrandt's précis of the Archives."[1] The need for his book was an obvious one. Whereas these scholars had performed the necessary research, their published record was voluminous and detailed beyond the scope of the general reader and beginning student. So far, however, no one had undertaken to reduce this material to a point at which it could be employed with some facility. Scully saw the need and attempted to fill the vacuum which existed.

What Scully has produced avoids two approaches he must have been tempted to use. Thinking of the general reader and elementary student, he very well might have been inclined to make his book interesting by presenting "The Story of South Africa." As an experienced fictionist, he would have found no difficulty in employing this method. What he would have sacrificed, however, was quantity of historical fact in the process of securing narrative flow. Had he decided to follow a "story" approach, he would have encountered another and more subtle temptation—to shape the material in a way which would express his own point of view. Both temptations have been avoided. The result has given a very dull book but a volume in which one can place considerable trust. It would be difficult to imagine a history of three hundred pages which offers more facts.

Limitation of space has made impossible a treatment of complex events. In his preface the author calls attention to this deficiency. He personally would have been pleased to present the rise of the Zulu Power under Tshaka and the devastation that it inflicted upon the Bantu tribes. At least three hundred pages would have been required to depict this violent eruption and all that flowed from the initiating source. Thus, though Tshaka is not ignored (he appears in no less than four different places in the book), the author did not allow himself to start into something he could not develop properly. Even more complex than the dislocations caused by Tshaka were the intricately intertwined events which led up to the Boer War and the difficult process of receding from the conflict itself. Not even three hundred pages would have been sufficient for even a superficial treatment of that era of South African history. Naturally, many of the actions and events related to this war appear in the book, but only as facts; they are not developed as to cause and effect.

What, then, is the kind of book Scully has written? He has offered dates, characters, and events. The organization is chronological. During the first half of the book, everything is focused from the Cape. Then, as the other areas begin to develop, he turns to each in its place. The history of Natal, the Orange Free State, and the Transvaal is given separately. Near the end, of course, they merge as events point towards war and finally union.

Because of the plan of the book, isolated events can be recorded very briefly, without any transition before or after necessary to connect these happenings with others. One learns, swiftly and easily, of every "first" as it occurs: the first regular religious services to be conducted, the first hospital, school, military protection, settlement outside of the Cape Town area itself, mail service, use of steamships—indeed, any of the developments which revealed the growth of the country. The result of every census is recorded. Individually many of these details are given very little space, yet cumulatively they assume considerable significance. The accumulation takes place in the reader's mind and does not require the author to use his pages to effect this result. Another chain of events, treated similarly is the Kaffir wars, of which there were nine, the first in 1779 and the last 1876. None of these is given extensive treatment, yet when a reader is told that this is the "First Kaffir War" he knows he is being prepared for more than one conflict. As the series continues, he becomes increasingly sensitive to similarities and differences.

More concentrated than any other event of South African history which Scully handled was his presentation of the Great Trek. Twelve consecutive pages are given to this event, or rather series of events, for the Great Trek was not a single unified effort. There were a number of leaders, starting from different points, at different times (covering several years), and with different destinations. The chapter devoted to the Great Trek may be used as a test of Scully's ability to condense a confused mass of material into a few pages which give a reasonably clear impression of what happened. Even in a poem on the subject, writtin in celebration of the hundredth anniversary of the occasion, Francis Carey Slater filled a hundred and fifty-six pages.

Introducing his reader to the Great Trek, Scully quotes two opposing opinions of the kind of people who initiated and carried out this important movement. Thousands of miles away in London, the Secretary of State, Lord Glenelg, insisted that "The motives of the migration were the same as had in all ages impelled the strong to encroach upon the weak, and the powerful and unprincipled to wrest by force or fraud, from the comparatively feeble and defenceless, wealth, or property, or dominion." The Governor, Sir Benjamin D'Urban, who had been in touch with the frontier conditions, said of the "Voor-Trekkers" that they were "a brave, patient, industrious, orderly, and religious people, the cultivators and defenders and the taxpayers of the country."[2]

Even in the few pages Scully allows himself, one becomes familiar with the names of the leaders. The first trek group was led by Louis Triechard and Hans van Rensberg. The trek swerved far to the north and finally came to a stop in the region known as the Zoutpansberg. After a brief stay, Van Rensberg led his trekkers to the east for purposes of exploration. Not a single member of the party was ever seen again. Information gathered from the natives suggested the trekkers had been massacred by the Makwamba tribe. In an attempt to establish communication with Lourenço Marques, Triechard and his companions were almost wiped out by fever. Among the other prominent leaders were Hendrick Potgieter, Gerrit Maritz, Pieter Uys, the Liebenbergs, and the Krugers. The son of Casper Kruger, Paul, then a boy of ten, was later to become president of the South African Republic, the Transvaal. Potgieter and his followers suffered grievously from the attacks of the Matabele and the Liebenbergs were massacred almost to the last person. Later Pieter Uys and his son died from Zulu spears. About this time Pieter Retief reached the scene of all of these activities and became the accepted leader, at least for the time being. Exploring into Natal, Retief established relations with Dingaan, King of the Zulus. Assuming that he had succeeded in negotiating an agreement with Dingaan, Retief with about sixty men met the King at his Great Place, Umkungunhlovu. Everything appeared to be going in a friendly manner during the period of negotiation, from February 3, to 6, 1838. When the trekkers went to bid farewell to Dingaan, they were asked to stack their guns outside the kraal before approaching to sit in friendship with the King. They did as requested. It was their last decision. At a signal from Dingaan, armed warriors rushed upon the trekkers, who were dragged to the place of execution and clubbed to death. That night an army was sent out to destroy every trekker family in the whole territory.

A force under Pieter Uys and Hendrick Potgieter came to the rescue from another area, only to be drawn into a trap by the Zulu army. An English force from Port Natal was also led into a position where it was caught between the famous horns of a Zulu attack. When all appeared utterly hopeless, Andries Pretorius, with a commando, arrived from Graaff Reinet. Steadily, but refusing to be tricked into an unfavorable fight, Pretorius moved towards Dingaan's capital. On December 15 he and his men camped beside a river into which a deep donga (narrow steep-sided ravine) led. Already protected on two sides, the trekkers carefully fortified the remaining sides. On December 16, at first light they saw before them a massive Zulu army moving to the attack. Before the end of the day, the river ran crimson with Zulu blood. Three thousand dead were left on the field. The encounter became known as the battle of Blood River, and December 16 is celebrated as Dingaan's Day. Pretorius and his men moved on to Umkungunhlovu, which they found in flames. Dingaan had fled. On Execution Hill they identified the remains of Retief and his companions. Among other things, Retief's leather bag was discovered with the Deed of Cession granted by Dingaan. Though one king's power was near its end, Zulu might still existed, and it was only one segment of total Bantu power. Lord Glenelg should have been present upon some of these occasions as the trekkers encountered the "feeble and defenceless" people of this country.

How a student may use the book can be demonstrated by gathering widely scattered materials for studying a subject like "The Governors of South Africa." Starting with Simon van der Stel, who assumed authority in the name of the Dutch East India Company, a sampling through the years will show the method Scully has employed. There are the facts of each person's administration. These vary with the length of his tenure and the kind of situation with which he dealt. Then the author gives a brief statement concerning each governor's

The Painful Growth of a Nation

character and something of his reputation. (It should not be assumed that the opinions expressed originated with Scully.) Simon van der Stel, 1679–1699, is certainly the best known of the Dutch governors of the Cape. He is presented as a man who had received an excellent education and had a distinct individuality. In his activities, he showed what is usually called common sense, and he had a winning personality. It was suggested that this influence upon South Africa would never disappear. During the period in which the European wars made it difficult to guess who would have control of the Cape during any given year, Du Pre Alexander, Earl of Caledon, was appointed Governor in 1807. The power granted him seemed unlimited. Yet when he returned to England in 1811, it could be said of him that "He had used his almost despotic power so fairly and judiciouly that his reputation among the colonists stood high."[3] The man who followed the Earl, Sir John Cradock, was claimed to be "a fair, just and open-minded man, and proved one of the best Governors who ever ruled the Cape Colony. One of his most useful measures was the establishment of free schools in the principal centres for poor European and coloured children."[4] The man who succeeded Sir John was given no such praise. Of him Scully wrote, and this was certainly not merely a personal opinion, "It is not too much to say that Lord Charles Somerset was eminently unfitted for his post. Proud, arrogant, and conceited, he regarded opposition to his will as the unpardonable sin, and acted as a tyrant towards all who dared to think independently."[5] Soon after the Orange Free State was organized, an advocate at the Bar of the Supreme Court in Cape Town was appointed President. Scully states that his wisdom and ability controlled the state for many years, which was indeed fortunate for a newly organized area. He gives praise to this man who did so much for the country: "Intellectually and morally President Brand stands high among his contemporary South Africans."[6] One of the best of all the governors sent to the Cape arrived in December 1854.

Sir George Grey was a many-sided man. He possessed great tact and had that faculty for dealing successfully with inferior races which is inborn and cannot be acquired. The guiding principle of his career was an intense desire to promote the welfare of whatever province lay in his charge. He was endowed with considerable physical endurance, and he invariably inspired his subordinates with strong personal regard. Moreover, he was an accomplished scholar.[7]

Sir George was said to be the first Governor who secured the affection and trust of all elements of the population: English, Dutch, and native. When, however, he dared to say to the officials in London that it was time to consider bringing the separate states of South Africa together under a government which could speak for the whole, he was recalled to England. "For the third time within a quarter of a century a Governor who had brought an open mind to bear upon South African problems and had successfully endeavoured to overcome the difficulties and disabilities under which the country laboured had been deprived of his office owing to want of understanding on the part of distant party politicians."[8] Surely with material of this kind a student would find it simple enough to write a paper on "Kinds of Officials Who Guided South Africa."

An essay on "The Influence of Missionaries on South Africa" would be far more difficult. The obliviousness with which Europeans approached Africa was introduced by an expedition of thirteen ships which left Portugal in 1500 under the command of Pedro Alvarez Cabral. "Cabral was instructed to offer peace and friendship to all he met on condition that they became Christians and consented to trade, but in case of a refusal, war was to be at once declared."[9] Another type of action reported in Europe's attempt to bring Christianity to Africans occurred when in 1736 the Moravian Society sent a missionary, George Schmidt, to Baviaan's Kloof for work among the Hottentots. One of the conditions required by the Dutch Company was that the missionary had to present his converts to the church at Stellenbosch for baptism. After five years Schmidt gave up in despair and returned to Europe. In 1792 the Moravians again tried to establish a mission at Baviaan's Kloof, and once more Stellenbosch objected. One complaint given the Council of Policy was that the ringing of the church bell on Sunday at the Moravian Mission disturbed the worship of the congregation at Stellenbosch. The distance by air between the two points was some thirty miles. Nevertheless, orders were given that the bell was not to be rung on Sunday.

Until the nineteenth century, missionary activities in South Africa were insignificant. In 1799 the London Missionary Society sent out the first workers. One of these was Dr. van der Kemp, who went first to Gaika's country. Among the Bantu he found the difficulties insurmountable and transferred to Graaff Reinet for work among the Hottentots. Several years later he "purchased a black slave girl and married her."[10] The London Society now established a station called Bethelsdorp, near Algoa Bay. To this Dr. van der Kemp moved, assisted by two other missionaries, with several hundred Hottentots.

The Painful Growth of a Nation

The future of Bethelsdorp was to be a turbulent one. Scully commented, "Whatever mistakes Dr. van der Kemp and his colleagues may have made, there can be no doubt that their unsuccessful attempts to conserve the remnants of the Hottentot race were dictated by the purest philanthropy."[11] One of Dr. van der Kemp's most serious deficiencies was his ignorance of the nature of the Hottentots (in fact the native races), with whom he had decided to work. Another liability was that he had no sense of proportion, of balance. Scully observed that "It is hardly too much to say that in his opinion the Hottentots could do no wrong, and the European could do no right."[12] The attitude which Scully accepted in this and other situations like it was expressed in one sentence with which he closes what he has been saying about Bethelsdorp. "Thus the generous but mistaken indignation of a group of ill-balanced enthusiasts weakened a righteous cause. . . ."[13]

Among the "ill-balanced enthusiasts" who "weakened a righteous cause" during the nineteenth century, Scully nominates Dr. John Philip for first place. In 1828 Dr. Philip published a book which he called *Researches in South Africa*. According to Scully, "The publication of the 'Researches' caused bitter indignation in South Africa, and aroused violent feeling on both sides, which has had a permanently bad effect. While giving Dr. Philip full credit for being passionately persuaded of the justice of his contentions, one cannot avoid admitting that his influence upon South Africa, and upon the cause which he had most at heart, has not been beneficial."[14] On one occasion when a committee of the House of Commons was taking evidence about the conditions of native races in British colonies, "Dr. Philip appeared before this committee with two natives. One, Jan Tshatshu, was a petty chief, the other a man of mixed race. . . . They were entertained by the highest in the land, and at banquets led titled ladies to the table. Tshatshu, it may be mentioned, became a sorry backslider. He took to drink, and was expelled from membership of his church."[15] The event which finally turned Dr. Philip from politics was hearing that "Jan Tshatshu, his former *protégé*, had joined Pato's murderous gang, which burned alive Fingo old men, women, and children who fell into their hands. . . ."[16] When he received this information, it was said that "he completely broke down."[17] There is more about Dr. Philip, other individual missionaries, and the situation in general throughout the entire book.

Though almost all of the facts and opinions of *A History of South Africa* can be traced to the author's sources, there are passages which are distinctly the result of Scully's experiences and attitudes—even though they may be in complete agreement with his sources. One paragraph which seems to belong very much to him speaks of the pioneer adventurers. The period of whick he writes is early in the eighteenth century. The author has paused in his reciting of facts to present a summary of life at that time in South Africa. First he describes what it must have been like to reside in the place which had come to be called "the tavern of the eastern seas," Cape Town. Then he moved away from the sound of waves and commerce to Stellenbosch where farming had prospered. Here town and farm were intricately related, and for a brief period existence attained a solidity and certainty seldom found in the history of civilization.

But there was a third class—one formed of the percentage in whom the leaven of desire for adventure worked—the restless spirits who gazed longingly at the mountain rampart beyond which lay the wonderland of the unknown. To such the voice of the veld, the call of the wide, unmapped, untrodden waste, was an imperative command. In heavy, strong, lumbering wagons, accompanied by mate and brood, these people went forth and subdued the wilderness. Only two things linked them to the conventional world: their weapons and their Bible. Naturally, the ideals of these wanderers diverged from the ideals of those who remained behind. Unfortunately, on the track of those who adventured for adventure's sake, went others—men who acknowledged no law and practised no restraint.[18]

Many of Scully's experiences had introduced him to descendants of those rare spirits who penetrated the wilderness seeking adventure, and, unhappily, the group that followed. Years as a magistrate had acquainted him with the undesirable element. Both found a place in his stories and novels, and finally some were named in his nonfictional books.

From time to time in the *History* a brief passage about the Bantu will suggest that the author was writing from experience as well as academic sources. In discussing early nineteenty-century border disturbances, he remarks that "War, hunting, and cattle-lifting were looked upon by the Bantu of the period as the only pursuits worth following, and there was probably hardly a Xosa within fifty miles of the border who had not participated in the plunder to which the farmers had for so long been subjected."[19] For the Bantu warrior, there was no moral problem of right or wrong in taking cattle. There was only one consideration: Was the attempt successful or unsuccessful? What needs to be stressed here is that Scully is not taking sides in

The Painful Growth of a Nation 151

the conflict. He is simply explaining what happens when two totally different civilizations impinge upon each other. Europeans have never considered changing their codes. Therefore, when their civilization comes into conflict with another, they must allow time for the other side to come to an understanding of a new code. The time needed might be very considerable, for some of the problems call for far greater change than any that might be needed in relation to cattle lifting. For example, at the end of the Seventh Kaffir War, eleven conditions were imposed. Scully says that nine of these were the ordinary ones, as "obedience to law." Two, however, were such that no one with any knowledge of the natives would expect them to be obeyed: (1) "To disbelieve in and cease to tolerate or practice witchcraft in any shape." (2) "To abolish the sin of buying wifes." Though Scully was passionately intent upon helping to eliminate witchcraft, he knew very well that it could not be abolished by a government order. The same was true of profoundly important social attitudes, such as that cited relating to traditional marriage arrangements. To Scully the most urgent change which needed to be made was in the Bantu belief which attributed sickness to spells cast by an enemy. A witch doctor was consulted, and because of his indentifications large numbers of innocent people received a cruel death. One very wise Governor of the Cape, instead of issuing an order, built a hospital for the natives. Nothing was to be said about witchcraft, but it might be hoped that slowly those treated would learn the nature of disease. Again, the indispensable requirement was time, long periods of time.

Students of South African history may often pause to wonder how any group of people could survive the agony of growth through which this land had been dragged during more than three centuries. Scully has not withheld details, but one does not close the book with a sense of despondency. The attitude results from the author's introduction of the good along with the bad. This is an extremely effective approach because ultimately the method establishes trust. A reader can finally say, "This is how it was, not how someone says it was."

CHAPTER 9

After Retirement from the Civil Service

RETIREMENT permitted Scully to consider travel in a sense never before possible. Time and circumstances had reduced the family to a manageable size. Elaine, the oldest daughter, had married.[1] Gerald was a lecturer at Stellenbosch University, and Ernest had entered the business world at Port Elizabeth. Miriam was an art student in London. This left only the younger girls—Lilla, thirteen, in school at Wynberg, and Betty, five, at home. It was decided that Mother and Betty would leave for England in July, and early in the New Year Father would follow with Lilla. It was 1914, and war between England and Germany (August 4) came while Mother and Betty were on the Atlantic. According to plans, Father and Lilla started their journey north early in the New Year. War destroyed all hope of an anticipated European vacation for the parents and a convent period for the girls at Lausanne, where one of Scully's sisters was a nun. Instead, the whole family sailed for the United States on the *S. S. New York,* a week after the sinking of the *Lusitania,* May 7, 1915. Scully was doing certain publicity work as they travelled across the States, touching many of the important cities but also being able to see some of the "interest spots" as they proceeded slowly towards the Pacific. Finally they reached Vancouver Island, and the family was established in Victoria, while Scully went alone to South America. Here, exploring a great forested area, he became ill but was cared for by Indians until they could get him to a town and into a hospital. Upon his return north, he collected the family on the shores of the Pacific, and all made their way east over the Canadian provinces. Back in England, Scully decided food was too scarce for them to add to the war burden of the English. Thus, after a few weeks they sailed for South Africa. It was now 1917. For the moment, they settled in Queenstown, where Mrs. Scully's mother lived. Here Scully continued his writing and experimented with the growing of roses. During one period of the War, he became acting magistrate at

After Retirement from the Civil Service

Lobatsi, in the Transvaal, to relieve a younger man for active duty. At last Scully was able to do something specific for the War effort. When the British empire had early moved into what was to become a world conflict, Scully tried to enlist for combat. At fifty-nine he did not accept gracefully his rejection because of age. Certainly the armèd forces had few men who could kill a racing oryx at three hundred yards. Yet the official verdict could not be set aside; so Scully had to wait his time to make a contribution to active duty indirectly.

When the great conflict was over, Scully purchased land (1919) at Somerset Strand and there built a house. Several years later, Lilla developed tuberculosis, and the family moved from their home beside the sea, for her health, and settled in the dry climate of Kimberly, 1923. In 1938 Lilla died, and the same year Scully broke a hip, at eighty-three. Two years later, 1940, the family returned to the coast, this time at Umbogintwini, where they were to spend their last days.

Though Scully had never been able to change the nature of bureaucracy, his intense desire to let the truth be known inpregnated his fiction from the earliest stories. In retirement, and after the end of World War I made publication possible again, he offered his final two novels, each written from the same impulse that would have motivated him to report his superior while he was still a very young member of the Cape Civil Service. In introducing each book, the author explicitly states that the fiction has been created to represent the historical facts of the particular situation. As novels, the two books use very different compositional methods.

I *"Take Heed to Thyself"*

Having been forced to become closely acquainted with certain aspects of the 1899–1902 South African War because of official duties, Scully confesses that some force was urging him to tell what he knew. The book toward which he was being driven was *The Harrow,* first written in 1904, rewritten in 1907, and published in 1921. "This book," he explained in a 1907 introduction, "is not my own so much as the creature of some influence working through me, some voice whose command has been as imperative as insistent. After a season of hesitancy—and even resistance—I became like a haunted man. Things great and small seemed to point out the path on which my duty lay. . . ."[2] About this time an old and dear friend shortly before his death said to Scully, "Let no one persuade you to suppress that book. Do not publish it now; keep it for ten years and then let it appear. Let people know the truth!"[3] Meanwhile the manuscript was kept in the strong room of the Standard Bank of London. During the waiting period war exploded upon most of what is called civilization. When the gas had blown away and the trenches were cleared, Scully decided that the time for *The Harrow* had arrived, and thus he proceeded with plans for publication. Along with the manuscript, he placed in the hands of the publisher *"a key to the story, giving a reference to the actual occurence upon which every one of the main episodes is based."*[4] This he did because he was sure it would be said that what he presented as fiction had no basis in fact. Of anyone making such charges, he said, "My only fear is that those who say so will content themselves with the mere assertion, that they will refrain from putting their words to proof. If my words are false, they can easily be disproved. . . . Taking the line I do, it would be not alone a disgraceful but a foolish thing to make any material misrepresentation."[5] Of one thing the author seemed sure, that "the measure of abuse and hatred which the book arouses will be the measure of its truth and its usefulness."[6]

What specifically had created in Scully the need to purge himself of certain memories is detailed in the 1907 preface to *The Harrow*.

Not alone have I closely and at first had examined the monstrosity denominated "martial law," but after the conclusion of the war I spent thirteen months as Chairman of a commission appointed for the purpose of taking evidence as to war losses and awarding compensation. In this capacity I visited and sojourned at . . . [more than sixteen locations, as Graaff-Reinet, Uitenhage, Somerset East].

When the Cape Government of the day refused to redeem its most solemn and reiterated pledge to hold an enquiry into the occurrences under martial law during the then recent hostilities, I conceived the idea of which this book is the outcome. This pledge was given when the Indemnity Bill came before the House of Assembly, and it was on the condition therein expressed that such Bill was allowed to become law.

The reason assigned for the breach of faith was the mendacious one that there was danger the enquiry might have the effect of unsettling the people. But the true reason was the knowledge of those in office that the revelations inevitable upon such an enquiry would . . . "stagger humanity."[7]

Because he was convinced that a large percentage of the population in both England and South Africa was ignorant of what had happened during the Anglo-Boer War, he wished to reach them through his novel.

After Retirement from the Civil Service 155

This book . . . is an honest attempt to shew British people what was done in their name and under their sanction in the terrible period to which the story relates. . . . I have, in common with most of my Dutch friends, sufficient faith in Great Britain to believe that if she had known what was happening, the nation would have recoiled in horror, punished the guilty instruments of her mistaken policy, and made all possible reparation. . . .[8] [but] . . . not one in ten of the British inhabitants of South Africa has even the remotest idea as to what took place. Often have I mentioned lamentable occurrences which I knew had indubitably happened, only to be met by a look of utter incredulity. The Dutch people know of these things and resent their unmerited sufferings being ignored, for they believe that the British possess similar knowledge. In this lies the root of that hostility which is so much to be deplored, but which will increase unless a common basis of understanding is reached.[9]

Once Scully had decided that he must write a book devoted to this particular phase of South African history, he began the practical task of considering what kind of book to write. Rather naturally his first thought was to write a systematic history in which he would name individuals, places, and give specific events and dates. Finally, however, he decided that a novel would reach a larger number of the audience desired than any other form he might employ.

Far more material was available than could be used. Selection was necessary and then organization. For the fictitious town of Jagersdorp, population six thousand, Scully combined four small towns of the Cape Midlands. This was the area which had been settled by the Dutch farmers and hunters a century and a half before the English arrived in considerable numbers. As created, Jagersdorp is typical of the place and time. In addition to the Dutch Reformed Church, there is an Anglican and also a Wesleyan church, presided over by the Reverend Augustine Gargoyle and the Reverend Theophilus Sparrowswerth, respectively. There, is, of course, a Resident Magistrate and when martial law is declared, a Commandant.

Rapidly the author sketches in all that might normally exist in a town such as Jagersdorp; then he begins the development which will make the book a novel. Into his setting he introduces characters who are not Dutch and who are strong enough to offer opposition to the existing situation created by the coming of martial law. The important non-Dutch characters created are Captain Benton, appointed District Commandant upon the declaration of martial law; John Marsden, English, Civil Commissioner and Resident Magistrate, and his daughter Laura; Dr. Terence Ryan, Irish and District Surgeon; Tom Parratt, English, a surveyor and the local satirical poet; Alexander Macgregor, a Scot, manager of the local branch of the Standard Bank; and Laurence van Sittart, English, engaged to Laura Marsden. Captain Benton, a man of experience with a disturbing habit of asking for facts when charges are made, is soon relieved of his command. John Marsden, who represents established law and administration, is more difficult to destroy. Headquarters will not remove him without evidence. Thoughout the action of the novel a number of attempts are made to trap him, yet he survives to the end—both he and his daughter Laura. These two and Dr. Ryan become involved in continuing action which finally assumes something of the proportions of a plot and even creates foreshadowing and suspense. John Marsden, Laura, and Dr. Ryan are all a part of the last tragic event, which is employed as the climax of the novel.

Discovery of diamonds and gold created the curse. Men who had made fortunes wanted still more, and with that they craved power. Being shrewd men and knowing what they wanted, they began to look for ways of achieving the desired end. They looked upon an England hypnotized by what it considered imperialism, and they knew that here was something they could use. To create a belief that the flag was in danger would serve them well. First they quietly purchased an interest in most of the papers of the Cape, having carefully noted that in an age of rush most people read little else and consequently received from the press the ideas by which they lived. Now commenced the news releases from Johannesburg, chiefly, to the Cape and to England. As a result, "In England the most preposterous assertions were taken as sober truth. President Kruger was accused of the most grotesque atrocities. One was of fastening a woman between boards and sawing her in two. A patriotic Anglican clergyman called attention on a public platform to the fact that this allegation had not been denied by the President and therefore must be true."[10] After the collective mind had been prepared, it could be made to believe that the British flag was in danger of being driven from South Africa. As might be expected, war resulted. Since the serious fighting was in the north and little more than occupation in the south, military competence went north and incompetence south. "Thus the unfortunate Dutch-descended inhabitants of the Cape Colony were laid prone under that harrow, the spikes whereof were incapacity, greed, race-prejudice and dishonesty. Their English brothers, drugged by the haschish of the purchased press closed their minds to reason and their hearts to pity."[11]

Physical combat had commenced in October 1899. Martial law was not declared in the Cape until early 1901. By that time organized fighting had ended, and only Boer commandos moved here and there, for the most part still in the north. A Commandant, however, was sent to each town, and Jagersdorp received Captain Benton, a veteran of Kaffir warfare. He arrived with a hundred men, who conducted themselves in an orderly manner. No disturbances occurred in the district. To certain "loyal" citizens this was quite unsatisfactory. A group went to Captain Benton and presented him with a list of Dutch townsmen accused of treason. The Captain took notes and traced each accusation to the vanishing point and then reported to the group that they had been mistaken. Next a meeting of the "loyal" business men of the town was held. They elected Aaronson as chariman. At the meeting a black list was made up. It named most of the Dutch business or professional men of Jagersdorp. They went to Captain Benton with the demand that all of these be deported. Again the Commandant found a lack of evidence. Captain Benton himself, however, was now on a black list. Aaronson made a visit to Hisch, one of the principal organizers of the Military Intelligence Department. His staff was drawn principally from the lowest class of his own race. "Of course Hisch knew the man just suitable for the post of Commandant at Jagersdorp. Ability? No, certainly not. Ability would be supplied by the Intelligence Department; in a commandant it would be distinctly superfluous. All that was wanted was 'loyalty.'. . ."[12] Next Aaronson visited General Christopher Wren for his approval of what Hisch had already decided. The following day Captain Benton received urgent orders to leave for Stellenbosch. Within twenty-four hours after the arrival of his replacement, most of the business men of Jagersdorp were deported to the loyal resort of Port Alfred. Business now resided in "loyal" hands, and large orders for merchandise were sent out at once. Loyalty became very profitable, and this was only the beginning and merely one area in which profit was to be made.

Quite soon Hisch sent two assistants to the Commandant of Jagersdorp, Captain Rice. Now it became clear why Hisch had said the Commandant needed no ability. The assistants held power not only over the people but over Captain Rice. He merely declared all persons brought before him guilty. No specific charges were made; no defence was allowed. There was a code of martial law supplied for the guidance of men such as Captain Rice (who had been a bank clerk), but in practice this was merely something to flourish in the face of the House of Commons when questions were asked, not rules which were to be followed. The two men sent by Hisch to spy on Captain Rice, as much as on the people, were Rennet and Keddelston. Rennet "suggested a ferret by his appearance as much as by his character and his methods. Keddelston was tall and thin, in appearance a kind of pinch-beck Mephistopheles."[13] The Dutch of Jagersdorp soon discovered that their destiny was held tightly in the hands of two very evil characters. To recite their cruelties and crudities would be profoundly depressing. The only relief might arise from contemplating which was more evil, the deeds or the manner in which the actions were performed—though ultimately the two could not be separated.

Only once in the novel is there respite from the crushing or tearing blows inflicted upon all Dutch and anyone else who does not accept the domination of the self-serving dregs who now control the life of the town and district. The one comic chapter, so intended by the author, as he admits in his introduction, gives an account of the most important of all of the soirees held under the auspices of the Loyal Ladies' League. For the occasion, the officers of the League have captured a visiting colonel, who very reluctantly has consented to attend. He arrives with two aides, young and feminine. In fact, it appears that the one way to find favor with the colonel is to have a young and pretty daughter who is willing to support the military life. In the midst of the evening, Dr. Ryan remarks to Laura Marsden that "there's nothing in Aristophanes or Molière, not to mention Gilbert and Sullivan, that comes near it."[14] In fact, Dr. Ryan himself a few moments after this remark makes a contribution which any of the writers named would have approved. The Wesleyan minister had requested from the visiting colonel copies of the Army's *New Testament* as a gift to his Sunday school. Publicly the colonel announces that books will be sent to the Reverend Mr. Larkspur, which he changes to Sparrowbeak, never quite making it to the correct Sparrowswerth. When that worthy man of God approaches the Doctor during the evening, he is greeted with,

"Hullo, Sparrowswerth . . . can it be true that you are going to put those blasphemous testaments that old satyr spoke about in the hands of your Sunday school children?"

"Blasphemous, Doctor?"

"Yes, blasphemous, flatly blasphemous against the Prince of Peace. Have you seen a specimen of the book?"

"Certainly! I have one; I use it daily."

"And do you mean to tell me that you, who claim to have been teaching charity and mercy in the name of Christ for a quarter of a century, can bear to see His message labelled with a prostituted text, a quotation torn from its context so as to make it appeal to the tiger instincts in man?"

"Dr. Ryan, this irreverence—"

"Irreverence, yes, irreverence of the worst kind. If it had been the Old Testament, it would not have been so bad, but the New Testament—the Gospel of Life. Sparrowswerth, I am ashamed of ye."

Mr. Sparrowswerth gaped in silent amazement.[15]

Neither Jehovah, Christ, nor John Wesley supplied this twentieth-century representative of the church with words.

Showing no favoritism, the author allows the Reverend Mr. Gargoyle, of the Anglican church, to give the final address of the evening. Mr. Gargoyle's wife is President of the Loyal Ladies' League. In his address, he assures Colonel Macleay, who seems more concerned with his aides, that Jagersdorp will completely "support the policy of bringing the whole of South Africa under the great and glorious Union Jack, beneath whose folds all men were equal, all men were free."[16] Laura Marsden might have had a few reservations to make about this statement of *equal* and *free,* knowing, as she did, all that had been done to trap her father. Then, too, Laurence van Sittart, to whom she was engaged, had seen his home, orchards, and horses destroyed because he had spoken for Aaronson's opponent in an election. Tom Parratt had had his arm shot off by a soldier on the streets of Jagersdorp because he had not given the countersign at seven, which was not supposed to be given until ten. Each of these men was English, van Sittart the nephew of a lord, and all moved beneath the folds of the flag to which Mr. Gargoyle referred. Not having observed any contradiction between his words and events in the community around him, the speaker concluded his address by showing in detail how the work of the Loyal Ladies' League had supported the "development of the policy which eventuated in this most righteous, most glorious and most Christian war. . . ."[17] Long before the thunderous applause poured over his oratorical effort, many aspiring writers must have been taking notes along with Aristophanes, Molière, Gilbert and Sullivan.

Exactly in the middle of the book, Scully devotes eight pages to an episode which convinces the reader there still exists in the world that which is clean and good. It is an adventure through which Dr. Ryan passed as he was returning to Jagersdorp one night after a visit thirty miles away. All was going well when the Doctor's ponies stopped suddenly and snorted. Surrounded by armed men and taken captive, the Doctor was blindfolded and placed on a strong horse. Off they rode at a sharp canter. The grade increased and then the riders entered the mountains. After almost two hours, all halted, and the blindfold was removed. Two men stepped forward: one tall, blond, and bearded; the other slight, of compact build, with dark hair and eyes. The latter spoke in fluent English, though there was a slight foreign accent. He apologized in the name of the Commandant for this treatment, but the truth was that his professional services were urgently needed, their surgeon having been killed the week before. The Doctor followed the two men to a cave, where the speaker gave way and allowed the Commandant and Doctor to enter. In Dutch the Doctor was told that the bullet had passed through the chest and then into the arm. As the doctor was removing the blood stained bandages, he stopped with a gasp. The patient was a woman. At that moment, someone handed the Doctor his instruments and medicine chest. There was, however, little that he could do.

"Come here, Doctor," said the patient, speaking English. . . .
The two men approached and bent down, one on each side of the patient. . . .
"I thought I would have to die from the moment I was wounded," she said. . . ." but my husband hoped there might be a chance for me."
The Commandant sobbed as if his heart were breaking, as it probably was. The woman lifted a hand with difficulty and offered it to the Doctor's grasp.
"Good-bye—and thank you," she said, and her voice was very weak.
The Doctor reverently raised the hand—it was small and refined in shape—to his lips. Then he withdrew, his eyes half blinded by tears.[18]

Again the young man with the foreign accent took charge of the Doctor and his equipment. Four horses were saddled and ready. As they paused to listen to the men of the Commando singing, the young man explained that he had written the words and composed the music.

"Ye did? Well, may the divil admire me if ye oughtn't to be proud of that same. Ah, well, its a quare world."
"I suppose there is no hope for her."
"None whatever. . . . God rest her brave sowl."
"I feared so. Hm—she is a noble woman; there's not a man here who would not have died to save the tip of her little finger."
"Why don't you bhoys go home? Ye've done your best? Surely ye don't think ye can pull this off now?"
"I? No, but I am only a soldier of fortune, a man without faith. But

these—they are religious men; they believe. 'Si Deus nobiscum, quis contra nos?' "
"That sounds like Heidelberg Latin."
"It is; I left Heidelberg two years ago."
"Ah," said the Doctor with a sigh, "it is two and forty since I left it."
"My father was there two and forty years ago."
"Then we may have drunk beer together. What was his name?"
"That, I regret to say, I may not tell you. . . . Here, Doctor, is your fee."
"Ah, the divil a fee I'll touch. . . ."[19]

After the Doctor had been blindfolded and mounted on his horse, the young man pressed a ring into his grasp. The two clasped hands, and then the horses started down the mountainside. When the group halted and the blindfold was removed, dawn was breaking. The ponies were harnessed to the buggy several miles nearer Jagersdorp than when stopped. The Doctor's medical chest was fastened into place, and the Boers silently withdrew. As he turned his ponies towards home, he felt little fatigue. A new day emerged in all its freshness. The Doctor drew the ring from his pocket. It was of heavy gold. On its bloodstone was carved a crest belonging to one of the noblest families of southern Germany.

Finally an action occurred that was so brutal it could not be ignored or excused. This tragedy turned the community back in search of its lost sanity. The beginning of the specific event was happy. Dr. Ryan had advised Laura Marsden to get away from town for a rest because she had exhausted herself nursing an ill mother, who was now much better. Since her father was going out into the district on business, Laura journeyed with him to visit the Jansens at "Elandsnek." Hessie, Mrs. Jansen, an orphaned girl, had grown up in the Marsden home as "mother's help." She had married Diederick Jansen and gone to live at his homestead built on a high "neck" between two mountain ridges. Here, even in summer, the air was cool and fresh—just the location for the needed recuperation. Grateful for many kindnesses she had received from the Marsden family, Hessie was delighted to have a visit from Laura. That first evening with Hessie, Diederick, and the children erased the lines of stress from Laura's face and gave peace to her mind.

Peace was to have a very short existance. At dawn Laura was awakened by the arrival of a commando of Free State Boers between the dwelling and what had been a shop—now without stores. It was her first close view of these strong, silent, armed men about whom she had heard so much. There, too, was Diederick explaining that his shop was without goods. He invited them to investigate. They did, since they were strangers from far away. Soon they mounted and rode off to the northeast. Laura dressed quickly and sought out Diederick, who would say no more than that he had given his oath not to speak of the visit. After breakfast, a British patrol approached the house. The officer in charge questioned Diederick, who had convinced him that he knew nothing, when a hawk-nosed man riding with the patrol reported that Boers had just passed. He had secured his information by distributing sweets to the Jansen children—ages six, five, and three—who were playing in the wagon house. By questioning the five-year old girl, he had learned what he wished to know. There was a swift change in the officer. He ordered everyone to be made a prisoner and brought before him one at a time. After Diederick was questioned, Laura walked forward in an attempt to help, identified herself officially, and explained the whole situation—including the fact that Diederick was under oath to maintain silence. All she could say was of no avail. Diederick was carried away under guard. Laura's father, who had been turned back from his official business, arrived very soon, and under military orders father and daughter proceeded to Jagersdorp.

Meanwhile, in an attempt to follow a shortcut indicated to them by their sergeant, the three troopers who were taking Diederick to camp as a prisoner became lost. They turned to their captive for directions, and he explained where they had made a wrong turn. When they reached the proper turn and started on the way, they were ambushed by Boer riflemen. Diederick was shot through the lower abdomen, from side to side. One of the troopers was struck in the hip and another through the arm. The third escaped and returned to the homestead for help. Hessie sent two messages to Jagersdorp, one to Dr. Ryan and the other to the Commandant telling him what had happened to his troupers. Then she and the driver started with the wagon to help her husband and the two wounded men. All were cared for and brought back to Elandsnek. There again she provided for their needs, not forgetting food for the troupers, who when they learned a report had been sent to Jagersdorp said they preferred to remain outside until picked up. Before sunset an ambulance cart and a surgeon arrived. The men were transferred to the cart, but no enquiry was made by the surgeon concerning Diederick.

When Dr. Ryan arrived and examined the patient, he told Hessie that the chances for recovery were slight. All he could do was to prescribe absolute quiet and at intervals liquid food in very small quantities. He promised to return the next afternoon. Diederick slept during the night, which Hessie believed was a good sign. With morning she began to feel that there was hope. The children were posted around the house to keep everything completely quiet. At ten o'clock, Willem tapped softly on the door to say horsemen were approaching from the direction of Jagersdorp. Hessie slipped from the house and saw not only a troop of mounted soldiers but seemingly they also were followed by a small mob of mounted civilians. She advanced into the road and with outstretched hand tried to signal silence and ask that they pass along the back of the dwelling. The men only turned their horses enough to avoid riding her down. All of the way to the front door they went. Hessie rushed through the crowd and to the front steps, where she turned and in a low voice explained that her husband was ill and begged them to make less noise and to depart. The response from the commanding officer was, "Remove that woman." As two soldiers advanced upon Hessie, she fled into the house. Troopers followed, seized Hessie, and pushed her into a room across the hall. Soon from the bedroom came angry voices.

. . . She heard one say: "Finish the ———— here." Another called gruffly: "No, do it outside." She heard a noise of struggling, of the bed creaking, of furniture being pulled about, then these words spoken loudly in the passage: "That will do; bring him out now."[20]

Huddled on a chair, Diederick was carried through the hall. Two men lifted the chair and another held him to prevent his falling.

They set the chair . . . down. . . . the officer came forward and urged Diederick to confess to having treacherously led his escort into an ambush on the previous day. But Diederick refused, absolutely. . . .

Then the officer informed Diederick that, confession or no confession, he was about to be incontinently shot and suggested that if he, Diederick, went before his Maker with a lie upon his already burthened head, the consequences might be serious. . . . He lifted his trembling hands and prayed to the God of his fathers, for the wife and children who were so dear to him, for the salvation of his own soul. Then . . . he asked to be permitted to say good-bye to Hessie and his children.

This was refused. A man in an intense state of excitement then ran forward and wildly besought Diederick to confess his guilt. . . . But Diederick Jansen lifted his right hand high so that all might see and spake in a loud voice that all might hear, calling on the God he was about to meet face to face to witness that he died innocent of the treachery laid to his charge.

There was tumult and a struggle. Hessie had escaped through the back premises and rushed round to the front. The troopers seized her, but she first *saw*. She saw for one abysmal instant the ghastly, swaying figure in the chair, the rifles at the "ready," the dripping blood from the re-opened wound staining the white blanket. . . . Her heart stopped beating. Then with a cry which, if justice reigns in Heaven or retribution dwells on earth, will reverberate for ever in the ears that heard it, Hessie fell—insensible—heavily to the ground. . . .

. . . The words "I am innocent" came, muffled but audible, from under the blanket. . . . Then the volley crashed. . . .

The three children upon hearing their mother's doleful cry had followed her out of the house. They now lay crouching beside her prone body. . . .

They flung the body of Diederick Jansen on the bed in which he and his wife had slept. . . .[21]

Because Dr. Ryan was delayed by a very serious case, he did not reach Elandsnek until darkness had covered the events at the homestead. He was welcomed only by silence. In front of the house he fell over a chair. Stepping inside the house, he struck a match and followed trampled stains of blood as far as the bedroom—where the match flickered and burned out. He struck another and entered.

. . . The corpse of Diederick Jansen lay on the bed where it had been flung. . . . On the floor, in the middle of the room, crouched a being that had once been a sweet and gracious woman, but was now an unsexed maniac—a creature in torn and dishevelled raiment full of dark-red stains. . . . As the Doctor gazed at this frightful figure, he felt as though he were, in very deed, turning into stone.

In a corner were huddled three silent, fierce-eyed human cubs—creatures flung by fate, in one of the most fiendish of her pranks, back across the gulf of unimaginable ages to the days of the cave-men.[22]

Against its will, Jagersdorp was forced finally to learn what had occurred at Elandsnek. Gradually "a feeling of undefined and speechless horror stole over the community."[23] At this time the Loyal Ladies' League held a soiree, but before the guests turned homeward it was quite definite that another would never be scheduled. Nebulously aware that something should be done for those of the Jansen family still living, the executive committee of the Loyal Ladies' League proposed getting up a subscription for Hessie and her children. When Dr. Ryan heard of the suggestion, he wrote a letter to the president of the organization. What was in the letter has never been revealed, but the lady to whom his words were addressed was driven into violent hysterics. Three days elapsed before she was able to rise from her bed. Changes now came rapidly. Rennet applied for a permit to return to Johannesburg, which was granted. Keddleston merely disappeared, though he took with him a large draft on a London bank. When last heard from, Captain Rice was a resident of the diamond fields, working as a barman in a low canteen. He had not shared in the plunder that went to Rennet and Keddleston. The officer in charge of the patrol that fateful day at Elandsnek took his own life, as did his immediate subordinate.

When the war finally came to a close, a last desperate effort was made to destroy the liberties of the people. A petition was circulated requesting the suspension of the constitution of the Cape Colony. Lord Milner gave strong support to the movement. In fact, it was assumed by many that it originated with him. At the time, the Colonial Prime Ministers were meeting in London and it was believed that their strong opposition saved the Cape from this action.

Now from press, platform, and pulpit came the sermons which said "forgive and forget." Scully accepts forgiveness but rejects the advice to forget.

. . . Forgiveness is a virtue; let us, therefore, try to practise it—even though we know that its full realisation may have to be for the present classed among counsels of perfection. Forgetfulness is however a weakness, and often a mischievous one. But let us, in the name of the Eternal that maketh for the Righteousness, brace our wounded spirits towards acting up to the first part of the text—let us try to forgive. In making this effort let us in all reverence take our guidance from the words of the tortured Christ, from that most sublime prayer, "Father, forgive them, for they know not what they do."

But, O imperialists, from beneath whose heavy, and sharp-toothed harrow we have just emerged with still-bleeding flesh, pray give us a reasonable time for the complete process of forgiveness. . . .

There really is, in spite of a systematic ignoring of the fact in the carefully selected literature which is all you read, quite a lot to forgive. . . .

As to forgetting—well, were South Africa ever to forget what happened during the three terrible years of her passion, she would richly deserve that similar things should happen to her again. . . .

No, we will never even try to forget; we will never try to commit that basest treason not alone against the dead, but against the less fortunate ones who, having passed adown the valley of the shadow of deepest woe, will bear through the weary remainder of life the indelible imprint which suffering leaves on the faces of those who endure beyond a certain degree. . .

Therefore, O fellow South Africans, let our wise forgiveness . . . be rooted in the soil of rich remembrance. . . . Let us forgive England by not forgetting the nobility of her past, by remembering that the terrible lapse from righteousness of which she stands guilty in our case was due to the most tremendous and elaborate conspiracy of deceit the world has ever seen [1899–1902]. . . . Let us moreover remember that when England awoke from the effects of the poisoned cup with which her enemies had drugged her, she made us what reparation the *Zeitgeist* permitted her to make. . . .

But pay no heed to those who continually emphasize the necessity for forgetting. As the Deuteronomist wrote:—"Only take heed to thyself and keep thy soul diligently, lest thou forget the things which thine eyes have seen, and lest they depart from thy heart all the days of thy life; but teach them thy sons and thy sons' sons."[24]

What has been presented in this discussion of *The Harrow* constitutes only a few of the measures imposed upon Jagersdorp and the surrounding district during the progress of the novel. One of the extensive, detailed, and varied aspects of the situation was the millions made by completely unscrupulous individuals because of conditions created by the presence of large numbers of troops in the country—but in the novel more specifically the period of martial law, when ruthless confiscation of many kinds was practiced. Another area was in the presentation of the methods used by Captain Rice, with Rennet on one side and Keddleston on the other. As the author suggested, the whole could have been considered a stupid, a ridiculous performance except for the fact that it was tragically real and that the vicious clowns had the whole might of the British Empire behind their decisions. Still an additional horror emerged from the gratuitous insults, humiliations, and unwise procedures. For example, one of the most widely-known and distinguished citizens of the region was arrested, sentenced, and imprisoned at hard labor. The man was then paraded through Jagersdorp, physically chained to the lowest available prisoner, performing the most degrading imaginable task. This was the first action which caused a number of the loyalists to begin having doubts as to the wisdom of the methods practiced. Probably the most completely unwise order issued during the entire period was that forcing all of the Dutch to attend the executions, often of relatives and close friends. Being required to sit a few feet away while dear ones were toppled into a grave was not likely to make it easy to accept the "forgive and forget" sermons soon to come. This and much more packed the pages of the book. Before the end of the novel, condemnation was complete.

Judicious readers of *The Harrow* will be assisted in various ways by remembering carefully certain chapters of *The Ridge of the White*

Waters. (See Chapter 7.) At both the time of composition (1904 and 1907) and the time of the publication (1921), Scully could presuppose a greater knowledge of the Rand than may be assumed after the passing of between half and three-quarters of a century. The history of South Africa has followed a complex process of development, yet the poems, stories, novels, and nonfiction of William Charles Scully have supplied much that is valuable in reaching an understanding of important events.

II A *Pleasant Interlude*

When Sir J. H. Meiring Beck died in 1919, Lady Beck asked William Charles Scully to write a memoir of her husband. He acceded to the request, and in 1921 published what he modestly called a compilation. The introduction was written by John X. Merriman, and a poem of tribute by Monseigneur Kolbe concluded the memorial volume. For Scully the task was a thoroughly congenial one. Not only was Dr. Beck a friend but Scully believed that he had made a number of valuable contributions to the life of South Africa. Naturally his medical work came first, but Dr. Beck was known for many other activities.[25] Very early he showed musical interest and aptitude, and ultimately he had considerable influence upon the music of the country. During his last twenty years, he was prominent in the political affairs of South Africa—as a senator and finally a cabinet member at a crucial period in the affairs of his country.

Love of South Africa was evident in all that Dr. Meiring Beck did. This was natural because his family had been a part of life in the Cape since late in the eighteenth century. His great-grandfather had come out from Thuringen as an official of the East India Company. Grandmother Beck had brought French Huguenot blood into the family. His father was Cornelius Beck and mother Johanna Elizabeth Meiring. Johannes, later known as John, was born at Worcester, November 28, 1855. Both his academic and musical education were started in Worcester and transferred to Cape Town when he was seventeen. Having decided upon a medical career, he sailed (1874) for England, with the University of Edinburgh as his ultimate destination. During the period devoted to medical training, he did not neglect music. Even vacations on the continent were spent at both medical and musical centers. Despite a brilliant academic record and excellent offers to remain in Scotland or England, he returned to South Africa in 1881.

During his years of medical practice, Dr. Beck did many things for the health of those around him. He was active in attempts to improve sanitation and have physiology taught in the schools. It was he who, after study in Paris, took the first X-ray photographs in South Africa. His last contribution was made during the great Influenza Epidemic of 1918. He offered his medical knowledge for the benefit of the public and spent as many hours as possible in the Pretoria hospitals.

Between the ages of seventeen and nineteen, while a student at Cape Town, John Beck took part in the performances of the Musical Society. When the scene became Edinburgh, he played first violin in programs of the Orchestral Society from 1874 to 1879. It was during this period, while in Germany, that he first heard and liked the Wagnerian operas. The Hungarian violinist Remenyi thought that Beck was a musical genius and should have made music his profession. Despite his decision to follow a medical career, his contribution to music in South Africa was important. It was he who convinced the Director of the Royal College of Music in London that examiners should be sent to Cape Town to raise the standard of excellence in the music being taught there. Dr. Beck was not only a promoter and performer but a composer and also skilled in improvising at the piano. Scully gives a list of forty-one compositions, twenty-three of them published.

Always interested in the agricultural development of the land, soon after he entered parliament Dr. Beck compiled statistics to demonstrate that the wealth derived from agriculture was greater than that from the mines. This came as a surprise to almost everyone, for few had stopped to consider the concentration of one source of wealth compared to the range of the other. Agricultural wealth included the production of grains, fruits, vegetables, sheep, cattle, wines—to give a partial list. When he moved to Tubagh, Dr. Beck himself became interested in producing a light wine in that vicinity. Experts advised against the attempt, but with care he personally selected what he considered possible varieties of white grapes and gave his own attention to the whole process of production. The result was the well known "Witzenberg," named for the mountains on the eastern side of the Tulbagh Valley.

Throughout his life Dr. Beck was active in helping preserve buildings and objects of historical value. The first building he helped save was the oldest of all South African structures—the Castle at Cape Town. When he was president of the Society for the Preservation of Objects of Historic Interest, he was active in saving many kinds of things—such as Bushman paintings, mysterious old beads in the vicinity of the copper mines at Messina, and Dr. Livingstone's first mission stations. Through his initiative in 1911 a valuable house and its contents in Cape Town were preserved and became a National Museum. One of the important restorations of his life was done for personal reasons. After some twenty years in the Cape Town area, the Becks decided to move into a rural setting. Search for a suitable place led to the century-old drostdy (office or residence of a landdrost) at Tulbagh. The building was begun by Governor Jan Willem Janssens and was intended as the administrative seat as well as the residence of the landdrost (land-or county-sheriff. A Boer magistrate in a rural district prior to the establishment of British administration). Purchased by the Becks just before it was to be converted into a wagon house and stables, "De Oude Drostdij" was completely restored. With the house went a thousand acres, also much neglected. This rich land was also returned to cultivation. The setting was a magnificent one—Great Winterhoek to the north, Obiquas Bergen the west, and Witzenberg east. Of special interest was the fact that the first minister of the Dutch Reformed Church at Tulbagh, the Reverend Arnoldus Mauritz Meyring, was Dr. Beck's great-great-grandfather. The third minister from Holland to this church was Mrs. Beck's great-grandfather, Abraham Johannes Kuys.

Perhaps the best known of Dr. Beck's contributions to his country was political. He first entered parliament in 1898. During 1908 he was selected by Prime Minister Merriman as a delegate to the National Convention which framed the Act of Union. When Union came in 1910, he was chosen by parliament as a senator. He entered the cabinet in 1916. Before this period, a knighthood had been bestowed upon him. Both in and out of parliament, Sir Meiring became widely known for his speeches, and it seems quite definite that he was one of the most admired, even beloved, men in South Africa. It was often said that he created happiness around him and that even his political opponents always liked him and believed in his integrity. His death, May 15, 1919, from pneumonia, in his sixty-fourth year, was widely mourned.

The memorial volume which Scully has created is fitting in every sense. Though filled with factual detail, the book never becomes dull. Both European and South African reaction to Dr. Beck is given almost entirely in the words of those who were acquainted with him most intimately. The testimony begins with that of the person who tutored him in Greek when he came to Cape Town at age seventeen. This is the same man who wrote the memorial poem with which the book ends. Many of the memories come from persons of great importance in the medical, musical, political, and social world, for from his youth Johannes Henricus Meiring Beck associated with those who held positions of leadership.

III *A Human Being With Rare Qualities*

Drawing from more than half a century of experiences with the Bantu tribes of South Africa, Scully made his last novel, *Daniel Vananda,* 1923, a serious study of the conditions under which the Bantu peoples were living between 1880 and 1920. The narrative starts with the birth of the chief character and carries him through a series of adventures, and ends with the images which pass through his mind as death comes. Events of the novel are chosen to illustrate various aspects of life during the time. Scully says that there is nothing in the novel which is not based upon fact. For several of the important episodes, he identifies the historical event being used. No small part of the book emerges from actions of which Scully had detailed personal knowledge.

Born without ever having known his father, who had died from the bite of a snake, Vananda grew up in the kraal of his grandfather, Kondolo, of the Quati Clan, living now under the rule of the paramount chief of the Tembus. Old Kondolo had an enormous store of historical information, and he knew the whole intricate system of Bantu law. At times powerful chiefs of other tribes asked for his ruling on difficult problems. As a child, Vananda showed an interest in and an aptitude for absorbing his grandfather's learning. The young and the old were drawn very closely together. Vananda grew in size, strength, and in the skills of his people. At fourteen, he was one of the strongest and most handsome boys in his vicinity and gradually became a leader among those with whom he lived.

Suddenly war changed everything. Because he attended the ceremonies with his grandfather, Vananda witnessed the slaughtering of the black bull, with all of its symbolic impact, and the anointing of the warriors in preparation for battle, though Vananda was too young for official combat. Alas, all was of no avail. In a few weeks the entire clan was either destroyed or scattered. Vananda alone survived from Kondolo's kraal. In a final desperate attempt to escape the enemy forces closing in on two sides, he was brought down by one of two assegais hurled from different directions. Surrounded by Fingo warriors, Vananda awaited certain death. Reprieve came with the arrival of a Cape calvary officer, who with his pistol stopped the

Fingos. He drew the assegai from Vananda's flesh, bound the wound, and ordered four of the Fingos to carry the boy on a litter to a tent in the valley. Soon a doctor came and attended the wound. When he had an opportunity to converse with the man who had saved his life, Captain Stephen Vardy, the boy learned that Europeans did not kill persons taken in combat. Complete astonishment enveloped him. How could the Amaquati chief have been mistaken in judging a people so powerful and good? As the captured youth began to strengthen, he attached himself to Captain Vardy in what approached worship. When the Captain's unit was ordered to Basutoland, he arranged for Vananda to be received at Rossdale Mission Station, near Butterworth, to be educated and taught a trade.

Following custom, the boy accepted the Christian name of Daniel and kept Vananda as a surname. His attempts to learn carpentry were a failure; in the academic areas, his progress was superior. Rossdale, however, was a training institution. When the boy did not develop in a trade, they could only send him on to King William's Town to work in a mercantile firm as a store-boy. His employer was pleased with his performance. Trouble came from the social world. Before war bereft him of home and family, Daniel felt no natural inclination towards girls. The tragedy and subsequent salvation which came to him dominated his mental processes for a considerable period. Then, too, at Rossdale rigid separation by sex was practiced. Now nature began to assert itself. As is frequently true, he found an accomplished coquette conveniently waiting. Briefly all was well; but when Maggie Zama discovered the depth of Daniel's feelings and seriousness of his mind, she fearfully rejected all advances. Understanding nothing of what had happened, Daniel was dangerously distressed and turned to brandy as something to deaden pain. His descent was rapid—loss of work, evil companions, an encounter with the police, then jail. Since he was not a criminal character in any way, he made a very poor prisoner—having no concept of the actual nature of the environment into which he had been hurled. Goaded by one of the warders, Daniel fiercely attacked the man with a force and grip which required four men to break. For this outburst he was flogged. The cruel blows were received without visible reaction, but the inner response was intense. As the strokes fell, Daniel stroke by stroke came to understand what had happened in his life. From that moment he turned back towards the clean and upright action which he had abandoned for only a brief period. When free again, Daniel left the town in which he had encountered evil and moved towards a new existence. One day he viewed for the first time the vast sweep of ocean waters. Soon he crossed the Bushman's River and found himself in a green valley. He was attracted by a white-walled farmhouse. Here, he felt, peace must dwell if it was to be found on earth. As he walked on, he observed a man several hundred yards before him. Intending to seek work here from the person he assumed was the owner, he increased his stride. When he approached the man he was trying to overtake, that person turned and revealed his identity. It was Stephen Vardy, the one person on earth who meant the most to Daniel. So great was the emotional release that he dropped beside the road and wept, which he had not done since childhood. Finally in control of himself, he went with Vardy to the homestead, Avalon, and told him what had happened at Rossdale and King William's Town. Now the man who had once saved his life offered him work on the farm.

With joy and energy, Daniel went about his assigned tasks, which were done faithfully and well. After six months, as all others on the farm were, he was offered a small piece of land on which he could grow a crop and have a few cattle and sheep. At the end of each half-year, Daniel accepted his pay in livestock. Thus he began to create a home of his own. His land was near that of a former servant of Vardy's, Songelwa, now almost blind. With him lived his wife, Nomani, and a widowed daughter-in-law with her three children—two boys and a girl. With this family Daniel made close friends. In the daughter Alice, Daniel found the opposite of Maggie Zama. Here was refinement and peace. "Love once more entered his life—not as before like a flaming sword, but rather as a sunbeam stealing between green leaves, gently warming that on which it fell. The girl was as shy as a forest bird, as virginal as the dawn in springtime—as evasive as the rainbow."[26] Deep affinities drew Alice and Daniel together. Before any words were spoken, each knew what was happening. Daniel spoke to Stephen Vardy, who approved of the match, and gave Daniel the day off to select and present the first payment of "labola" cattle.

While everything was in the process of going supremely right, suddenly everything went supremely wrong. Satan had entered the Garden of Eden not as a serpent but as a corporal of the Cape Police. Though the actions of Corporal Konza and the trial of Daniel Vananda for sheep stealing create the most exciting portion of the book, in these events Scully is very careful to identify his historical source. The author states that for this part of the narrative he has "drawn freely upon the main features of the notorious 'Fish Water Flats' case, which was tried before the Circuit Court at Port Elizabeth in 1909, and in the prosecution of which I, personally, took a leading part."[27] Because in Daniel's trial he was subjected to torture, Scully says, "With regard to the application of torture, I am prepared to reveal to the Minister of Justice of the Union (under adequate guarantees) the name of a retired sub-inspector of Police who will admit that torture, of the description detailed in this book, was often inflicted at the Police Station under his control for the purpose of inducing confession in cases where the evidence was regarded as insufficient to secure a conviction."[28]

Given the time and the place, the emergence of a Corporal Konza was essentially inevitable. In the preface Scully asserts "that at the end of the last Native war period (1881) the Bantu of the Cape Province finally abandoned all idea of opposing the White Man's domination, and settled down to peaceful pursuits."[29] In this state they became easy prey to natives operating against them under the authority of established government. Looked at in one way, these oppressors replaced the witchdoctors of a previous era. Scully had insisted that the witchdoctors were one of the most insidious forces present in Bantu life; now he offers his opposition to a practice which is being substituted for an evil which was already reduced and—hopefully—might soon be destroyed.

Though there was a detachment of Cape Police in the neighborhood to which Daniel Vananda had moved, the white population of the area was not the kind from which criminals grow. Neither were the Bantu criminally inclined. Obviously the police force had little work to perform. Under these conditions the native members of the force were likely to feel uneasy about the continuation of their employment. Therefore, they stimulated a few "criminal" actions, making it possible for them to arrest, prosecute, and convict the "guilty" persons. Sheep stealing was the most normal charge to manufacture. The process was quite simple. Native police planned or concurred while their accomplices did the stealing. In this particular area the police were Corporal Konza and his four privates. When enough thefts had been perpetrated to upset the farmers of the region, Corporal Konza and his men would make arrests. Often this meant arresting one of the accomplices, who could be sacrificed with safety, or someone against whom Corporal Konza held a grudge. The Corporal's methods were swift and thoroughly effective. The farmers looked upon him as a true friend and protector, and his superiors were oblivious of the fact that he actually ran the detachment, not they themselves. The natives understood very well what was happening but were unaware of how to submit their information to the awesome Cape government. A few individuals, such as Stephen Vardy, understood Corporal Konza's character and knew what he was doing. Vardy privately considered Konza as an "obnoxious scoundrel."

The forces of attraction which pass between the sexes are completely beyond explanation. Otherwise the second half of this novel might have a different plot. Corporal Konza, brutal and unscrupulous, saw Alice and was strongly drawn to her demure and gentle nature, though it should not be assumed that his intentions were the same as those of Daniel. Despite his feelings, Konza feared to employ his usual methods, knowing that he was dealing with Stephen Vardy's people. There was something about this frail, reserved man which made him afraid. He could, however, get rid of Daniel by his indirect method, this man who had married Alice and become the most trusted of Stephen Vardy's workers. Exactly as the witch doctors before him, Corporal Konza made it his business to know everything possible about persons with whom he might have to deal. As soon as he learned Daniel came from King William's Town, he had inquiries made. The reports supplied everything he needed. Daniel not only had been in jail, he had been flogged.

Because of developing consumption, Stephen Vardy was forced during the summer months to leave the hot moist air of the farm, lying near the sea, and stay with a friend in the mountains. On these occasions, Daniel was now left in charge. Corporal Konza saw to it that Vardy was absent from the farm when he started a period of sheep thefts. The farmers of the area called for more police protection. Daniel began to guard the Avalon flocks both day and night. Once when he heard the sheep being molested, he hurried to the spot and saw two men rise and flee. Next day his inspection revealed the footprints of booted men. One night soon after this discovery, he rose from his position as guard to investigate the source of a disturbance among the sheep and was felled by a heavy blow to the head. When he regained consciousness, he found himself handcuffed, his feet bound together, and his hands and clothing smeared with blood. Before him was a freshly slaughtered sheep. Sitting on a stone was Corporal Konza and with him two of his men. When the Corporal asked for a confession, Daniel refused. Prisoner and evidence were then moved to the police station, and Daniel was locked in a small dark cell. Late in the afternoon, he was brought before the Sub-

Inspector and asked to make a confession. Again he refused. Because of natural thirst, Daniel asked for water. Corporal Konza placed the water before him. As Daniel started to drink, the water was withdrawn, and he was told that he had to confess before he would be allowed to drink. Refusal sent him back to his cell and the police into conference. They feared Daniel's intelligence and considered Vardy a dangerous man with whom to deal. Finally they decided that a confession was necessary, despite the evidence they had carefully assembled. First they applied what was known as the *lesser question.* "An irregular block of iron weighing over two hundredweight was carried into the cell. This block was pierced by a hole with ragged edges, just big enough to permit of a man's arm passing through. One of the arms of the obstinate prisoner was drawn through the hole; the other was passed over the end of the block and the wrists were handcuffed together. Instead of being embraced, as in the case of the Iron Maiden of Nuremburg, the prisoner did the embracing; he had to remain crouched upon his knees, in a strained position; he could neither lie down nor get up. . . ."[30] After five hours, he was again brought before the Sub-Inspector, the water placed, and the confession requested. Though he was unable to speak, he moved his head to give a negative reply. Now the *greater question* was applied. The prisoner was suspended by his wrists from a rafter, with his toes just touching the floor. Having extinguished all light, the inquisitors left the room.

Meanwhile Alice had learned of Daniel's arrest and accusation. Under protecting darkness, she was watching when he was brought from the cell after enduring the *lesser question.* She counted the men as they entered and then as they filed out of the office. One was missing, Daniel. Softly she slipped into the office and found him hanging by his wrists. First she brought water. Then, as she was searching for something with which to cut him away from the rafter or lift him from the floor, she was discovered because the Sub-Inspector returned. Daniel's bearing in the rejection of all demands for confession had destroyed the man's assurance that he was dealing with a guilty though obstinate prisoner. Now, with his own knife, he released Daniel and watched as Alice rubbed his arms to restore circulation. He left and soon returned with a blanket in which the prostrate one could be wrapped. When Corporal Konza burst into the room and stared in amazement, the Sub-Inspector simply pointed towards the door. Daniel was now lifted to his cell, where a bed of straw waited, along with water and food. Intuitively Alice understood that for the moment he was safe. There would be no more torture. Hurriedly she made her way home and thence to the village of Alexandria, where she found one who could reach Stephen Vardy by telegram. Three days later, when Daniel was brought to trail before the magistrate in Alexandria, even Corporal Konza's poise failed when a solicitor from Grahamstown stood up and announced that he was there to represent the defence. At his request the case was postponed for a week. Meanwhile Vardy returned. After careful consideration, the lawyer decided not to introduce the details of the torture to which Daniel had been subjected. Because there were no marks on the body, he felt it might weaken his chance for a verdict of not guilty in connection with the official charge.

Having rehearsed their story as in past cases, the three men who had arrested Daniel were completely unprepared when cross-examination began. They contradicted each other on every question asked—regardless of how simple. Accustomed to testifying in the presence of each other, they were thoroughly confused when separated. When Corporal Konza was asked what happened to the meat that was taken as evidence, he said it had been destroyed. Questioned as to the method, he floundered terribly. Finally, he remembered that the meat had been given to a native constable, one not present at the trial. The next witness testified that the meat had been divided among the three making the arrest. Though the third initially declared that he knew nothing of the matter, he finally admitted he had eaten a "little bit."

When the prosecution had completed its case, the lawyer for the defence proposed to the magistrate that the witnesses be kept separated, that the court adjourn to the location of the alleged crime, and there re-hear the Corporal and his men while each was out of the sight as well as hearing of the others. The magistrate agreed. Standing where he said the arrest had been made, Corporal Konza gave a dramatic account of the event, even pointing to some of the blood that he said could still be seen on the spot of the slaughter. He had, however, selected the wrong spot. The actual arrest was made some distance from the place to which he had guided the court. The second witness, far behind and not knowing where his corporal had guided the magistrate, chose a location several hundred yards away from that identified by his superior. In addition, he claimed that the police had closed in on Daniel from the opposite direction than that stated by Konza. The third witness contradicted both who had preceded him. At this point the magistrate declared Daniel innocent and arrested

Corporal Konza and his men for perjury and conspiracy. Tried before a jury of local farmers, they were acquitted. Then followed a departmental investigation. At the end, the Police Commissioner dismissed Corporal Konza and his subordinates from the service. Then he removed the police detachment from the district. Stock-stealing ceased completely. This is not Scully giving an effective twist to the conclusion of an event in his novel. It is an author employing in fiction what had happened in a famous case in which he had been involved because of his own position as an official of the Cape Civil Service.

Granted his freedom, Daniel returned to Avalon. His position was essentially that of overseer, and his own herd and flock increased until by native standards he was a rich man. All, however, was not well. Each time Stephen Vardy came for the brief visits he was now permitted in the cool season, Daniel could see that he was weaker. Soon there would be a farewell without another welcome. Then, too, deep within his being Daniel knew that Alice had never recovered from the ordeal through which she had passed at the time of his tortures. In addition, it became evident that she too had started the fight against consumption. Refusing to leave Daniel for a high and clear climate, Alice's struggle against the disease ended before that of Stephen Vardy. As Daniel walked home from Alice's grave, he knew that the Master of Avalon would not be long in seeking that mysterious country. He was correct.

With the death of Stephen Vardy, Avalon passed to the hands of the nearest cousin—a man in every possible way the opposite of Stephen. Within a few days after his arrival, he reduced both Daniel's status and pay to that of an ordinary laborer. As soon as an opportunity presented itself, he dismissed Daniel and gave him three days to leave the farm with his sixty cattle and two hundred sheep. The period was one of drought, and the novel now depicted the tragic odyssey of Daniel and his family until not a single head of cattle or one sheep remained, the end coming in a heavy storm upon a spur of the Great Winterberg. The final event of this phase of the narrative was the death of his son, for whom life on the road had been more than his small body could endure.

After the death of little Tyali, Daniel again became a wanderer in the land. Feeling that hard work was very necessary for his state of mind, he turned towards the coast and took a place on the cargo boats at Port Elizabeth. The pay was small and the work was hard, but neither disturbed Daniel. What horrified him, however, was the miserable living conditions. Scully was quite knowledgeable about the details of the situation, for his last appointment in the Civil Service took him to Port Elizabeth. Lack of any possible comfort came first from the type of building used for housing. Most dwellings were of corrugated iron, unlined. In winter, if the temperature dropped to freezing outside, it was little better inside. In summer the same principle operated. If it was extremely hot outside, the inside was equally hot, or even hotter, for the heated air was trapped. Huts to which the native was accustomed resisted external changes of temperature in either direction. Another aspect of the environment was ultimately far more serious. Going to and from work, the native passed twenty public houses designated as hotels but which were quite simply liquor shops. The author observed that Port Elizabeth contained more churches in proportion to its population than any other town in South Africa, yet licensed these "hotels" knowing very well that they were carrying on an illegal business. Daniel was not tempted by brandy, but he was deeply saddened by the conditions under which thousands were forced to exist. After seeing the disintegration of one solidly respectable family with whom he had become friendly, he started for Johannesburg.

Because Daniel does not in any way become a part of life in Johannesburg, he is able to serve as a detached recorder. His first employment is as a worker in the gold mines. Again here, as with all physical labor in the past, he enjoys the healthy use of his muscular body. Among other things, hard work brought sound sleep at night—something for which he longed at this time. Neither work nor sleep dulls his powers of observation. Through him a reader hears of life in the mines, and the compounds, and the hospitals. Finally Daniel, as thousands before him, succumbs to miners' phthisis. When he asked to be seen by a doctor, he was examined. Then he was paid up to date and dismissed. Before this time, he had met an acquaintance of the King William's Town days. This person found him a place as a house boy for a couple living on Hospital Hill, above Joubert Park. His employees were Roumanian, a Mr. and Mrs. Stepan Flotov. The husband was a "jackal" who followed one of the "lions" of Commissioner Street and Park Town. Eventually Daniel found himself almost trapped into the same position occupied by Joseph in the home of Potiphar. He fled just in time. The person hired to fill his place was not so fortunate and was sentenced to hang. The jury did not even leave the box to consider the verdict.

Following his escape from the Flotov home, Daniel secured work in the kitchen of a restaurant—doing the rough and heavy work there.

After Retirement from the Civil Service

The hours were very long and the work monotonous, but there was an abundance of food, and when his labors were ended he slept soundly. There came a day, however, when he knew that the phthisis infection was winning the assault upon his lungs. Memories of the past began to fill his mind. Under their influence he left Johannesburg and started towards the land of his childhood, his grandfather's kraal. Slowly and painfully he made his way to the beloved spot. He could find only one kinsman, an aged uncle, who was very poor. With the coming of winter Daniel's cough was constant, and the body rapidly weakened. He gave his uncle all of the accumulated savings from the Ridge of the White Waters. Now a doomed man, he sat waiting.

The Present faded—became less and less real; the Past closed in upon Daniel Vananda like a tapestried curtain. The crises of his life seemed to re-enact themselves,—the killing of the black bull—the escape from the Fingo spears—the torture at the Police Camp—the long, cruel pilgrimage and the death of his cattle in the snow-drift. . . .

But when the last stage of all came, it was only the gentle face of Alice that the eyes of his soul saw against the background of darkness.[31]

Oblivion descended upon one who had known great sorrow but had also experienced loves which were their own rewards: love of his grandfather for his knowledge and command of the past, love of Stephen Vardy for his selfless humanity, and love of Alice for the peace which they shared.

Much of the strength of the book results from the author's creation of memorable scenes and characters. Some of the scenes a reader does not forget are brief and seemingly of little importance, but cumulatively they exercise considerable impact. A scene of this kind is an early one of Vananda in Kondola's kraal. When his grandfather was discussing tribal history, giving detailed accounts of ancient events, the child noiselessly slipped to a place within hearing and pretending sleep, curled up under his kaross (rug made of skins, used also as a garment), as if he were a hedgehog. Though the child assumed the practice was unobserved, his grandfather knew he was listening. Nothing was said, but the old man was pleased with the action. As events of this kind continue, a reader comes to appreaciate the bond developed between Kondola and this unusual and lonely grandchild. Thus, when the moment of death comes for the old man, readers feel with Vananda a sense of loss.

Flashing through the novel are scenes of many kinds. Although he is not in the combat zone during the war period, old Kondola, his hut, all livestock, and every human being except his grandson are swept from the land, leaving no trace. Mention has already been made of Vananda's attempt to escape through the battle lines and being brought down by a Fingo assegai. Perhaps more intense than any of the scenes of the war period is that in which Alice rescues Daniel from the police torture. In the midst of violence and tragedy, however, there are scenes of peace and happiness. It was during his years on the Vardy farm that important changes occurred.

Daniel often carried his burthen of memories and dreams to the sea at night. The phosphorescent flashes from the breaking water, the whispering undertones audible through the resonant booming of the surf, seemed to tell of another life—a sphere to which man must, whilst in the flesh, remain a stranger. . . .

The scorched garden of this lonely man's heart through which love, elemental and terrible as sudden flame from a sleeping volcano, had swept so destructively, once more became verdant. With the change came back the old longing for human companionship.

The pensive, gentle face of Alice . . . haunted his walking dreams. . . .

One night Daniel slept at old Songelwa's kraal. The girl lay next to her grandmother; Daniel at the opposite side of the hut. He remained sleepless throughout the greater part of the night; his acute sense told him, through the girl's breathing, that she, too, was awake.

It was midsummer. At grey dawn Alice arose, took a large calabash and stole out of the hut. All the others were still asleep. Daniel followed her. He saw her disappear between the trees which lined the curved pathway leading to the stream. He found her bending over a clear pool at the foot of a small cascade, filling the vessel. At the sound of Daniel's footstep she leaped to her feet—wide-eyed—trembling—infinitely alluring in her shuddering modesty. . . .[32]

With brevity and reserve Scully handles the scene which follows, an event leading to an altogether satisfactory marriage.

Naturally the title character of any novel written as a biography must have a prominent part in what happens, but he will achieve significance only in relation to the human element with which he is surrounded. For example, certain characteristics of Daniel Vananda can be elicited only in relation to the women who are close to him. The youthful attractions of Maggie Zama showed the innocence and immaturity of Daniel at this early period, yet offered glimpses of depths to be revealed later. The evil and passionate beauty of Lydia acted as a foil in displaying qualities which otherwise would never have been seen. Contact with Lydia gave Daniel an opportunity to

After Retirement from the Civil Service

develop some understanding of himself. Finally, Alice made very clear the ultimate strengths found in this lonely man. Maggie is in every way trivial, but Lydia and Alice are thoroughly decisive characters—in totally opposite ways.

Among all of the other characters of the novel, regardless of how interesting and important, none is more necessary for Scully's purpose than Stephen Vardy. Entering the story early, he remains until his death, which brings to a conclusion Daniel's years at Avalon. Of this character, the author says,

> Vardy was one of that tragic band of human creatures who are cursed with vision clear enough to enable them to see just a little farther than their fellows, and who are consequently doomed to permanent estrangement from their kind. . . .
> The little farm . . . gave him enough for his simple needs,—and something more. It had been Vardy's habit for a quarter of a century to visit Europe every fourth Spring. In the course of his various trips he had sojourned in every important European city. Languages he seemed to absorb without an effort. He had picked up the Kaffir tongue colloquially when a child. Later he perfected this knowledge until he spoke every dialect found between Natal and the Cape Province far better than nine-tenths of the Natives themselves. Moreover, he had a deep and sympathetic knowledge of the Native character.[33]

Though Stephen Vardy is not present in the narrative except when he is needed as a part of the action, he is obviously a very useful person to Scully in developing various attitudes.

Despite Scully's intention to write a novel in which he depicted the relation existing between the white and black races in South Africa, the finished work transcends the original purpose. The title character is not merely the Daniel or the Vananda of his name. Before the end of the book, he has been established as one of the rare human beings of the earth who must live outside of the realm of normal society because of certain qualities of his innermost being. The child's grandfather understood the incipient characteristics which were to distinguish this boy from his associates. Neither Maggie Zama nor the men of her environment could understand the region through which Daniel Vananda moved; Lydia, however, knew enough to grasp the existence of something very unusual, something she wanted for herself. Daniel, however, rejected the evil world that surrounded Lydia. He fled not alone from Lydia and what was close to her but from the whole environment in which he had been briefly lost.

Daniel was seeking the purity which he finally discovered in Alice. From the qualities symbolized by Alice he never departed, despite evil men who took his possessions and the infection which wasted his body. The significance of all of this is that the most powerful parts of the novel reveal Daniel Vananda surrounded by his own race, though except for Alice his own know him not.

IV What Now?

When *Daniel Vananda* was published, its author was sixty-eight. Though Scully had no way of knowing how many years stretched before him and with what they would be filled, he was to have twenty, most of them to be spent in Kimberley, where the family had moved in 1923. As might be expected, even the move to Kimberley did not signal a return to the past for rest, rememberance, and peace. Only death could completely retire William Charles Scully to a world of repose—if that was the state which was to be visited upon man. Not only did he stay in touch with events in South Africa but with world affairs.[34] At one time during these years he was very active in reviewing books of a wide variety. There were biographies of Henry VIII of England; Peter the Great of Russia (also Catherine); Louis XIV of France; the House of Fugger, a sixteenth-century equivalent of the Rothschilds; and of Ambroise Paré (1510–90), a French barber surgeon of unusual qualities. He reviewed volumes concerned with naval geniuses, American psychology, and affairs in India. Considerable attention was given to a book depicting crime in Chicago during the first quarter of the twentieth century. A publication which stirred a deep interest in him was entitled *Twelve Against the Gods*, a study of the philosophy of adventure. The person among the twelve who was, he felt, most successfully handled by the author was Woodrow Wilson, compared with Alexander of Macedon. This selected list reveals the variety of material with which his mind was being stimulated. Meanwhile he engaged in reading of his own choice, which was tending more and more towards philosophy. Though the ultimate questions were never answered for Scully, the search continued.

V Pharmacy and Politics

In 1937 Scully issued a pamphlet which he called *Scopalomine in Africa, or Pharmacy and Politics*. According to a Prefatorial Note, he was reading Aldous Huxley and encountered a passage which influenced him in a strange manner. Huxley suggested that "The propagandists of the future will be chemists and physiologists as well as writers. A cachet containing ¾ of a gramme of chloral and ¾ of a gramme of scopalomine will produce in the person who swallows it a state of complete physiological malleability, akin to the state of a person under complete hypnosis. Any suggestion made to the patient while in this artificially induced trance penetrates to the very depths of the sub-conscious mind and may produce a permanent modification of the habitual modes of thought and feeling."[35] That night Scully slept with unusual soundness and had a vivid and detailed dream. Having awakened from this experience, he recorded the whole in all of its completeness. When he read what he had put down as a dream, he felt great uneasiness. "The sequence of occurrences seemed so real, so characteristic, that I began asking myself: Is it possible that this can be other than true, from beginning to end?"[36] After assuring the reader that it was a dream, though perhaps a prophetic one, he proceeds with the narrative.

Secretly six members of the Cabinet of the South African Union are meeting in an inconspicuous building in the southern section of Pretoria. Lights are dim and windows heavily curtained. Each member who arrives is cloaked and visored in black velvet. A particular rap is given and a password whispered. Those who form this cabinet within the Cabinet are the Prime Minister, General Hertzog, who presides; General Smuts, Mr. Havenga, Mr. Hofmeyr, Mr. Pirow, and Colonel Deneys Reitz. The purpose of the gathering is to decide what to do about a serious situation which has developed. Dr. Malan and Colonel Stallard have been nibbling from opposite sides at the structure of the state, which has begun to wobble. Now the two appear ready to combine and attack as a unit. Cabinet spies have reported a meeting planned for the night following this gathering of the important six.

Since his colleagues already know something of the effects achieved with a new drug, "Scopalomine," the Prime Minister reads a cable just received from M. Chautemps, Premier of France. The Premier announces that "Further experiments give more and more astonishing results. Yes, may be used hypodermically or through digestive tract. Former method invariably successful, latter occasionally fails. Soup best medium. Have treated several Nazis captured at frontier. They now weep at sight of Swastika. Instead of former Nazi salutation they now employ a gesture hitherto unknown in France—placing their thumbs beneath their noses and shouting 'Bile Hitler!' "[37]

With a minimum of discussion it is decided necessary for the good of the country to take Dr. Malan and Colonel Stallard into custody and administer Scopalomine, together with the needed influences to redirect their attitudes and thinking. Detention at the point of rendezvous is effected, and the two are flown to an isolated spot where a doctor and two nurses are ready for the expected guests. Generals Smuts and Hertzog are present to proceed with the desired reeducation, General Smuts reading from his book *Holism* and General Hertzog playing Afrikaans tunes on his violin. Two days later the generals return to Pretoria with a report of their success.

After a political meeting at which the loyalty of Dr. Malan is demonstrated by making him the principal speaker, further experiment is planned at a banquet to be given for the Chamber of Mines and the principal mining magnates. The guest list is carefully sifted, only those known to eat soup being invited. There is one exception. Sir Abe Bailey sometimes takes soup and sometimes does not. He is, however, far too important not be be included. Throughout the evening all goes as planned, except for one thing. Sir Abe decides not to have soup. Thus, when the time comes for him to speak, he rises to offer violent opposition to what is being said and accepted. His associates, having eaten the soup, shout until he cannot be heard and can only rush from the hall. Alas, he rushed into the hands of myrmidons in the employ of the Prime Minister and his five associates. Soon Sir Abe is escorted aboard the special plane which bears guests to that medical center deep in the veld, where the doctor and two nurses await. The doctor is not needed, Sir Abe being more sensible than former patients. He elects soup and is soon sleeping peacefully and listening to a lecture about gold, super tax and profits, and all of the benefits which result from certain practices. The next day he awakens on a bench in his own garden. What has happened during the past forty-eight hours is a complete mystery to him. When a few days later representatives of government meet with the mining interests and propose a ten percent increase on gold profits, the request is graciously approved.

Again the Prime Minister has called the Inner Cabinet into session, this time at the secret spot in the veld. For the occasion, the doctor and nurses have been given a brief vacation. The subject being discussed is the establishment of a National Scopalomine factory.

They feel practical details, though troublesome, can be handled; yet there is one serious problem. General Smuts asks if they have the correct formula and a man who knows how to use it. The Prime Minister admits that everything depends upon the answer to these two questions. Then he explains that he has in the Central Prison of Pretoria three men who claim to be experts. They are French, Russian, and Czechoslovakian. The Prime Minister says, "The Frenchman I rather distrust; he sleeps most of his time and only wakes up to shout for absinthe. I would not suggest for a moment that Chautemps is double-crossing us, but he is, after all, only human. He is making a lot of money out of us and insists upon being paid in gold. And we know the franc is unstable. The Russian was sent by Stalin, with a strong recommendation. We have had to import for his use a large quantity of vodka. I fear—judging from the rate of consumption—that a further supply will soon be needed. It has to be cleared through the Customs as hair-wash." ("More Machiavellianism," growled Mr. Hofmeyr.) "The Czechoslovakian is not, I am afraid, all that Benes certified him to be. Now, Gentlemen, can you make suggestions as to how the competence of these men might be tested?"[38]

Immediately it is proposed that each man be given a laboratory and that his Scopalomine be tried on a suitable subject. The ministers then make a little game of suggesting likely subjects. General Smuts says that an attempt might be made to convince a Wellington or Paarl wine farmer to advocate total abstinence. Mr. Hofmeyr feels that a proper test would be to induce an Anglican High Church Bishop to publish a pastoral favoring easier divorce. Colonel Reitz believes they should try to get a Western Free State Farmer who pays workers five shillings a month to agitate for a twenty shilling minimum wage. When all proposals have been given, the Prime Minister observes that the tests are indeed severe but fair. He says he will set up what has been suggested.

Acrimonious discussion now develops in an attempt to decide upon a custodian of whatever Scopalomine is on hand. The Minister of Finance believes that the greatest treasure of all should be in his possession, but the Minister of Defence and Railways insists that he has a desperate need for the drug in order to silence the demands of the railwaymen for higher wages. Before now these two had been close friends; now each fears the other plans to Scopalomize him. Attention is diverted from this conflict by Colonel Reitz, who announces that swarms of locusts are moving south at an alarming rate and something must be done. He believes the answer has been found.

"I have been reading 'Holism,' that remarkable book written by my friend the Minister of Justice, and have been struck by the essential organic connection which exists between various groups of animals. . . .

"That is involved in the Holistic Conception of the Universe," remarked General Smuts complacently.

"But we are here to discuss Scopalomine; there is nothing about locusts or 'Holism' on the agenda," said Mr. Hofmeyr.

"I am coming to that," rejoined Colonel Reitz. "I have a theory which I want to test. To carry out the necessary experiments I shall require a small quantity of Scopalomine. . . . I propose to establish contact with a moderately-sized swarm, treat it with Scopalomine and convince it that its proper course is north-westward. Then I will send selected individuals—missionaries, as it were—to the advancing hordes to persuade the latter that it is not alone their duty, but to their interest to return to their more suitable environment, which is undoubtedly the Kalihari."[39]

With swarms of locust flying through his dreams, the author is startled back into the waking world.

Literature has always been an art in which one thing is depicted in terms of another. A poet such as Aristophanes created whole new worlds to present what he wished to say. An author's claim that what he offers came to him in a dream also has a long and honorable literary history. Scully made no apologies, nor did he need to, for the methods employed in *Scopalomine in Africa*. It has ever been the practice of satire to use indirect methods, and it has always been the intention of satirists to reform that which they feel is in error. Clearly William Charles Scully was concerned with the practice of South African politics and was having his say.

One detail of *Scopalomine* is most unusual. Scully has made no attempt to disguise the names of the principal political characters in South Africa at that time. General Hertzog, General Smuts, Mr. Hofmeyr, Dr. Malan . . . . all are present. Here is something very special. Did the author proceed with their knowledge and approval? At least this much is true: several years later General Smuts wrote an introduction to Scully's final book and argued strongly for the author's right to be heard on South African subjects. Had General Smuts been offended, would he have offered the praise given Scully in such generous measure? Also, it should be observed that during the next year Stellenbosch conferred upon Scully an Honorary Doctorate of Literature. Mrs. Gray says, "I think the majority of the people mentioned in *Scopalomine* were amused, reacting as politicians do to the comic cartoons in Punch—but, of course, some were mortally offended."[40]

VI My Task Is Done

Five months before death, now in his eighty-eighth year, Scully held in his hands a copy of *Voices of Africa*, 1943, the last of his books. It was a War Publication, royalties going to the South African Red Cross. The volume was a collection of ten stories and eight poems. All of the stories except four had appeared in one of the early volumes, and the remaining four in magazines. Seven of the poems were from what Scully had written after he turned from verse to prose. The dust jacket states without qualification that "W. C. Scully stands unchallenged as the patriarch of South African literature." It then continues, "Time has no more dimmed his technique than it has dimmed the technique of Luke, the beloved physician . . . . In all writing such as this, put down under a deep sense of compulsion, where there is meaning and purpose, there is a freshness and power that knows no recession." Allowing for all of the exaggeration expected from dust jackets, this is still a statement of significant approval. As a reader opens the book and examines the dedication, he is pleased to discover that though almost ninety Scully still has a clear wit. Offering the book to his "Domestic Censor," he explains she might be looked upon as a combination of "St. Monica, St. Ceclia, Jane Austen and Mrs. Gummidge, with a handful of Mrs. Fairchild thrown in for luck.".

Written in 1899 and used at the beginning of *By Veld and Kopje,* 1907, "Voices of Africa" becomes the title poem of this last volume. It offered an important statement of Scully's thinking at the turn of the century and continued to represent his attitude as the years passed. The tone of the whole is projected by the words of the Sahara.

> Time, like a little child, amid my sands
> Builds and unbuilds with feeble, listless hands.

Time and change, that is to say change in the passage of time, have been, are and will be the rulers in Africa. After the Sahara, Egypt speaks, saying, "The young world listened, breathless, when I spoke."

Time past reigns in memory as Mount Atlas whispers that

> Pan walks with Faunus through my dreaming woods,
> And Dryads pace my leafy solitudes.

After Ruwenzori, which Ptolemy had called the "Mountains of the Moon," has a say, followed by the great central lakes, the author moves south. The Zambezi recounts a natural cycle, a return to the source as time measures elemental change.

> The spoils the sky had of the world-wide main
> I bear, new-gathered from ten thousand rills
> To where the thund'rous gates my steps unchain,
> Clogged with the wastage of a million hills.
> Thence, breaking forth in triumph, full and free
> I render back my booty to the sea.

Zimbabwe was and is, yet here change remains a mystery. ". . . No rumour speaks my birth, No legend shrines my death."

With the emergence of the voices into the modern world, history becomes prophecy as Kimberley, Johannesburg, and the White Commonwealths speak.

> Black, echoing chasm, whence the bright diadems
> Of half Earth's thrones are furnished, I can hear
> The lost souls wander, wailing, far and near.
>
> A maenad seated on a golden throne;
> My plaything is a nation's destiny;
> My feet are clay, my bosom is a stone;
> The princes of the Earth are fain of me,
> But, stark, before the splendour of my gates,
> The grim Boer, leaning on his rifle, waits.
>
> Blind to the lurid writing on the wall,
> Deaf to the words Fate's warning lips let fall.[41]

Ominous indeed are the words which issue from the great hole at Kimberley and the golden throne built by the flow from beneath the Ridge of the White Waters. In ancient days when Belshazzar saw the handwriting on the wall of his palace, it was already too late—even though there was a Daniel to tell him the meaning of the words. Did Scully assume it was already too late in 1899? Obviously he did not believe that all was well. Yet as a man of fortitude, the author did not end his writing life in an atmosphere of gloom. Rather, he chose a sun-flooded valley fenced by the stately and graceful Drakenstein, scene of "A Stellenbosch Reverie." The closing stanzas of the poem will serve well as the author's valedictory.

> God made this land of ours to be
> A wonder and a mystery—
> Deep as the changing, changeless sea . . .
>
> We have our record—light and shade—
> Mean, noble, terrible—inlaid;
> Of such mosaic is history made.
>   When carping critics urge our blame
> Ask where that stainless land may be—
> Beneath what sky, washed by what sea,
>   Whose page reads not the same? . . .
>
> Two mighty nations, each a star
> In Freedom's crown, our parents are—
> And we a nation-child. Afar
>   We strayed as our strong brothers strayed
> To brighten earth's most darksome ways,
> To labour through unthankful days—
>   Watchful and unafraid. [42]

By birth Scully was Tipperary-County Clare Irish, but he had in spirit become pure South African, loyal to the memory of the mother countries but true to the land that was home.

How thoroughly Scully had oriented himself in the region of the earth to which his family moved is revealed again and again in all that he wrote. In *Voices of Africa* the four stories never before collected and which represent the author's last efforts as a prose fictionist show him still deeply concerned about South African history and continuing to find mental stimulation in South African events. "The Flood," of course, depicts a natural phenomenon and reveals few special affinities with any particular part of the world. The other three stories, however, emerge from that which is South African. Then all three move firmly towards the universal. "Laughing Is no Laughing Matter" starts with something that happened at a concert in a village of the Eastern Cape. The performance was given to aid the school, and the participants were all natives. Because they were genuinely sympathetic, the Europeans of the village had come to watch in considerable numbers. The principal soloists were brother and sister, one with a pleasant baritone voice and the other performing with some skill on a small organ. During one of the solo numbers, the European part of the audience, or much of it, burst into uncontrollable laughter. The performers did not take offence, but the incident disturbed the narrator and motivated him to pursue a serious investigation of the nature of laughter and the reason for this seemingly unwarranted outburst. Though he brings Herbert Spencer and Bergson into the discussion, he does not believe that their explanations of the nature of laughter explain the event he had experienced. Indeed, he himself admits he can not find a solution. What he does insist upon is that laughter is a subject for serious consideration.

Written with a distinct undercurrent of the comic, "On Picket, An Episode of the South African War" introduces the question of revenge, which is indeed a serious subject. The picket is composed of three men: Jan Viljoen, son of a once-wealthy Free State farmer, a veteran at twenty-one; a Swede named Frithyof, who had been in South Africa only three years; and a powerful Irishman, nicknamed "Blaasbalk" by the Commandos. As a youth he had sworn an oath that he would be revenged upon the English because his family had been dispossessed of their house for not having paid the rent. Yet to his friend Jan he says that through the years he has learned " . . . vengeance is always a mistake."[43] Then he proceeds to offer an analysis of his own situation.

> The difficult thing about revenging oneself is that you can hardly ever get within striking distance of the right person. In my own case, for instance; now who can I hold responsible for my mother's death? Was it the Sheriff, or was it the officer in charge of the soldiers who was sorry for me and offered me half-a-crown and who, I am sure, hated the job he was sent to do? Was it the agent, who was acting for the landlord's lawyer, or was it the landlord himself, who had never seen the property, but who had got into debt and whose estate had been put in the hands of a receiver? Why, the blame splits up and runs away like quicksliver when you try to pick it up. I might even shift the responsibility to one of the Popes of Rome who gave Ireland as a present to an English king 800 years ago. I might even go back to the creation and blame the Almighty for placing England and Ireland alongside each other and populating one with Anglo-Saxons and the other with Celts.[44]

A reader chuckles, though he understands the speaker (and the author) is serious. Later in the story Blaasbalk gives Jan another bit of "wisdom," this aimed towards Jan rather than himself.

> My friend, when your people colonised this country the Devil, knowing

that gold and diamonds were under the soil, must have laughed heartily at the thought of what was coming. What you are fighting against is not so much the English as what is known as "the spirit of the age." You Boers were asleep and your dreams were of two hundred years ago. It was a pity, but the waking had to happen. If the English had not done it, the Germans or some other up-to-date people would. You had to be brought up-to-date. Not a good thing, mind you, from my point of view, but inevitable. You will be defeated, but not turned out of your kraal; no fear of that—your blood is too red and your bone too solid. But you will mix with those you hate, and become a new people.[45]

As a whole, the story is not one of talk but of action. Yet Scully has availed himself of the opportunity to express two opinions which were important to him. The author was, of course, having Blaasbalk say certain things which were already an accomplished fact. Other aspects of the statement remained in the realm of opinion.

Farewell to Tshaka was said in "The Battle of Ezinyoseni." A note remarks that "In main details the narrative may be regarded as literal history."[46] The author obtained the more dramatic aspects of the materials from "a very ancient native" who as a boy had been an attendant in the "great place" of Umsilikazi, the Matabele chief, on the day of the Zulu attack.[47] The battle was fought near the present site of Potchefstroom, oldest town in the Transvaal and today an important educational center. Potchefstroom was established by one of the Voortrekker leaders, Hendrick Potgieter, December 1838. Only a few years before this date it had been the kraal of Umsilikazi. A commander in Tshaka's forces, he had fled north in 1820 and established an independent tribe, known now as the Matabele. Making war upon the tribes of the whole area, Umsilikazi soon became ruler of the region to which he had gone. The Matabele had inflicted serious losses upon Potgieter and his men before the arrival of Gerrit Maritz and Pieter Retief in the area. In November 1837, a combined force under Retief made a carefully planned attack upon the Matabele. The battle lasted for some days. Finally, the rifles of the Voortrekkers convinced the Matabele that the course of wisdom was again towards the north. The tribe crossed the Limpopo and took possession of the area, thence called Matabeleland, later Rhodesia. Umsilikazi named his "great place" Bulawayo, the "place of slaughter," in imitation of Tshaka.

For years after Umsilikazi had broken away from the Zulu king, Tshaka had sent an impi to attack him and his rebellious tribe. After

Tshaka's death in 1828, Dingaan continued the practice. The present story opens with the Matabele chief watching vultures circle above the kraal.

Umsilikazi regarded them with sombre eye. He felt bored. For some months no fighting had taken place, for the sufficient reason that all the tribes within a circle of 200 miles had been either destroyed or scattered. Life, for the nonce, had lost its savour. In his present mood Umsilikazi was as dangerous as a hungry lion.[48]

Indeed the king is in a dangerous mood. His wrath falls upon Kalipa, Head Induna, who has sent the fighting men to the fields because the corn crop is a rich one and the grain already overripe. It is beyond the powers of the women to harvest in time to save everything. Suddenly a breathless man approaches and literally throws himself at Umsilikazi's feet. Finally his voice returns and he wails, "The Zulus . . . O my Chief . . . The Zulus."[49] All turn in the direction he indicates. Only five miles away from the Zulu advance was to be seen dust. With something to do, the chief becomes decisive in every nerve and muscle. Orders to assemble were given. The women shrilled the war-cry. "The land for many miles around became like a disturbed ants' nest."[50] Next the chief turned to the commander of the army, who was now in disgrace because of his failure in defence.

"Kalipa," said the chief, and the induna stiffened to attention. "Take my shield and spear and go forth with these, my boys, to meet the Zulus. Ask if Tambuza be the leader; it may be well for you if he is. Say this to whoever the leader may be: 'You have come to fight men, not women and children. The men are scattered among the fields. Stay your attack until they can be collected!' I will remain here alone."[51]

Making straight for the "forehead" of the Zulu formation, Kalipa approached to within three hundred yards. Here he stopped, stuck his spear in the ground, threw down his shield, and waited. Soon surrounded by the Zulus, he asked for a word with Tambuza—or with the person commanding. Tambuza appeared and received Umsilikazi's message, then retired for a conference with his captains. To Kalipa he announced the decision: "Until the sun reaches *there* [he pointed with his spear to the position of the sun in mid-afternoon], no attack will be made."[52] When Kalipa reported to his chief, he was told, "To-day you will remain behind with the women. I will direct the battle."[53] Direct the battle he did! Just before darkness would bring an end to the fighting, Tambuza gave the order to retreat and with several hundred veterans cut a way of escape from the circle of spears in which they had been caught. It should be remembered that this was intramural war—Zulu against Zulu. Umsilikazi and Tambuza had received the same combat instruction and developed under the same dicipline. The difference on that day of the battle was probably the result of the fact that Tambuza and his men went into combat immediately after days of marching over difficult country. Even under these conditions, they had agreed to give their opponents time to prepare. Also, they had with them a number of young, untried men at the tips of their horn formation. Umsilikazi knew all of these facts and therefore when and where to attack and press. Ultimately "The Battle of Ezinyoseni" was more important as an example of Zulu combat methods and attitudes than as a significant segment of history. The battle decided nothing except Kalipa's fate. His chief was so pleased with the results that his induna was soon restored to favor. Then, too, those around Umsilikazi benefitted because the battle relieved his boredom and made him easier to live with, at least for a few months.

The longest and one of the finest of the stories in Scully's first collection, "The Quest of the Cooper," presented Tshaka at the time of his most awesome destructiveness. In "The Battle of Ezinyoseni" the author shows that his interest in Tshaka followed the Zulu king's influence even after he was gone.

CHAPTER 10

Conclusion

NOTHING suggests William Charles Scully thought of himself as a representative of the Renaissance ideal which resulted from the union in man of the active and the contemplative. Yet the facts of his life certainly reveal a character in whom action and thought were always present. For full half a century Scully filled his years with hard work of many kinds. Admiration for men of action is represented both directly and indirectly in what he wrote. He also began to admire men of intellect early in his career. To them he listened intently.

Having received only a few months of formal schooling before he reached the age of twenty-one, Scully then began his pursuit of all human wisdom recorded in the literature of the world. Shakespeare became one of his first interests, along with the Psalms, Prophets, and Apostles. Regularly he read through the *Bible,* alternating it with Gibbon's *Decline and Fall of the Roman Empire.* During his late twenties he also reached out seriously into the area of science. Extensive reading in English literature appears to have started with the Renaissance. In addition to Shakespeare, he shows an awareness of such diverse works as *The Faerie Queene, Paradise Lost,* and *The Duchess of Malfi.* From this postion in time, his references reach to the twentieth century. In one of his books he quotes a poem by a younger contemporary South African writer. As related in Chapter 1, his introduction to Wordsworth had come early and in a special way. He pursued both Latin and Greek authors in the original, though it is not unlikely that he also read in translation. He displays at least some acquaintance with American literature, more with German, which he read in German. French had also been added to his languages and at least a smattering of Italian and Spanish. In addition to his reading knowledge of languages, Scully spoke Afrikaans and several of the Bantu tongues. An early friend had developed in him an interest in and some knowledge of Mohammed. His final choice of reading material for his journeys into the Bushmanland desert was the Vedic Hymns.

During the last twenty years of his life Scully turned to philosophy, giving special attention to Swedenborg and Spinoza.[1] In 1930 Scully wrote, "In philosophy I follow Schopenhauer; I think his 'World as Will and Idea' is the most satisfactory philosophical work ever written. What religion I have is based on three texts, two from the Gospels and one from Micah. (1) 'The Kingdom of God is within you.' (2) 'Whoso loveth his life shall lose it,' and (3) 'What doth the Lord require of thee but to do justice, and to love mercy and to walk humbly with thy God.'"[2] One of his close associates during the final years was the Reverend Mr. Gahn, as Anglican priest, with whom he discussed many subjects, among them the eternal mysteries. The Anglican friend insisted that anyone who could write "The Prayer of the Cattle" must believe in God. To this the author of the poem replied with a gentle and quizzical "Perhaps."[3] Though to the end of his life he continued his search for answers, he never claimed to have solved the riddle of life. In a letter written in 1936, he confessed that his long period of philosophic enquiry had been essentially futile and had led "along a lonely road into an infertile region."[4]

When Scully had passed into his eighties, he received from Francis Carey Slater (along with a copy of *Dark Folk and Other Poems*) a letter lamenting their failure to meet with each other on a particular occasion. In offering his appreciation for the book, Scully added, "Yes,—it was unfortunate our missing each other, and yet, I do not know. People who have admired my books seem to be invariably disappointed when they meet the author."[5] There is an appealing wistfulness about the statement, yet Scully must have known there were good reasons for this type of reaction. From fourteen to twenty-one he had lived in a world of action, not talk, especially social chatter. During those years he almost invariably was the youngest in every group of which he became a part. This forced upon him the role of listener and observer. The experience was excellent training for a writer and also for his thirty-eight years of work as a magistrate. Both of these activities demanded that he continue to listen and observe. Thus he had retired before there was much opportunity for normal social affairs.

Early in life Scully had been introduced to both the fact and the theory of human loneliness. During his years of retirement he wrote, "We all are lonely individually. I think I am lonelier than most."[6] Of her father's "lonely" times, Mrs. Gray says, "All my life he would go off every so often, into the 'bundu' and live rough. Several times, during my early teens, [middle 1920s] he took me with him to the Diamond Fields on the Vaal River, where we lived in a wood and iron shack, and he indulged in his passion for 'digging' . . . while I pretended to keep house. But more often he would go off on his own. One day he would arrive home looking like a tramp, but fit and happy. Mother was very understanding about it—you see, she was an artist too, and also liked being alone sometimes."[7]

In addition to the direct evidence, in his fiction Scully also develops the theme of human isolation powerfully. "The Madness of Gweva," written in the middle 1890s, shows the first characters who become a part of this theme. So intense, and complete, and enduring is the love of Gweva and Nomasaba that they defy Bantu custom and accept total isolation (banishment) from their civilization that they may have each other. Written later, "Afar in the Desert" starts by using the title of Thomas Pringle's famous isolation poem. At the conclusion of the story, the principal character decides that he must "be for ever a stranger among the sons and daughters of men."[8] In the same volume, another character who had lived in isolation for twenty years testifies that "The wild animals seem to know me, for they never attempt to do me any hurt. I do not think I am unhappy, for I can sleep when I like, and in my dreams I go over the past again and again. They used to teach me that another life comes after death. I do not know. . . . I know that if the soul lives when the body dies, our souls will be together. . . . But now I dream . . . and dream. . . . "[9] Other examples appear in the novels and in *Lodges in the Wilderness* Scully expresses his devotion to the purifying solitude of the great Bushmanland desert. Though some of his fictional characters totally reject civilization—from strength, not weakness—Scully himself revealed a powerful dualism. Despite his understanding of the values of isolation and his desire to make these a part of his life, he also had within him a love of human companionship.

Physical memorials did not appeal to William Charles Scully. His hope was that the work he had done might be a memorial.[10] Looking back upon what he did and what he wrote, a biographer and critic can say with assurance that the areas in which he labored have accorded honor to his name. In the performance of his routine duties as a magistrate, he was never merely a routine officer. Thousands of the inarticulate, especially among the natives, whose territories he administered for a number of years, must have blessed his name. Beyond his routine, the various special studies he made as a member of the Cape Civil Service and also particular investigations for which he was appointed have become a part of the public records of South Africa. Another obvious contribution may still be seen in important herbaria of three continents. Finally, his published books have become a memorial.

At the beginning of his career as a writer, he offered more than a hundred poems to an infant South African literature. In an article published in 1915, John Clark, himself a poet and for many years Professor of English Literature at the University of Cape Town, called for a greater availabilty of Scully's poems to the general reader and for students the accessibility of poems "in bulk." Though the request was not fulfilled, Professor Clark was making an important critical judgment. His evaluation was immediately supported with examples of Scully's work and detailed analyses of what he wrote. Unusual attention was given to Scully's metrical practices—which the analyst looked upon with favor, observing the range and the harmony between meter and thought. Along with the formal patterns the critic presents with approval, he shows admiration for the poet's *thought*. Indeed, he identifies its source as none other than the inspiration of Apollo. At times his comments use the word *thought*, as ". . . enshrines a noble thought with power, and truth, and mysticism. . . ." ". . . possesses assertive thought and genuine workmanship. . . ." Even when the *word* is not used, the critic implies an intellectual content because of what he says. He remarks that the sonnet on Immanuel Kant "has an interesting, and, I should think, not very common subject." As might be expected, much of the emphasis upon *thought* came during his consideration of the sonnets, five of which were selected for comment. One of the best of the five, however, was an image poem; yet the critic accurately discussed it from this point of view. He writes, "*Namaqualand* . . . conveys finely by expressive phrase, and concrete detail, and two powerful terminal lines [also images] the impressions made on the responsive mind by a land of lethargy."

Though John Clark may never have seen Namaqualand, he had for many years lived with Table Mountain as a part of his environment. Thus, from personal experience, he could say, quite simply, of Scully's verses on the famous stone mass, "I regard the poem as a summation of the charm of the mountain." Though writing with personal bias, as a critic he was not insensitive to the reasons for any reader's reaction. Much of the strength and effectiveness of "Table Mountain," he observes, derives from the fact that it is not one but five poems (see Chapter 3), each written from a different point of view and each employing a meter and stanza form appropriate to the intention of the moment. Rather than being *over*-written, as one might fear, the critic insists that Scully creates the impression that "a reserve exists," that in truth the author is *under*-writing.

While "Namaqualand" and "Table Mountain" emerged from details with which Scully had extensive and intimate contact, "St. Benedict" was created from historical materials with which the author had no physical experience. Yet Professor Clark feels that the resulting poem is one of the author's best. Scully, he believes, has succeeded in dramatizing the ideas and attitudes appropriate to the sixth century monastic setting; yet he says that the austerity of the age has been "touched into charm, and blown upon by the wind of poetic power. . . . " Even more significant is his claim that a religious point of view perhaps not congenial to many in the modern world has been in certain areas made to reveal "a side that has universal appeal."[11] Thus Scully has raised his poem above the narrow grasp of a particular period or an individual theology.

Published without either introduction or conclusion, Professor Clark's discussion of Scully's poems does not attempt to place him in South African literature; but the critic indicates that he considers this author worthy of serious attention—certainly more than he received between 1886 and 1915. Now, however, the world had suddenly gone to war and little time was left for the type of poetry Professor Clark had been analysing. After men returned to at least a relative sanity, Scully's poems were perhaps more forgotten than remembered.

Almost half a century later, in making a study of South African poetry in English, G. M. Miller and Howard Sergeant appraised *The Wreck of the Grosvenor and Other South African Poems* as "the most distinctively South African book of verse to be printed up to that date. . . . It is not that the subjects are exclusively South African. . . but that the poet identifies himself with the country in an unmistakable manner. His experience has been seen through South African eyes. One can discern where he was influenced by Shakespeare, by Shelley, Tennyson and Swinburne, yet the attitude to life is that which has grown out of his own adolescence and manhood."[12] Perhaps because of this fact it can be said that "for the ordinary people of South Africa he is remembered for the *Poems* almost more than any other book."[13]

Despite the historical importance of the position accorded his

Conclusion

poems and despite the South African memory of him as a poet, Scully's most significant contribution to literature was his prose. Between 1895 and 1923, the short stories, novels and nonfictional prose gave South Africa and the world something that should not be forgotten. Of *Kafir Stories*, Scully's initial volume of prose, one critic years after its publication wrote that "As a sheer piece of literature, dealing with our natives, it is worth fifty of the ordinary 'best South African novels.' "[14] A review of *Between Sun and Sand* offered the following observations in June 1898: "Mr. Scully has 'trekked' for himself, and left the conventional paths of the ordinary stereotyped South African fiction. So his writings have, to begin with, the advantage of entire novelty. And added to the novelty of the surroundings and unusualness of the types, we welcome a most engaging literary style, with quite a distinction of its own—terse, strong, restrained, and condensed." Another reviewer said that "Many writers have lately given in novel form accounts of unfamiliar regions, to which it is impossible to accord more than a *success d'estime*. Mr. Scully's personages hold the attention, while he imparts without effort a store of information in a manner that impresses it on the memory." A third wrote, "Strong, simple, direct in his method. Broad is the touch, instant and quickening the effect. With the least possible expenditure of material, the effect produced is wonderfully vital and enduring."[15]

During the second decade of the twentieth century, Scully entered the nonfictional field with his memories of life in South Africa from 1867 to 1900. Two volumes were published, in March and September of 1913. Many reviews of the second volume referred to the first. From London, the *Sunday Times* commented, "The broad sympathy, the geniality, and the freshness of outlook which distinguished his earlier 'Reminiscences' are equally manifest here and combine with the natural ease of his narrative style to keep the reader's interest." At the same time another reviewer was saying. "The Muse who rules the copious literature of modern biography knows quite well that half the books of reminiscences published suffer from the hampering fact that their authors have really very little to 'reminiss' about. This is where Mr. Scully scores. His first installment of South African recollections, which ceased at the time of his entry into the Civil Service, after seven years of wandering, was an admirable example of all that a book of pioneering reminscences should be; and the present series, which includes adventures and experiences for the period from 1876 to 1899—the year of the South African War—is no less striking." A third added these observations, ". . . his intellectual gifts are of the highest order; he has exceptional powers of observation, for the exercise of which he has had great opportunities; his literary style is perfect; and the result is a book that is fascinating in a high degree, full of facts, scenes, and experiences that are new and fresh, and presenting phases of South African life which hitherto have been scarcely touched by literature."[16]

Though only a tiny sample, the passages above show something of the approval with which Scully was received by the reviewers. Nothing, however, guarantees that once a reputation is created it can be maintained. Among other things, Scully's literary position, soon after it was achieved, had to sustain the upheaval of a world war. More important, however, is the fact that early in his life as a fictionist, Scully was designated as a "local colorist"—though even the first reviewers realized there was something about his fiction that was different from that usually called local color writing. (See Chapter 1.) Indeed, the difference was there, and it was fundamental. South African materials were employed freely; but they were organically incorporated, not pasted on as decoration. Thus, though a novel like *Between Sun and Sand* is an accurate and powerful depiction of Bushmanland and its inhabitants, it is a study of temptation, crime, and punishment. Few, however, have given even the slightest attention to South African literature as universal rather than local. Consequently, when with the passage of time the local color designation lost its impact, there seemed nothing to replace it in the general consciousness. There is, however, much more than local color to be examined. What Scully wrote about the northwest Cape will furnish an excellent guide to his achievement. Two major full-length books may be used: *Between Sun and Sand* and *Lodges in the Wilderness*, a novel and a nonfictional book, both concerned with experiences in the Bushmanland desert.

Something has now happened that will cause the settings of Scully's writings to be regarded in historical rather than local color terms. During the 1970s, the desert which Scully celebrated for its purifying solitude was invaded by heavy-mining machinery with the expectation of extracting reserves to the worth of R 8 600-million in zinc, R 2 000-million in lead, R 1 000-million in copper, and R 500-million in silver. There are also diamonds, manganese, iron, and "the world's only reclaimable blue asbestos."[17] The region is probably destined to become important in South African economy; many animals will die out; the tents of the scattered inhabitants will disappear; in fact these inhabitants will become part of the general change to come. Yet human nature will not be destroyed. Hate and love, grief and joy, prejudice and understanding, materialism and idealism, pettiness and magnanimity as seen in *Between Sun and Sand* are universal traits and will withstand the erosion of the years. Gert Gemsbok as a Hottentot belongs to the area at a particular time; as a human being he belongs to mankind. Koos Bester was a Trek-Boer. Scully, however, was much less interested in blood than behavior. The skill with which Oom Schulpad played the violin was unrelated to any of the characteristics of the Bushmanland desert. Indeed, little of serious importance in the novel can be called what is normally spoken of as local color. Scully's subject was human lives as they impinged upon other lives.

Writing two years before the publication of *Lodges in the Wilderness*, a reviewer from London had suggested that one of the most "attractive features" of Scully's *Reminiscences* was his "occasional excursions into the philosophy of things."[18] *Lodges*, which could have been the authors's greatest temptation to write a local color book, became indeed an excursion into the philosophy of things. Bushmanland forced anyone who had ventured out upon its vast spaces to learn first to respect the desert or never return to reveal the failure. This, however, is an elementary aspect of the desert. Once a human being comes to understand that survival must come first, he may find that the environment into which he has moved will allow him to think, in fact will encourage him to contemplate the nature of things if he has it in him to proceed in that direction. None of the petty activities of the outside world will be there to distract him, nor will any man beside him—one who has earned his own survival—interfere by breaking in upon his thoughts. Under these conditions, any thoughts that come will be universal. Whether or not a man offers his thoughts to others is not the significant fact, though Scully was articulate and did leave this admirable volume for those who wish to make excursions into the philosophy of things.

Whether or not Scully could have maintained the creative intensity which was his during the 1890s is a question that cannot be answered. War enveloped the country and made normal activities impossible. When what was called peace came, men with Scully's information and sensitivity could not tear the war years from the calendar and pretend nothing had happened. In an agony of the spirit, he conceived and wrote *The Harrow*. Though the book contains some of the author's finest passages and scenes, here Scully dedicated himself to historical accuracy. Perhaps the best way to suggest what the author has achieved is to say that no one who has read the entire volume carefully will ever feel the same again about this particular period in South African history. Regardless of the ideological position from which a reader starts, he will not escape from the events of this book. One person may come to hate the man who has developed such a novel, but he will not be able to erase the actions from his memory. Another person will bless the man who created the book and will retain the events among his memories. Scully has done his work with remarkable effectiveness.

Having written *The Harrow* in 1904, revised it in 1907, and published a collection of short stories in 1907, Scully then started a period of nonfictional writing. *Unconventional Reminiscences* was given monthly magazine publication from 1910 to 1912. This was followed by *The Ridge of the White Waters*, 1912; *Reminiscences of a South African Pioneer* and *Further Reminiscences of a South African Pioneer*, 1913; *A History of South Africa* and *Lodges in the Wilderness*, 1915. As these last two volumes were moving through the press, World War I interrupted almost everything that might be considered normal life for a large part of the earth's population.

Scully returned to the tasks of the writer when global combat was terminated. In 1923 he offered his last major book, *Daniel Vananda*. Perhaps few have ever approached this volume for any purpose other than to examine a study of race relations in South Africa. Yet there is more than ample reason to study the novel as a presentation of problems created by the presence of the unusual person in any society during any period of history. As a child Vananda preferred to listen to his grandfather's rendering of Bantu stories and legends rather then engage in the play of the children around him. At fourteen he was the acknowledged physical and intellectual leader among his associates but said to be "more respected than liked by his companions."[19] When war destroyed the Quati Clan, Vananda alone sat beside his dying grandfather, who had been for this lonely child "the embodiment of wisdom and of power."[20] After his grandfather died, a strange turn of events placed Vananda at the Rossdale Mission Station. When he came to understand the use of the alphabet, he entered a world which previously he had not even imagined. The literature of the *Bible* moved him deeply, as did music. "Daniel had grown tall and strong, with limbs and body of almost perfect symmetry. His features were of that Egyptian cast which, among the Natives, so often accompanies a hue of dark bronze. His cheek-bones were high and his nose finely cut and slightly aquiline. . . . as time went on he became more and more reserved and introspective."[21] Any such nature as that developing in Daniel Vananda is destined to have tragic encounters with what is spoken of as "the world." The passing years brought a supply of clashes with those around him. Though upon various occasions Daniel lost to the world on its terms, he was not, after maturity, changed from the course he set for himself. To the great sea beside which he lived while at Avalon, Daniel took his questionings. "All unbidden had arisen in the mind of this intellectual exile from his kind, a craving for some key to the riddle of being—some clue to the purpose of existence. To such souls, whether their garment of flesh be black or white, the all-pervading, impersonal voices of Nature . . . are ever full of deep meaning."[22] Very clearly, Daniel Vananda stands beside the author who has brought him into being as both search for the meaning of life. High above the chaos of racial strife ascends the spirit of Daniel Vananda in its quest for understanding and peace.

A consideration of his integrity is important in an evaluation of Scully as a writer. This quality becomes extremely significant when an author attempts to handle controversial issues, which is certainly the kind of material Scully employed in many of his books about South Africa. Most obvious of the controversial issues was that created by the coming of European settlers into an already complex native situation. The powerful Bantu tribes had originated somewhere in the central areas of the continent and had pushed towards the continental tip, having moved south and finally west. Much earlier the Bushmen and then the Hottentots had moved into and occupied the southernmost areas of Africa. Though Bushmen and Hottentots were unable to stop the movements of the Bantu tribes, European powder and shot could, and ultimately did, prevail against the most powerful of the warlike groups. However, victory brought problems even greater than those originally existing because of certain other developments. Inevitably there was the necessity of replacing the concepts of one civilization with those of another. Had the transition been under the direction of knowledgeable leaders with a sincere desire to do the proper things, it still would have been exceedingly difficult. Actually the transition was not a planned one, and leaders were often completely unprepared for the conditions with which they had to contend. The results were frequently nothing short of chaotic.

Regardless of the difficulty of handling this kind of material, Scully endeavored to present the existing situation rather than a particular point of view. A consideration of all of his books as a unit shows that he has not been for or against any group. He has not tried to answer difficult questions of racial relations by saying that the white man should never have approached Africa. He does not take the side of black against white, or white against black. Problems, he believes, must be solved in terms of what actually exists. What is needed is patience and understanding. When he moves from the struggle between the Bantu and Europeans to the conflict between Afrikaner and English, he proceeds without taking sides. Even in *The Harrow* he was asking England and the English South Africans to examine what had happened in their name. If they would do that much, he trusted their sense of justice to do the right things. Finally, he was not for the traditional against innovation or innovation against the traditional. He reasoned that time brought change, whether good or bad, and that man should attempt to resolve difficulties instead of opposing them or pretending they do not exist. No man or group, he was convinced, could block the flow of civilization. The best possible action was to adjust wisely to that flow.

Eventually even a man with Scully's strength was forced to accept, in a personal physical sense, what the passage of time decreed. Immobilized by a broken hip and entering a shadowy world because of dimming sight, he could no longer move about at will or write. One day in 1942, he called Betty to his side and dictated to her a poem which he called simply "Rondel." The use of one of the French fixed forms when relying only upon memory is a tribute to the quality of his mind at the very end. According to Mrs. Gray, her father recited the whole without hesitation, even instructing her where to put the punctuation marks.[23] All evidence suggests that this was his last poem, now published for the first time.

> When tir'd Spring slept—the Year's bright daughter
>   Frail flow'r wraiths decked her drooping head
> Till Earth in his safe breast had wrought her
>   So fair, a soft and sleeping bed
> Where whisper'd winds and wand'ring water
>   Low dream tones through her slumber shed.
>   When tir'd Spring slept
> Kind Summer gently came and brought her
>   Soft plumy grass: rich berries red
> Staid Autumn bore, mild days besought her
>   To rise, and scented blossoms shed.

> She stirr'd, but Winter's cold hand caught her
> And chill'd her till she lay as dead
> And tir'd Spring slept.[24]

As a reader ponders the lines, he cannot avoid associating what the poet is saying with the fact that the germinal and growing seasons of the author's life were ending and now winter was upon him.

After seventeen years at Kimberley, the Scullys moved to Umbogintwini, where they could be near their eldest son, Gerald, and his wife, Muriel. On the Natal South Coast, fifteen miles from Durban, Scully spent his last years, 1940 to 1943. The body had been exhausted by the long days and short nights, the battles with fever, and the countless tests of endurance through which he had passed. Here with a loving wife and visits from the children and grandchildren, he dozed and dreamed. His daughter Betty reports that one of the joys of this period was the short drives on which they took him. She says, "He loved us to drive and park where he could see and hear and smell the sea."[25] With her mother during the last moments, Mrs. Gray speaks of her father's death as a "quiet withdrawal."[26] The end came while the night hours of August 25 passed. It was winter. The cold, however, was behind, and before him was the soft, warm air from the Indian Ocean, whose waters seventy-five years earlier had brought him to this land.

Notes and References

Chapter One

1. William Charles Scully, *Reminiscences of a South African Pioneer* (London, 1913), "Foreword," p. 12.
2. William Charles Scully, *Voices of Africa* (Durban; 1943), first page of the introduction, not numbered.
3. The reviews quoted, in the order given, are from the following: *The Athenaeum, The Daily Chronicle, The Graphic, The Academy, Black and White, The World*.
4. Edward MacLysaght, *Irish Families* (Dublin, 1957), p. 263.
5. *Reminiscences of a South African Pioneer*, p. 23. Elsewhere Scully says Middle Gardiner Street. Concerning the date of birth, he explains that the baptismal records were not available to him. Most of the material of this type has been taken from Scully's two autobiographical volumes.
6. *Irish Families*, p. 99. Mrs. Betty Gray gives the spelling as Creigh.
7. *Reminiscences*, p. 40.
8. *Ibid.*, pp. 48–49.
9. *Ibid.*, p. 53.
10. *Ibid.*
11. *Ibid.*, p. 54.
12. *Ibid.*, p. 87.
13. *Ibid.*, p. 89.
14. *Ibid.*, p. 126.
15. *Ibid.*, pp. 128–29.
16. William Charles Scully, *Further Reminiscences of a South African Pioneer* (London, 1913), pp. 248–49.
17. *Reminiscences*, pp. 175–76.
18. *Ibid.*, pp. 264–65.
19. *Ibid.*, pp. 310–11.
20. *Ibid.*, p. 311.

Chapter Two

1. *Further Reminiscences of a South African Pioneer*, pp. 26–29.
2. *Ibid.*, p. 69.
3. *Ibid.*, p. 84.
4. *Ibid.*, p. 153.
5. William Charles Scully, *Poems* (London, 1892), p. 93.
6. *Further Reminiscences*, p. 165.

7. *Ibid.*, p. 188.
8. *Ibid.*, pp. 192–93.
9. *Ibid.*, p. 196.
10. *Ibid.*, pp. 199–200.
11. *Ibid.*, p. 202.
12. *Ibid.*, p. 189.
13. Letter to the author, March 2, 1977.
14. *Further Reminiscences*, p. 221.
15. *Ibid.*, p. 222.
16. *Ibid.*, p. 251.
17. William Charles Scully, *The Native Question* (Lovedale, South Africa, 1874), pp. 2, 3, 19.
18. *Ibid.*, p. 18.
19. *Further Reminiscences*, pp. 373–74.
20. *Ibid.*, p. 343.
21. *Voices of Africa*, pp. 31–32.
22. *Kafir Stories, The White Hecatomb, Between Sun and Sand, A Vendetta of the Desert.*
23. *Further Reminiscences*, p. 350.
24. *Ibid.*, pp. 366–67.

Chapter Three

1. *Poems*, p. 165.
2. *Ibid.*, pp. 83, 86.
3. *Ibid.*, p. 87.
4. *Truditur dies die,* Day is pushed forth by day.
5. *Further Reminiscences of a South African Pioneer*, p. 158.
6. *Poems*, pp. 46–47.
7. *Ibid.*, p. 67.
8. *Ibid.*, p. 96
9. *Ibid.*, p. 181.
10. *The State*, August 1911, pp. 155–56.
11. *Poems*, pp. 111–23.
12. *Ibid.*, p. 59.
13. *Ibid.*, p. 62.
14. *Ibid.*, pp. 98–99.
15. *Ibid.*, pp. 157–58.
16. *Ibid.*, p. 190.
17. *Ibid.*, pp. 151–52. Three of fifteen stanzas quoted.
18. *Ibid.*, pp. 146–47.
19. *Ibid.*, p. 188.
20. *Ibid.*, pp. 144–45.
21. *Ibid.*, p. 134.
22. *Ibid.*, pp. 127–29.
23. *Voices of Africa*, p. 106.

Chapter Four

1. Letter to the present author, March 2, 1977.
2. William Charles Scully, *Kafir Stories* (London, 1895), p. 92.
3. *Ibid.*, pp. 119–20.
4. *Ibid.*, pp. 123–25.
5. *Ibid.*, p. 126.
6. *Ibid.*, pp. 126–27.
7. *Ibid.*, pp. 159–60.
8. *Ibid.*, p. 134.
9. *Ibid.*, pp. 157–58.
10. *Ibid.*, pp. 177–78.
11. Ibid., pp. 167–69.
12. *Ibid.*, p. 183.
13. William Charles Scully, *The White Hecatomb and Other Stories* (London, 1897), p. 249.
14. *Ibid.*, p. 122.
15. *Ibid.*, p. 46.

Chapter Five

1. William Charles Scully, *Between Sun and Sand* (Cape Town, 1898) p. 1.
2. Self-created.
3. *Between Sun and Sand*, pp. 3–4.
4. *Ibid.*, p. 28.
5. *Ibid.*, p. 24.
6. *Ibid.*, pp. 4–5.
7. *Ibid.*, p. 16.
8. *Ibid.*, pp. 18–22.
9. *Ibid.*, pp. 35–39.
10. *Ibid.*, p. 57.
11. *Ibid.*, p. 51.
12. The Communion Service of the Dutch Reformed Church. These services frequently became a time for social activities and for the performance of other services (as weddings) and in addition acquired commercial aspects.
13. *Between Sun and Sand*, p. 134.
14. *Ibid.*, p. 211.
15. *Ibid.*, p. 225.
16. *Ibid.*, p. 226.
17. This story fills the last fifty-six pages of *Between Sun and Sand*.
18. William Charles Scully, *A Vendetta of the Desert* (London, 1898) p. 15.
19. *Ephesians* 6:17, . . . the sword of the Spirit, which is the word of God.
20. *A Vendetta of the Desert*, pp. 16–17.
21. *Ibid.*, p. 37.

22. *Ibid.*, p. 19.
23. *Ibid.*, p. 21.
24. *Ibid.*, p. 28.
25. *Ibid.*, p. 51.
26. *Ibid.*, p. 56.
27. *Ibid.*, p. 84.
28. *Ibid.*, p. 85.
29. *Ibid.*, p. 98.
30. *Ibid.*
31. *Ibid.*, p. 99.
32. *Ibid.*, pp. 108–109.
33. *Ibid.*, p. 111.
34. *Ibid.*, p. 113.
35. *Ibid.*, p. 116.
36. *Ibid.*, pp. 185–86.
37. *Ibid.*, p. 204.
38. *Ibid.*, p. 205.
39. *Ibid.*, p. 206.
40. *Ibid.*, p. 193.
41. *Ibid.*, p. 175.
42. *Ibid.*, p. 184.
43. *Ibid.*, p. 53.
44. *Ibid.*, p. 49.
45. *Ibid.*, pp. 49–50.
46. *Ibid.*, p. 50.
47. William Charles Scully, *By Veld and Kopje* (London, 1907), pp. 51–52.
48. *Ibid.*, p. 59.
49. *Ibid.*, pp. 63–64.
50. *Ibid.*, p. 77.
51. *Ibid.*, pp. 141–42.
52. *Ibid.*, pp. 35–36.
53. *Ibid.*, p. 30.
54. *Ibid.*, p. 193.

Chapter Six

1. "Unconventional Reminiscences," *The State of South Africa*, 3, No. 6, (June 1910), 926.
2. *Reminiscences of a South African Pioneer*, p. 112.
3. *Ibid.*, pp. 207–08.
4. *Ibid.*, pp. 226–27.
5. *Ibid.*, pp. 258–59.
6. *Further Reminscences of a South African Pioneer*, p. 274.
7. *Ibid.*, pp. 157–62.
8. *Ibid.*, pp. 218–20.

9. *Ibid.*, pp. 251–52.
10. *Ibid.*, p. 278.
11. *Ibid.*, pp. 350–51.
12. *Ibid.*, pp. 352–54.

Chapter Seven

1. William Charles Scully, *The Ridge of the White Waters* (London, 1912), p. 92.
2. *Ibid.*, pp. 95–96.
3. Greek mythology: the gloomy space through which souls passed to Hades.
4. *The Ridge of the White Waters*, p. 159.
5. *Ibid.*, p. 156.
6. *Ibid.*, pp. 151–52.
7. *Ibid.*, p. 150.
8. *Ibid.*, p. 112.
9. *Ibid.*, p. 230.
10. *Ibid.*, p. 208.
11. *Ibid.*, pp. 238–41.
12. *Ibid.*, p. 242.
13. *The Bantu Speaking Tribes of South Africa*, Edited by I. Schapera (Cape Town, 1956), p. 69. Quoted from N. J. van Warmelo, 1931, p. 11.
14. Make haste slowly.
15. *The Ridge of the White Waters, p. 263.*
16. William Charles Scully, *Lodges in the Wilderness* (London, 1915), p. 249.
17. *Ibid.*, p. 194.
18. *Ibid.*, p. 22.
19. *Ibid.*, pp. 137–38.
20. *Ibid.*, pp. 36–37.
21. *Ibid.*, p. 54.
22. *Ibid.*, pp. 80–81.
23. *Ibid.*, p. 24.
24. *Ibid.*, p. 133.

Chapter Eight

1. William Charles Scully, *A History of South Africa* (London, 1915), p. v.
2. *Ibid.*, p. 154.
3. *Ibid.*, p. 104.
4. *Ibid.*, pp. 109–10.
5. *Ibid.*, p. 111.
6. *Ibid.*, p. 196.
7. *Ibid.*, p. 273.
8. *Ibid.*, p. 285.

Notes and References

9. *Ibid.*, p. 10.
10. *Ibid.*, p. 93.
11. *Ibid.*, p. 94.
12. *Ibid.*, p. 103.
13. *Ibid.*
14. *Ibid.*, p. 141.
15. *Ibid.*, p. 148.
16. *Ibid.*, p. 257.
17. *Ibid.*
18. *Ibid.*, pp. 54–55.
19. *Ibid.*, p. 118.

Chapter Nine

1. Material for this section furnished by Mrs. Betty Gray.
2. William Charles Scully, *The Harrow* (Stellenbosch, 1921), p. viii.
3. *Ibid.*, p. xiii.
4. *Ibid.*, p. xi.
5. *Ibid.*
6. *Ibid.*, p. x.
7. *Ibid.*, pp. vii–viii.
8. *Ibid.*, p. x.
9. *Ibid.*, p.xiv.
10. *Ibid.*, pp. 5–6.
11. *Ibid.*, p. 12.
12. *Ibid.*, p. 23.
13. *Ibid.*, p. 29.
14. *Ibid.*, p.87.
15. *Ibid.*, pp. 87–88.
16. *Ibid.*, p. 93.
17. *Ibid.*, p. 94.
18. *Ibid.*, pp. 99–100.
19. *Ibid.*, pp. 101–102.
20. *Ibid.*, pp. 181–82.
21. *Ibid.*, pp.182–84.
22. *Ibid.*, p. 186.
23. *Ibid.*, p. 187.
24. *Ibid.*, pp. 193–98.
25. All information is taken from the *Memoir*. William Charles Scully, *Sir. J. H. Meiring Beck* (Cape Town, 1921).
26. William Charles Scully, *Daniel Vananda* (Cape Town, 1923), p. 103.
27. *Ibid.*, p. xiii.
28. *Ibid.*, pp. xii–xiii.
29. *Ibid.*, p. ix.
30. *Ibid.*, p. 118.
31. *Ibid.*, pp. 219–20.

32. *Ibid.*, pp. 102–04.
33. *Ibid.*, pp. 90–92.
34. Information from clippings supplied by The National English Documentation Centre, Thomas Pringle Collection for Research Purposes.
35. William Charles Scully, *Scopalomine in Africa, or Pharmacy and Politics* (Kimberley, 1937), Preface and pages unnumbered.
36. *Ibid.*
37. *Ibid.*, p. 10.
38. *Ibid.*, p. 29.
39. *Ibid.*, pp. 30–31.
40. Letter to the author, March 19, 1977.
41. *Voices of Africa, pp. 10*–14.
42. *Ibid.*, pp. 113–14.
43. *Ibid.*, p. 119.
44. *Ibid.*
45. *Ibid.*, p. 120.
46. *Ibid.*, p. 29.
47. Variously: Umsiligazi, Mzilikazi, Mziligazi, Moselekatse, Moselekatze, Masulikatse, Masulikatze.
48. *Voices of Africa*, p. 21.
49. *Ibid.*, p. 22.
50. *Ibid.*, p. 23.
51. *Ibid.*, p. 24.
52. *Ibid.*, p. 25.
53. *Ibid.*, p. 26.

Chapter Ten

1. This and several of the direct statements of the paragraph (especially concerning knowledge of language) come from the letters of Mrs. Gray to the author.
2. *The Sjambok*, Mar. 28, 1930, from papers furnished by The National English Documentation Centre, Thomas Pringle Collection.
3. Letter to the author from Mrs. Betty Gray, March 2, 1977.
4. Francis Carey Slater, *Settlers' Heritage* (Lovedale, South Africa, 1954) p. 253.
5. *Ibid.*
6. *Ibid.*
7. Letter to the author from Mrs. Gray, April 30, 1977.
8. *By Veld and Kopje*, p. 215.
9. *Ibid.*, p. 251.
10. Letter to the author from Mrs. Gray, March 2, 1977.
11. All quotations are from "A South African Poet: Certain Poems of W. C. Scully," by J. Clark, *South African Quarterly*, 1, No. 5 (June-July-Aug. 1915), 116–19.

12. G. M. Miller and Howard Sergeant, *A Critical Survey of South African Poetry in English* (Cape Town and Amsterdam), p. 43.
13. Letter to the author from Mrs. Gray, May 27, 1977.
14. *The Sjambok*, Aug. 23, 1929, from papers furnished by the Documentation Centre.
15. *The Bookman*, from papers furnished by the Documentation Centre; *The Morning Post; The Daily Chronicle*.
16. *Sunday Times*, Sept. 21, 1913; *The Daily Chronicle*, Sept. 20, 1913; *The Dundee Advertiser*, Sept. 24, 1913.
17. *South African Panorama*, Jan. 1977, p. 1.
18. *Sunday Times*, Sept. 21, 1913.
19. *Daniel Vananda*, p. 23.
20. *Ibid.*, p. 40.
21. *Ibid.*, p. 57.
22. *Ibid.*, pp. 102–103.
23. Letter to the author, March 14, 1977.
24. Sent by Mrs. Gray, March 19, 1977.
25. Letter to the author, May 27, 1977.
26. *Ibid.*

Selected Bibliography

PRIMARY SOURCES
(Chronological Order)

1. Books

The Wreck of the Grosvenor and Other South African Poems. Lovedale, South Africa: Printed at the Institution Press, 1886. The author's name does not appear. Paper cover, 84 poems, 134 pages.

Poems. London: Unwin, 1892. Some thirty poems from the Lovedale volume are included in this book of 120 poems, 247 pages.

Kafir Stories. London: Unwin, 1895. Published in Unwin's Autonym Library; New York: Holt, 1895. Contains seven short stories.

The White Hecatomb and Other Stories. London: Methuen, 1897. Published in Methuen's Colonial Library; New York: Holt, 1897. Contains thirteen short stories.

Between Sun and Sand, A Tale of an African Desert. Cape Town: Juta, 1898; appears to have been printed at Woking and London: The Gresham Press, Unwin Brothers, Ltd. One of two novels published in 1898. Contains the long story called "Noquala's Cattle." In a first edition of the volume Scully wrote, "This book has not appeared in America—nor was it published finally in England, W. C. S." (Information furnished by Mrs. Gray.)

A Vendetta of the Desert. London: Methuen, 1898. Issued in Methuen's Colonial Library. One of the two novels published in 1898.

By Veld and Kopje. London: Unwin, 1907. Published in Unwin's Colonial Library. Contains thirteen short stories, one poem ("Voices of Africa") and an essay on Kaffir music, the last done in collaboration with his wife.

Unconventional Reminiscences. Cape Town: *The State of South Africa*, Vol. III, June, 1910; Vol. IV, July-Dec., 1910; Vol. V, Jan.-June, 1911; Vol. VI, July-Dec., 1911; Vol. VII, Jan.-June, 1912; Vol. VIII, July-Dec., 1912.

The Ridge of the White Waters ("Witwatersrand") or Impressions of a visit to Johannesburg, with some notes of Durban, Delagoa Bay, and the Low Country, with forty-three illustrations in half-tone. London: Paul, 1912. (Undated.)

Reminiscences of a South African Pioneer. London: Unwin, 1913. Sixteen illustrations. Seems to have appeared in March. Starts with Scully's childhood in Ireland and ends with his acceptance of a place in the Civil Service of the Cape Province, 1855–1876.

Further Reminiscences of a South African Pioneer. London: Unwin, 1913. Sixteen illustrations. Seems to have appeared in September. Starts with the beginning of Scully's life in the Cape Civil Service, 1876, and continues to the coming of the South African War, 1899.

Lodges in the Wilderness. London: Jenkins, 1915. Published in the Herbert Jenkins Indian and Colonial Library; New York: Holt, 1915. (Undated.) Looks back to Scully's experiences in the Bushmanland Desert.

A History of South Africa, From the Earliest Days to Union. With 45 maps and illustrations. London and New York: Longmans, Green, 1915.

The Harrow (South Africa, 1900–1902) A Novel. Beperkt, Capetown, Stellenbosch, Bloemfontein, Piertermaritzburg: De Nationale Pers, 1921. The book was written in 1904 and rewritten in 1907.

Sir J. H. Meiring Beck, A Memoir, with an Introduction by the Rt. Hon. John X. Merriman. Cape Town: Miller, 1921. (Undated.)

Daniel Vananda, The Life of a Human Being. Cape Town: Juta, 1923. Scully's last novel.

Scopalomine in Africa, or Pharmacy and Politics. Kimberley: printed by Creer & Co., 1937 (Undated.) Paper cover, thirty-one pages, nine pages of front matter. Illustrations had been created by David Saunders, but the expense made it necessary to drop them. (Information from Mrs. Betty Gray.)

Voices of Africa, with an introduction by Field-Marshal J. C. Smuts. Durban: Knox, 1943. Ten short stories and eight poems, published for the benefit of the South African Red Cross. There is a picture of Scully as an elderly man.

2. Anthologies

A Treasury of South African Poetry and Verse, collected from various sources and arranged by Edward Heath Crouch. London and Felling-on-Tyne: The Walter Scott Publishing Co., Ltd.; New York and Cape Town: Juta, 1907. Fourteen poems included.

A Treasury of South African Poetry and Verse, collected from various sources and arranged by Edward Heath Crouch, 2nd ed., enl. London: Fifield, 1909. The same poems were used as in the above, to which were added "Voices of Africa," all sixteen "voices" being printed.

Sonnets of South Africa, selected by Edward Heath Crouch. London: Fifield, 1911, Fifteen sonnets were selected.

Gold Dust: Siftings from South African Poems which most closely reflect the Life, Scenery, Fauna and Flora of South Africa, selected by E. H. Crouch. London: Fifield, 1917. One poem included, "The Nahoon." In his four anthologies, Crouch used almost twice as many poems from Scully as from Thomas Pringle.

The Centenary Book of South African Verse, 1820–1925, chosen and arranged by Francis Carey Slater. London: Longmans, Green, 1925. Seven poems included, the choice good. In giving biographical details

Slater shows a lack of information. The titles of two prose volumes were incorrectly recorded.

The New Centenary Book of South African Verse, chosen and arranged by Francis Carey Slater. London: Longmans, Green, 1945. Seven poems included, two different from the above. Slater increased the accuracy of the bibliographical details. He made one of his rare comments upon the authors included in his anthology. He says of the Scully volumes he has listed, "None of these books is as well known as it deserves to be. . . ." p. 225. He gives Scully credit for five volumes of short stories, instead of three.

3. Articles and Lectures

The Native Question, Delivered before the Lovedale Literary Society, February 23, 1894. Reprinted from "The Christian Express." Lovedale, South Africa: Printed at the Mission Press, 1894. Paper cover, twenty pages.

"The Lore of the Honey Bee," *The State of South Africa*, 8 (July-Dec. 1912), 150–53.

"Some South African Snakes," *The Atlantic Monthly*, March 1919, pp. 357ff. A study of the snakes of Southern Africa.

"The South African Chacma Baboon," *The Atlantic Monthly*, Dec. 1919, pp. 809ff. In Scully's hand, a note explains, "When I sent this article to the 'Atlantic Monthly' it was accompanied by a photograph showing the baboon at his work as pointsman [at the important railway junction of Uitenhage]—Mr. Ellery Sedgwick, the Editor, said that had it not been for the photograph, he would have had difficulty in believing the story."

"The Life of the African Ostrich," pp. 318–328 in an unidentified magazine. The pages withdrawn from the magazine are among Scully's papers, The National English Documentation Centre.

"The Pygmy Cave Dwellers of South Africa," a study of the Bushmen, publication unidentified. Among Scully's papers, The National Documentation Centre.

SECONDARY SOURCES
(Chronological Order)

1. Comment in Books, Magazines, and Newspapers

The State of South Africa, 6 (Aug. 1911), 155–56. A discussion of the development of the sonnet in South African literature, by Edward Heath Crouch, at the time of the publication of his *Sonnets of South Africa*.

"A South African Poet: Certain Poems of W. C. Scully," by J. Clark, *South African Quarterly*, 1, No 5 (June-July-August 1915), 116–19.

Christian Science Monitor, 1916, a feature on Scully and a review of his *History of South Africa*, written as an interview when he was in the United States.

"Stories of Kimberley Pioneers," *Diamond Fields Advertiser,* Kimberley, Sept. 2, 1939. An account of Scully's experiences in the fields.
"W. C. Scully, 'n Waardering, duer C. Louis Leipoldt," in *Die Huisferoat,* Sept. 24, 1943.
Synman, J. P. L. "The South African Novel in English" (1880–1930). Potchefstroom University, 1952.
Feature article by Betty Gray in *The Cape Argus,* April 16, 1955. Published in celebration of the centenary of Scully's birth.
Miller, G. M. and Sergeant, Howard. *A Critical Survey of South African Poetry in English,* Cape Town: Balkema, 1957, pp. 42–43. The discussion of the poetry is entirely satisfactory, but there is a lack of awareness of what Scully achieved in prose—unless the authors considered comment completely outside their province. They credited him with the authorship of five novels (instead of four) and two volumes of short stories (instead of three), and left unmentioned his six volumes of nonfictional prose (except to comment that he wrote an excellent autobiography, from which they give facts of his life). There was no reference to a satire and his articles.

2. Obituaries

The Star, Aug. 26, 1943.
The South African Printer and Stationer, Sept. 19, 1943.

Index

Abbeyview, 18
Aberdeen, 35, 36
Abraham, 129
Adamastor, 57
Africa, 17, 22, 35, 45, 63, 128, 148, 187, 203, 204
African(s), 17, 18, 41, 58, 125, 129, 140, 148
Afrikaans, 184, 194
Afrikaner, 204
Alaska, 120
Alexander of Macedon, 182
Algoa Bay, 48, 148
America, 35
American, 71, 182, 194
Anglican, 155, 156, 159, 185, 195
Anglo-Boer War, 112, 154
Anglo-Saxons, 190
Apollo, 197
Apostles, 194
Arabs, 82, 135
Aryan, 41
Atlantic, 138, 152
Australian, 28
Authors named:
  Aristophanes, 158, 159, 186
  Austen, Jane, 187
  Bergson, Henri, 190
  Browning, Elizabeth Barrett, 52
  Camoens, vas de, Luiz, 57
  Campbell, Roy, 57
  Gibbon, Edward, 194
  Gilbert and Sullivan, 158, 159
  Goethe, von, Johann Wolfgang, 133
  Heine, Heinrich, 48
  Huxley, Aldous, 182, 183
  Molière, 158, 159
  Pringle, Thomas, 46, 47, 196
  Schopenhaur, Arthur, 195
  Shakespeare, William, 30, 47, 61, 194, 198

Shelley, Percy Bysshe, 198
Slater, Francis Carey, 145, 195
Spencer, Herbert, 190
Spinoza, Benedict, 195
Swedenborg, Emanuel, 195
Swinburne, Algernon Charles, 198
Tennyson, Alfred, 198
Wordsworth, William, 22, 194
Avalon, 172, 174, 177, 181, 203

Bantom Berg, 91, 139, 140
Bantu, 41, 42, 48, 59, 72, 79, 93, 112, 122, 128, 129, 132, 134, 136, 148, 150, 170, 173, 194, 196, 202, 203, 204
Barkly West, 24
Basutoland, 36, 70, 80, 83, 171
Battle of Blood River, 146
Belshazzar, 188
Bible, 150, 194, 202
Biscay, Bay of, 20
Boer(s), 81, 85, 88, 90, 96, 110, 111, 120, 124, 130, 141, 157, 161, 162, 169, 188, 191
Boer War, 144
Breakwater Convict Station, 83
British, 103, 113, 129, 149, 153, 155, 156, 162, 169
British Empire, 138, 166
Bushman, 58, 100, 102, 104, 107, 108, 121, 141, 168
Bushmanland, 81, 84, 88, 142, 195, 200, 201
Bushmanland Desert, 19, 36, 37, 40, 58, 81, 84, 85, 127, 128, 129, 131, 139, 196, 200, 201
Bushmen, 41, 48, 58, 81, 84, 108, 118, 121, 131, 203

Cain and Abel, 110
California, 120
Canadian, 152

219

Canary Islands, 21
Cape Civil Service, 31, 33, 36, 81, 118, 123, 127, 152, 153, 177, 178, 197, 199
Cape (Colony or Province), 19, 20, 21, 25, 29, 38, 39, 40, 43, 45, 46, 54, 56, 57, 63, 79, 81, 83, 96, 105, 110, 137, 144, 146, 147, 151, 156, 157, 165, 167, 170, 173, 181, 200
Cape Copper Company, 40
Cape Government, 40, 154, 174
Cape Midlands, 155
Cape Mounted Riflemen, 24
Cape of Storms, 56
Cape Police, 174, 173
Cape Town, 21, 26, 30, 34, 35, 37, 38, 39, 49, 50, 79, 83, 88, 96, 97, 99, 101, 102, 103, 108, 109, 111, 130, 138, 144, 147, 150, 167, 168, 169
Cape Town Rangers, 36
Cape Town, University of, 197
Cashel (Ireland), 18, 19, 45
Castle, Cape Town, 168
Celts, 190
Chicago, 182
China, 134
Chinese, 135
Christ, 159, 165
Christian(s), 76, 87, 93, 94, 105, 136, 148, 159, 171
Christianity, 94, 148
Clare, County, 18, 189
Clark, Prof. John, 197, 198
Coloureds (Cape), 41
Comic Cuts, 130
Congo, 128
Crassulas, 127
Crouch, E. H., 51
Czechoslovakian, 185

Da Gama, Vasco, 57
Daniel (Old T.), 188
Delilah, 109
Deuteronomist, 166
Diaz, Bartholomew, 57
Diko, 122
Dingaan's Day, 146
Disa orchids, 127
Dryads, 188
Dublin, 18, 19, 20, 21, 45
Durban, 29, 130, 131, 205

Dutch, 41, 42, 79, 82, 100, 103, 110, 132, 135, 147, 148, 155, 156, 157, 158, 160, 166
Dutch East India Company, 146, 148, 167
Dutch Reformed Church, 97, 155, 169

Eastern Cape, 189
Eastern Province, 40
East Indian, 48
East London, 30, 34, 131
Edinburgh, 168
Edinburgh Orchestral Society, 168
Edinburgh, University of, 35, 167
Egypt, 85, 187
Egyptian, 129, 140, 202
Emjanyana, 118
England, 62, 132, 147, 148, 152, 156, 165, 166, 167, 190, 204
English, 20, 26, 30, 41, 42, 46, 48, 54, 73, 79, 103, 130, 132, 146, 148, 152, 154, 155, 156, 159, 160, 190, 191, 194, 198, 204
English lakes, 22
English Literature, 51, 197
Englishman, 79
Eumenides, 69
Europe, 35, 44, 45, 132, 148, 181
European(s), 47, 57, 70, 72, 83, 94, 102, 104, 114, 129, 134, 135, 136, 147, 148, 149, 151, 152, 169, 171, 181, 189, 190, 203, 204
Everyman, 51
Exodus, 121

Fairchild, Mrs., 187 (Mrs. Mary Martha Sherwood)
Falmouth, 20
Finistere, Cape of, 20
Fish Water Flats case, 172
Fleet Street, 129
France, 184
French, 167, 185, 194, 204
Frenchman, 185
Funchal, 20

Gahn, The Rev. Mr., 195
Gaika Rebellion, 23
Gaika Reserve, 23
Garden of Eden, 128, 172

Index

Gardiner Street, Dublin, 18
German(s), 48, 82, 191, 194
Germany, 152, 161, 168
Ghoda (Ghoda Bush), 72, 73, 74
Graaff Reinet, 34, 146, 148, 154
Grahamstown, 21, 39, 176
Gray, Mrs. Betty, 39, 62, 187, 195, 204, 205
Great Britain, 155
Great Trek, 144, 145
Greece, 69
Greek, 169, 194
Gummidge, Mrs. (*David Copperfield*), 187

Hatton Gardens, 24
Hebrew, 133
Hebrew Scriptures, 139
Heidelberg, 161
Henry VIII of England, 182
Holland, 96, 169
Hottentot(s), 41, 87, 88, 91, 92, 98, 104, 121, 141, 148, 149, 201, 203
House of Commons, 138, 149, 157
House of Fugger, 182
Huguenot, 167
Hungarian, 168

Illustrated London News, 25
India, 139, 182
Indian(s), (of India), 41, 132, 135
Indian Ocean, 205
Indians of South America, 152
Indra, 139
Ireland, 17, 24, 45, 190
Irish, 18, 20, 26, 32, 46, 155, 189
Irishman, 46, 190
Isaiah, 130
Islam, 79
Israel, 107
Italian, 194

Jagersdorp, 155, 157, 158, 159, 161, 162, 163, 164, 166
Japanese, 135
Java, 79
Jewish, 88
Jew(s), 41, 82, 86
Johannesburg, 130, 131, 132, 135, 136, 137, 156, 165, 178, 179, 188

Johannesburg Art Collection, 132
Joseph (Old T.), 178
Jove, 57

Kaffir(s), 22, 58, 59, 69, 112, 134, 135, 144, 157, 181
Kaffirland, 63
Kaffir, Seventh . . . War, 151
Kalihari, 140, 186
Kanya-veld, 140
Karoo, 84
Katberg forests, 35
Killarney, 45
Kimberley, 24, 25, 26, 31, 47, 83, 118, 124, 127, 153, 182, 188, 205
King William's Town, 21, 22, 24, 171, 172, 174, 178
Koch discovery, 42
Koranna-Griqua rebellion, 83
Koranna Hottentot, 82
Kruger Game Reserve, 28

Latin, 161, 194
Lausanne, 152
Leyden, 105
Literary works mentioned:
  Dark Folk and Other Poems (Slater), 195
  Decline and Fall of the Roman Empire (Gibbon), 194
  Duchess of Malfi (Webster), 194
  Excursion, The (Wordsworth), 22
  Faerie Queene, The (Spenser), 194
  Holism, (Smuts), 184, 186
  Jock of the Bushveld (Fitzpatrick), 21
  Lusiad, The (Camoens), 57
  Paradise Lost (Milton), 194
  "Rounding the Cape" (Campbell), 57
Livingstone, Dr. David, 47-8, 169
London, 45, 48, 129, 130, 132, 145, 148, 152, 165, 199, 201
Londoner(s), 129, 130
London Missionary Society, 148
London's East End, 82
London's East End, 82
Louis XIV of France, 182
Lourenço Marques, 122, 131, 145
Lovedale, 41
Lovedale Literary Society, 41
Loyal Ladies' League, 158, 159, 164

Machiavellianism, 185
Madeira Islands, 20
Makaula, 122
Malay(s), 21, 79, 132
Marah, Bitter Waters of, 121
Matabeleland, 191
Meneris butterflies, 127
Mephistopheles, 158
Micah (Prophet), 195
Military Intelligence Department, 157
Miller, G. M., 198
Mohammed, 194
Moravians, 148
Moravian Society, 148
Mountains of the Moon, 188
Mount Atlas, 187
Mount Erebus, 133

Nachtmaal, 88, 90, 97
Namaqualand, 37, 39, 40, 48, 55, 56, 127, 137, 138, 141, 197
Namies, 84, 85, 87, 88, 89, 90
Narcissus, 127
Natal, 29, 70, 144, 145, 181
Natal Mounted Police, 70
Natal South Coast, 205
Native Territories, 26, 41, 42, 43, 63
Native words used:
  gqira, 94, 95
  ikempe, 64
  imfeketu, 73
  imishologu, 76, 114, 115
  inhlonipu, 42
  kohlisi, 73
  munyu, 114
  ukushwama, 72, 74
  umdhlemnyana, 76
  umgwenya, 72, 74
Nazi, 183
Nesbitt's Horse, 36
Netherlands, 96
New Testament, 158, 159
Niger, 128
Nimrod, 101
Nuremburg, 175
'Nyatele Regiment, 64

Old Testament, 159
O'okiep Copper Mines, 37
Orange Free State, 144, 147, 161, 190

Pacific, 152
Palestine, 111
Pall Mall Magazine, 122
Pan, 188
Paraguay, 38
Parè, Ambroise, 182
Paris, 132, 168
Peter the Great (and Catherine) of Russia, 182
Pharoah, 85
Pondoland, 25, 41, 48, 74, 114, 115
Port Alfred, 157
Port Elizabeth, 21, 116, 130, 131, 152, 173, 177, 178
Portugal, 148
Potiphar, 178
Powerscourt, Lord, 19
Pretoria, 130, 131, 168, 183, 184, 185
Prophets of Israel, 47, 194
Psalms, 47, 130, 194
Ptolemy, 188
Punch, 187

Queenstown, 24, 152

Rand, 24, 131, 133, 134, 136, 137, 167
Rand Club, 132
Raphael, 82
Red Sea, 85
Renaissance, 194
Researches in South Africa, 149
Retief, Pieter, 145, 146, 191
Rhodesia, 191
Richards, Mr. (Mrs. Scully's father), 39
Richards, Mrs. (Mrs. Scully's mother), 152
Robben Island, 38, 99, 105, 106, 111
Rome, 82, 190
Rossdale Mission Station, 171, 172, 202
Roumanian, 178
Royal College of Music, London, 168
Russians, 185
Russo-Turkish War, 25
Ruwenzori (Mountains of the Moon), 188

Sahara, 187
Saracens, 111
Satan, 172
Scotland, 46, 47, 116, 167
Scot or Scottish, 20, 46, 156

Index

Scully, William Charles (1855-1943):
Biographical, Family, birth, early life in Ireland, 18-20; voyage to South Africa, 20-21; arrival at the Cape and eventual settlement in King William's Town, 21-22; first "adventure," 22; in charge of the family's sheep, 22-23; working for a trader, 23; life in the diamond mines, 23-26; years in the gold fields, 26-29; period with the Boating Company, then appointment to the Cape Civil Service, 30. Thirty-eight years with the Civil Service, 31-45. First marriage, 34-35; second marriage, 39; children, 152. After retirement, trip with wife and two of the children to the United States and alone to South America, 152; finally settles at Kimberley, 153; mental activities while at Kimberley, 182; reading, 194-95; exchange of letters with Slater, 195; attitude towards loneliness, 195-96; rejection of physical memorials, 196-97; integrity as a writer, 203-4; last days, 204-5.

Scully's Family, father John Joseph, 18, 20, 21, 22, 30; mother Elizabeth Mary Creagh (Creigh), 18; first wife Ellen Doveton, 34, 35, 39; Ellen's only child, Elaine, 34, 35, 152; second wife, Honoria Emily Richards, 39, 152, 205; son Gerald, 39, 152, 205; son Ernest, 152; daughter Miriam, 152; daughter Lilla, 152, 153; daughter Betty, 152; Scully's sister who became a nun, 152; Gerald's wife, Muriel, 205.

NOVELS:
Between Sun and Sand, 18, 81-92, 199, 200, 201
Daniel Vananda, 170-182, 202
Harrow, The, 153-167, 201, 202, 204
Vendetta of the Desert, A, 96-112

VOLUMES OF SHORT STORIES:
By Veld and Kopje, 112-122, 187
Kafir Stories, 48, 63-74, 199
Stories in *Voices of Africa*, 189-193
 "The Battle of Ezinyoseni," 191-193
 "The Flood," 189

 "Laughing is no Laughing Matter," 189-190
 "On Picket, An Episode of the South African War," 190-191
White Hecatomb, 74-80

VOLUMES OF POEMS:
Poems, 46-61, 198
Poems in *Voices of Africa*, 187-89
Wreck of the Grosvenor and Other South African Poems, The, 47, 48, 198

MISCELLANEOUS PROSE:
Further Reminiscences of a South African Pioneer, 31-45, 50, 81, 92, 132, 202
History of South Africa, A, 143-151, 202
Lodges in the Wilderness, 36, 131, 137-141, 142, 196, 200, 201, 202
Reminiscences of a South African Pioneer, 17, 18-30, 124, 126, 199, 202
Ridge of the White Waters, The, 131-137, 166, 202
Scopalomine in Africa, 182-187
Sir J. H. Meiring Beck, 167-170

SHORT STORIES:
"Afar in the Desert," 119-20, 196
"Aiala," 79
"Battle of Ezinyoseni, The," 191-93
"By the Waters of Marah," 119, 120-21
"Case for Psychical Research, A," 116
"Chicken Wings," 115-16
"Eumenides in Kafirland, The," 62, 69
"Flood, The," 189
"Forgotten Expedition, A," 122
"Fundamental Axiom, The," 63, 71
"Ghamba," 63, 70-71
"Gquma; Or The White Waif," 74-75
"Gratitude of a Savage, The," 121-122
"Imishologu, The," 76-77
"Kaffir Music," 112, 122
"Kellson's Nemesis," 63, 71-72
"Laughing Is no Laughing Matter," 189-90
"Lepers, The," 118
"Madness of Gweva, The," 196
"Mr. Bloxam's Choice," 116-17
"Noquala's Cattle," 44, 92-96
"On Picket . . ." 190-91

"Quest of the Copper, The," 63-69, 193
"Rainmaking," 114-15
"Return of Sobèdè, The," 75
"Seed of the Church, The," 75-76
"Tommy's Evil Genius," 121
"Tramp's Tragedy, The," 79
"Ukushwama," 63, 72-74
"Umtagati," 63, 70
"Vengeance of Dogolwana, The," 77-79
"White Hecatomb, The," 79-80
"Wisdom of the Serpent, The," 112-14
"Writing on the Rock, The," 118-19

POEMS:
"Aceldama," 60
"Bushman's Cave, The," 58
"Cattle Thief, The," 58-59
"Compass Berg," 57
"Dead Airman, The," 61
"Good and Evil," 51-52
"Home of the Ferns, The," 51
"Immanuel Kant," 48, 197
"Namaqualand," 52, 55, 197, 198
" 'Nkongane," 60-61
"Prayer," 50-51
"Prayer of the Cattle, The," 44, 195
"Rondel," 204-5
"St. Benedict," 54-55, 198
"Song" (As water flowing), 49
"Song" (We stood at dawn), 49
"Song" (O when the white . . .), 49
"Sonnets from the German," 52-54
"Stellenbosch Reverie, A," 189
"Table Mountain," 56, 197, 198
"Thomas Pringle," 47
"To Elaine," 35
"Traditur Dies Die," 49-50
"Voices of Africa," 112, 187-89
"Witch-Doctor, The," 59
"Wreck of the Grosvenor, The," 48

Characters in the novels: Aaronson, 157, 159; Alice, 172, 174, 175, 176, 177, 179, 180, 181, 182; Captain Benton, 155, 156, 157; Koos Bester, 82, 88-92, 201; Mrs. Koos Bester, 91; Willem Bester, 83, 88; The Rev. Philip Brand, 106; Jim Coki, 178; Uncle Diederick, 98, 100, 101, 106; Gert Dragooner, 97, 98; Mr. and Mrs. du Plessis, 105; Gertrude du Plessis, 105; Helena du Plessis, 106; Elijah, 93-96; Aunt Emerencia, 100, 101; Mr. and Mrs. Stephan Flotov, 178; The Rev. Augustine Gargoyle, 155, 159; Mrs. Gargoyle, 159; Gert Gemsbok, 82-92, 201; Old Schalk Hattingh, 82, 84, 86, 89; Mrs. Hattingh, 85, 86; Susannah (Hattingh), 82, 85, 86, 87; Hisch, 157, 158; Jacomina, 100, 101; Diederick Jansen, 161-64; Hessie Jansen, 161-164; Willem Jansen, 163, Jansen Children, 161-64; Kanu, 100-104, 106, 108-110; Keddleston, 158, 165, 166; Old Kondolo, 170, 179, 181, 202; Corporal Konza, 172-177; Ksoa, 109; Lydia, 180, 181; Alexander Macgregor, 156; Colonel Macleay, 159; Makalipa, 93, 95; John Marsden, 155, 156, 161, 162; Mrs. Marsden, 161; Laura Marsden, 155, 156, 158, 159, 161, 162; Lord Milner, 165; 'Ndakana, 94, 95; Nomani, 172; Noquala, 93-95; Tom Parratt, 156, 159; Rennet, 158, 165, 166; Captain Rice, 157, 158, 165, 166; Dr. Terence Ryan, 155, 156, 158, 159, 161, 162, 164; Oom Schulpad, 82, 87, 89, 90, 91, 201; Old Songelwa, 172, 180; The Rev. Theophilus Sparrowsworth, 155, 158, 159; Max Steinmetz, 82, 85-90; Nathan Steinmetz, 82, 87-92; Little Tyali, 177; Daniel Vananda, 170, 172, 174-82, 202, 203; Tyardt van der Walt I, 96; Cornelius van der Walt, 96; Tyardt van der Walt II, 96, 111; Stephanus van der Walt, 97-102, 106-8, 110-12; Marta Venter van der Walt, 97, 99, 101; Elsie van der Walt, 75, 99-111; Sara van der Walt, 101, 110; Gideon van der Walt, 97-102; 106-112; Aletta du Val van der Walt, 97, 101, 106, 107; Adrian van der Walt, 101; Laurence van Sittart, Stephen Vardy, 170, 171, 172, 174-77, 179-81; 156, 159; Maggie Zama, 171, 172, 180, 181; Zingelagahle, 93.

Characters in the Short Stories: Aiala, 79; Alida, 120, 121; The Rev. Peter Bloxam, 116, 117; The Boy, 119, 120; Lourens Brand, 79; Pres. T. F. Bur-

Index

gers, 122; Danster, 121; Dan the Reefer, 119; Dogolwana, 77, 78, 79; Corporal Francis Dollond, 71; Dumani, 121, 122; Faku, 115; John Flood, 113, 114; Dirk Fourie, 120; Anna Fourie, 120; Trooper James Franks, 71; Ghamba, 70, 71; Gqomisa, 77, 78; Jim Gubo, 69; Gweva, 196; Isaac, 116; Kalaza, 69; Kalipa, 192, 193; Kèlè, 77, 78; Kondwana, 63-69; Kreli, 113, 114; Kungayè, 75; Trooper George Langley, 70, 71; Mahlokoza, 78, 79; Maliwe, 69; Mampitizili, 75; Manciya, 75; Mangèlè, 118; Miss Stella Mason, 116, 117; Matshaka, 76; 'Mbopè, 75; Major M'Donald, 122; 'Ncapayi, 115; 'Ndepa, 75; 'Ndondo, 77; Nolala, 121, 122; Nomalie, 72, 74; Nomandewu, 121, 122; Nomasaba, 196; Nomayeshè, 77; Notemba, 77, 78; Numjala, 72, 73, 74; Lukwazi, 72; Philip, 78, 79; Mr. Donald Ramsay, 116, 117; Senzanga, 67-69; Miss Lavinia Simpson, 117; Sobèdè, 75; Songoza, 77-79; Tambuza, 192, 193; Tshaka, 58, 59, 60, 63, 64, 65, 67, 68, 69, 70, 79; Umdava, 70; Umgwadhla, 114, 115; Umquikela, 114, 115; Umsoala, 77; Sarel van der Merwe, 118, 119; Jan Viljoen, 190, 191; Vooda, 70; The Rev. Mark Wardley, 116; Lucy Westbrook, 121, 122; Mr. and Mrs. Westbrook, 121, 122; Miss Matilda Whitmore, 116; Trooper Hiram Whitson, 71; Mr. and Mrs. Windwood, 121; Tommy Windwood, 121; The Rev. Samuel Winterton, 116; The Rev. and Mrs. Josiah Wiseman, 116, 117; Xolilizwe, 72, 74.

Names in poems: Atlantic, 55; Boer, 188; Cape of Storms, 56; Chaka, 60; Dingaan, 61; Dryads, 188; Egypt, 187; Faunus, 188; Fusi, 59; Hesper, 57; Icarus, 61; Johannesburg, 188; Kimberley, 188; Mount Atlas, 187; 'Nkongane, 60; Noniese, 59; Pan, 188; Paul, 50; Phosphor, 57; Ruwenzori, 188; Sahara, 187; Tshaka, 60; Zambezi, 188; Zimbabwe, 188.

Persons named in miscellaneous prose:

Further Reminiscences of a South African Pioneer, G. F. Scott Elliott, 35; Lopez, 38; Prof. P. MacOwan, 34, 35, 37; Major Nesbitt, 36; Charles Rubidge, 34; Col. Wavell, 36. *A History of South Africa,* President Brand, 147; Pedro Alvarez Cabral, 148; Prof Cory, 143; Sir John Cradock, 147; Du Pré Alexander, Earl of Caledon, 147; Sir Benjamin D'Urban, 145; Lord Glenelg, 145, 146; Sir George Grey, 147; Casper Kruger, 145; Paul Kruger, 145, 156; Leibbrandt, 143; Liebenbergs, 145; Gerrit Maritz, 145, 191; Pato, 149; Dr. John Philip, 149; Hendrick Potgieter, 145, 146, 191; Andries Pretorius, 146; George Schmidt, 148; Lord Charles Somerset, 147; Louis Triechard, 145; Jan Tshatshu, 149; Pieter Uys, 145, 146; Dr. van der Kemp, 148, 149; Simon van der Stel, 146, 147; Hans van Rensburg, 145. *Lodges in the Wilderness,* Brunhild, 137; Andries Esterhuizen, 141; The Rev. Mr. Hein, 138; Hendrick, 141; Siegfried, 137. *Reminiscences of a South African Pioneer,* H. C. Becher, 24; Marquis of Bute, 20; Archibald Campbell, 25; Lord Carnarvon, 30; Col. Carrington, 36; Major Drury, 24; Sir Drummond and Mrs. Dunbar, 29; Reginald Fairlie, 25; Judge and Mrs. Fitzpatrick, 21; Sir Percy Fitzpatrick, 21; Norman Garstin, 25; Jimmy Kinsella, 19, 20; 'Ntshindeen, 29; George Paton, 24, 25; Cecil John Rhodes, 24, 25, 26; Frank Rhodes, 25; Herbert Rhodes, 24, 25; Mr. Samuel, 22; Sir Sydney Shippard, 26; Dr. Thorne, 24; Tiyo Soga, 22; Toby, 22, 23; "Tommy" Townsend, 25; H. C. Seppings Wright, 25. *The Ridge of the White Waters,* Hoggenheimer, 133. *Scopalomine in Africa,* Sir Abe Bailey, 184; Eduard Benes, 185; Camille Chautemps, 183, 185; Mr. Havenga, 183; Gen. Hertzog, 183-186; Hitler, 184; Mr. Hofmeyr, 183, 185, 186; Dr. Malan, 183, 184, 186; Mr. Pirow, 183; Col. Deneys Reitz, 183, 185, 186; Gen. Smuts, 183-186; Col.

Stallard, 183, 184. *Sir J. H. Meiring Beck,* Cornelius Beck, 167; Sir Johannes Henricus Meiring Beck, 167-170; Lady Beck, 167, 169; Johanna Elizabeth Meiring Beck, 167; Gov. Jan. Willem Janssens, 169; Monseigneur Kolbe, 167; The Rev. Abraham Johannes Kuys, 169; John X. Merriman, 167, 169; The Rev. Arnoldus Mauritz Meyring, 169; Remenyi, 168.

Sergeant, Howard, 198

Sketchy Bits, 130

Singapore, 79

Society for the Preservation of Objects of Historic Intent, South Africa, 168

Somerset, Colonel, 79

South Africa, 17, 19, 20, 26, 32, 35, 37, 40, 41, 45, 46, 47, 49, 54, 55, 59, 60, 62, 63, 60, 70, 72, 79, 80, 81, 82, 84, 112, 113, 114, 116, 118, 123, 127, 130, 132, 137, 143, 146, 147, 148, 149, 150, 152, 154, 155, 156, 159, 165, 167, 168, 169, 170, 178, 181, 182, 186, 190, 197, 198, 199, 202, 203

South African, 17, 21, 22, 24, 26, 27, 46, 47, 48, 49, 52, 55, 56, 74, 79, 119, 130, 144, 147, 148, 151, 155, 165, 168, 186, 189, 194, 198, 199, 200, 202, 204

South African Bushmen, 45

South African hospitality, 21

South African literature, 197

South African poetry, 198

South African Red Cross, 187

South African Republic, 145

South African Union, 183

South African War, 153, 199

South America, 35, 39, 120, 152

Southern Africa, 156

Southern African:

Tribal Chieftains, Chief of the Bomvana, 113; Chaka or Tshaka, 58, 59, 60, 63, 64, 65, 67, 68, 69, 70, 79, 127, 132, 144, 191, 192, 193; Dingaan, 60, 61, 145, 146, 192; Faku, 115; Hintza, 113; Makalaka Chief, 65, 66, 67; Moshesh, 80; Sandile, 23; Sekhukhune, 122; Umhlonhlo, 71; Umquikela, 114, 115; Umsilikazi, 191, 192, 193. *Clans or Tribes,*

Abambo, 63; Amabaca, 80, 129; Ambaca, 115; Amangwane, 79; Amaquati, 171; Amaswazi, 64; Baca, 72, 73, 115; Balotsi, 65, 66; Bapedi, 29, 122; Fingo, 149, 170, 171, 179, 180; Gaika, 148; Gcaleka, 114; Hlubi, 93; Makalaka, 64, 65, 66, 67, 69; Makwamba, 145; Matabele, 136, 145, 191, 192; Pondo, 25, 70, 136; Quati, 170, 202; Shangaan, 136; Swazi, 28, 29, 129, 136; Tembu, 136, 170; Tshomanè, 74, 75; Xhosa (Xosa), 136, 150; Zulu, 58, 60, 63, 64, 65, 66, 67, 69, 129, 136, 144, 145, 146, 191, 192, 193. *Mountains,* Amatole, 128; Compass Berg, 48, 57; Drakensburg, 64, 95, 126, 140; Drakenstein, 189; Great Winterburg, 177; Great Winterhoek, 169; Intsiza, 80; Lebomba, 28, 30, 64; Obiquas Bergen, 169; Roggeveld, 96; Sneeuwberg, 34; Witzenberg, 169; Zoutpansberg, 145. *Place names,* Alexandria, 176; Bashee Hoek, 36; Baviaan's Kloof, 148; Bethelsdorp, 148, 149; Bulawayo, 191; Butterworth, 171; Clarkbury, 36; Colesburg, 35, 37; Commissioner St. (J'burg), 178; Delagoa Bay, 64, 122; Elandsfontein, 96; Elandsnek, 161, 162, 164, 165; Fort Beaufort, 26, 35, 39, 41; Great Kaap Basin, 28, 126; Groote Schuur, 25, 26; Hospital Hill (J'burg), 178; Imbulumpini, 79; Inhambane, 128; Inkruip, 91; Joubert Park (J'burg), 178; Katberg forests, 35; Kuboos, 138; l'Agulhas, 140; Lobatsi, 153; Lydenburg, 24, 26; Maclean, 21; Matatiele, 122; Messina, 169; Mombasa, 128; Mount Frere, 41, 122, 127; New Scotland, 28; Nqamakwe, 35, 42; O'okiep, 40; Paarl, 185; Park Town (J'burg), 178; Peddie, 40, 62; Pietermaritzburg, 70; Pilgrim's Rest, 26, 27, 28, 29, 31, 47, 79, 118, 119, 120, 122, 127; Port Natal, 146; Port Nolloth, 37, 40; Potchefstroom, 191; Pretorius Kop, 125; Richtersveld, 138; Ron-

debosch, 104; Seymour, 37; Somerset East, 154; Somerset Strand, 153; Springbokfontein, 37; Stockenstroom, 35; Tarka, 30; Tarkastad, 30, 31, 32, 34, 35, 117; Tembani, 23; Tulbagh, 168, 169; Tutura, 22; Uitenhage, 154; Umbogintwini, 153, 205; Umkungunhlovu, 146; Wellington, 186; Worcester, 167; Wynberg, 152. *Rivers*, Bushman's, 172; Crocodile, 28, 29, 122; Gariep (Orange), 138, 140; Kei, 43; Kobonqaba, 22; Komati, 28, 30, 122; Letaba, 28; Limpopo, 28, 64, 66, 67, 69, 191; Olifant, 28, 120; Orange, 79, 83, 120; Pilgrim's Creek, 27; Tanqua, 96; Umtati, 74; Umzimvubu, 48; Upper Tugela, 70; Vaal, 83, 196; Zambezi, 25, 188.
Spanish, 194
Springfield, 19, 45
Stalin, 185
Standard Bank of London, 154
Standard Bank of South Africa, 156
State of South Africa, The, 123
Stellenbosch, 96, 97, 148, 150, 157
Stellenbosch, University of, 187
Strand (London), 129
Sudan, 128
Sunday Times, 199
"Sunny Slope" (farm), 21
Swastika, 183
Swaziland, 28, 126
Swede, 190

Table Bay, 21
Table Mountain, 48, 50, 55, 56, 57, 79, 103, 127, 128, 197
Tembuland, 36
Tembu War, 36
Templars, 129
Temple Church (London), 129
Teneriffe, Mt., 21
Tertullian, 75
Theal, G. McC., 22, 143
Theta Mine of Transvaal Gold Mining Estates Co., 29

Thetis (sea-nymph), 57
Thurigen, 167
Tipperary, 17, 18, 45, 189
Titan, 57
Tower of Babel, 101
Transkei, 22, 36
Transvaal, 21, 28, 79, 144, 145, 153, 191
Trek-Boer(s), 81, 82, 83, 84, 85, 87, 88, 90, 201
Tulbagh Valley, 168
Twelve Against the Gods, 182
Typhon, 140

Unconventional Reminiscences, 123, 202
United States, 62, 152
United States Army, 122
Unwin, T. Fisher, 48, 63

Vancouver Island, 152
Vedas, 139
Vedic Hymnist, 139
Vedic Hymns (Ludwig translation), 139, 195
Victoria (B. C.), 152
Voortrekker(s), 145, 191

Wagnerian operas, 168
Wales, 20
Wesleyan Church, 155
Wesleyan minister, 158
Wesleyans, 73
Wesley, John, 158
Western Orange Free State, 185
Wicklow, 19, 20, 45
Wilson, Woodrow, 182
Witwatersrand, 26, .54, 131, 132, 135, 137
Witzenberg Wine, 168
World as Will and Idea (Schopenhauer), 195
World War I, 153

Yankee, 71

Zululand, 64
"Zulu Pictures," 58